D0900879

Philosophers in the Classroom

Essays on Teaching

Edited by Steven M. Cahn,
Alexandra Bradner, and Andrew P. Mills

Hackett Publishing Company, Inc.
Indianapolis/Cambridge

Copyright © 2018 by Hackett Publishing Company, Inc.

All rights reserved
All essays included in this volume have been reprinted by the publisher with the written permission of the essayists.
Printed in the United States of America

21 20 19 18   1 2 3 4 5 6 7

For further information, please address
    Hackett Publishing Company, Inc.
    P.O. Box 44937
    Indianapolis, Indiana 46244-0937

    www.hackettpublishing.com

Cover design by Maura Gaughan and Brian Rak
Composition by William Hartman

Library of Congress Cataloging-in-Publication Data

Names: Cahn, Steven M., editor.
Title: Philosophers in the classroom : essays on teaching / edited by Steven M. Cahn, Alexandra Bradner, and Andrew P. Mills.
Description: Indianapolis : Hackett Pulishing Company, Inc., 2018. | Includes bibliographical references.
Identifiers: LCCN 2018010518 | ISBN 9781624667442 (pbk.) | ISBN 9781624667459 (cloth)
Subjects: LCSH: Philosophy—Study and teaching.
Classification: LCC B52 .P47 2018 | DDC 107.1—dc23
LC record available at https://lccn.loc.gov/2018010518

The paper used in this publication meets the minimum requirements of American National Standard for Information Sciences—Permanence of Paper for Printed Library Materials, ANSI Z39.48–1984.

∞

Contents

Preface

Steven M. Cahn

The origin of this book lies in a session sponsored by the American Philosophical Association's Committee on the Teaching of Philosophy at the 2017 Eastern Division Meeting in Baltimore. The theme was work I have done over the past two decades with Oxford University Press executive editor Robert Miller that has resulted in seventeen anthologies for classroom use. After our initial presentation, questions and comments from the audience revealed considerable interest in teaching philosophy, and I was struck by the passion of many who were seeking to enhance their methods of instruction.

When the session ended, I spoke with Deborah Wilkes, president and CEO of Hackett Publishing Company, which forty years ago had published my anthology *Classics of Western Philosophy*, now in its eighth edition. As she and I talked, we were joined by her editorial assistant Maura Gaughan, who had attended the meeting and, like me, was impressed by the pervasive concern for teaching. I suggested that perhaps a book could be developed that would contain thoughts on teaching philosophy by those who excelled at it. That idea struck all of us as worthy, but I soon recognized that the project was not one I could handle alone. Thus I wrote to Alexandra Bradner, chair of the Committee on the Teaching of Philosophy, who had organized and chaired our American Philosophical Association session, to ask whether she might be interested in joining me. She enthusiastically agreed and suggested that Andrew Mills, president of the American Association of Philosophy Teachers, would be an excellent choice to complete our editorial team. He was delighted to participate, and soon we formulated our plan.

We announced on many sites that we would welcome nominations and self-nominations of college and university faculty who had won teaching awards or been recognized in some analogous way for the quality of their instruction. The response was impressive. We then reviewed the list of submissions and issued invitations, almost all of which were accepted.

Each author understands the importance of preserving the anonymity of students, and every effort has been made not to infringe
on anyone's rights. Furthermore, the opinions expressed are those
of the authors and do not represent the views of their institutions.

Some of the participants are well-known researchers, others not.
The key point, however, is that while excellence in scholarship and
teaching are not at odds, knowing a subject does not guarantee the
ability to communicate it effectively, and that skill is not easy to
acquire. The number of master teachers is as small as the number
of outstanding scholars, and this book provides the opportunity to
learn about teaching from some of the finest philosophy instructors
at institutions, large and small, throughout the country.

I thank my coeditors Andrew Mills for his insightful suggestions,
and Alexandra Bradner, who did the bulk of the editorial work expe-
ditiously and effectively. We all appreciate Deborah Wilkes for her
guidance and support, Laura Clark for her conscientiousness, and
Maura Gaughan for helping in so many ways. Most of all, we are
grateful to those outstanding teachers who chose to participate in
the project and share their thoughts on the magic they perform in
turning classrooms into scenes of inspiration.

·

STEVEN M. CAHN, Graduate Center of the City University of New
York; former chair, American Philosophical Association Committee
on the Teaching of Philosophy; former president, the John Dewey
Foundation.

Introduction

Alexandra Bradner and Andrew P. Mills

If our experiences are not unique (and conversations with friends and colleagues over the years lead us to think they aren't), many of us didn't head off to college intending to be philosophy majors. Maybe because we didn't know what philosophy was or maybe because we had our hearts set on other pursuits, we found our way to philosophy by accident. We took a course (because we had to or because it fit our schedule) and got hooked. We majored, we flirted with law school, and then we headed to graduate school. Despite the array of forces driving us away from philosophy, we were bewitched by its puzzles. Whether in metaphysics or ethics or feminist theory or philosophy of science, we were taken by the problems and determined to spend our time grappling with them in graduate school and beyond.

Yet, we suspect that, for the authors of this volume (and perhaps for many of its readers), another accident happened: we were gripped by the problems of *teaching* philosophy. Whether because we found ourselves teaching material we did not know, found ourselves in jobs that did not support our research, found ourselves teaching hundreds of students a semester, found ourselves teaching students who didn't have the preparation we thought they should have, or because we found ourselves fascinated by the teaching problems themselves, we started caring more and more about how we could become better teachers of philosophy. We were still captivated by problems, but the problems that captivated us shifted.

The essays in this volume come from a wide cross-section of North American academic philosophers. There are those who are near or at the end of their professional careers, and there are those who are closer to graduate school than they are to retirement. Some authors work at departments with graduate students, although most are at undergraduate institutions. Some are at elite institutions teaching undergraduates who come from the best high schools, and others are teaching underprepared students at institutions with open enrollment. Some authors were trained in the "analytic" tradition and others in the "Continental" tradition. Their areas of specialization run the gamut, but what is notable is that nearly all of the authors in this volume, when asked to think about themselves as teachers of philosophy, talk, by and large, not about teaching graduate students or majors but about teaching introductory-level philosophy courses pitched to "gen-ed students"—those students who find their way into our classrooms not out of a love of philosophy but to meet a graduation requirement. Our authors write about trying to help those gen-ed students appreciate both the intrinsic value and the practical utility of philosophy during college and after graduation. They write about helping students find connections between their own interests and the questions of philosophy. They write about the bonds they have formed with these gen-ed students—bonds that remain long after the last day of class. The authors in this volume represent our discipline's award-winning teachers, so it's interesting to note that our best teachers spend their time wrestling with the problem of how to reach the "captive student" and not the high-flying major.

Maybe one reason so many of us—not just the authors of this volume, we suspect—spend so much time wrestling with the problem of how to teach gen-ed students is that we are teaching so many of them. In a survey Andrew Mills conducted in 2015, nearly 60 percent of the respondents who were full-time faculty (tenured, tenure track, or non-tenure track) taught at least 91 gen-ed students every year. More than 30 percent of those full-time faculty were teaching at least 126 gen-ed students every year. And it's not just that there are a lot of them; it's that gen-ed students form the vast majority of the students we teach every year. According to that same survey, 71 percent of the full-time faculty reported that at least 60 percent of the students they taught in an average year were gen-ed students, and 41 percent of those full-time faculty reported that 80 percent or more of the students they encountered every year were gen-ed students.[1] In other words, most of the students the majority of us teach are not graduate students and are not philosophy majors or even minors. Accordingly, we hope, the essays in this volume will speak to typical academic philosophers who spend their semesters

---

1. Andrew Mills, "What's Valuable about Philosophy Courses: Content vs. Skills." Paper presented at the American Association of Philosophy Teachers 21st International Workshop-Conference on Teaching Philosophy, Saginaw, MI, June 2016.

consumed with introductory-level courses filled with students who might not want to be there.

Another reason so many of us spend so much time thinking about how to reach the gen-ed student is, perhaps, that, as philosophers, we like tough problems. It's fairly easy to figure out how to teach a seminar room filled with well-prepared, eager, interested philosophy majors who know how to write an argumentative essay and come to class having done the reading. How challenging can that be when held up against the problem of connecting with a lecture hall full of students who don't want to be there, whose precollege education has left them ill prepared for college-level reading and writing assignments, and who see little value (at least on day one) in what our discipline has to offer? We don't mean to imply that teaching upper-level philosophy majors is without its own challenges: determining how to construct a historically responsible, sufficiently contemporary, and personally engaging syllabus is difficult, as is the development of properly sourced argumentative writing. We only mean to suggest that the greater challenge is in facing the problem of how to help our gen-ed students see the value of the very enterprise of philosophy.

In this respect, perhaps, we are sailing in Socrates' wake. As Socrates struggled to make the Athenians see the value of the examined life, so we struggle to help our Applied Ethics, or Critical Thinking, or Introduction to Philosophy class see the value of spending a semester thinking about Cartesian doubt, moral relativism, or the problem of evil. As Athens was Socrates' sluggish horse, perhaps the classroom full of business majors is ours.

Also, like Socrates (someone who, perhaps unsurprisingly, is mentioned in many of the chapters in this volume), many of our authors write about the love, care, and concern they have for their students. Such feelings might not be sufficient for bringing about the changes we hope to see in our students (as Socrates found out the hard way), but, judging from the essays in this volume, it certainly seems to be necessary. Perhaps only if one is moved by love—for philosophy, yes, but also for one's students and how we think philosophy can improve their lives—does one dedicate time to figuring out better ways to teach the rafts of students, many of whom will never take a philosophy course ever again.

In some respects, the problem of how to teach the gen-ed student presents an even greater challenge than the canonical problems of philosophy: the "teaching problem" involves real human beings, hundreds of them, who are all different from one another, with complicated sets of needs, values, beliefs, and desires. The abstract conceptual problems and paradoxes of philosophy (Gettier, Sorites, Ravens, mind-body, etc.) are formidable. But we can circumscribe those problems. They are "neat" problems, which we can address by drawing distinctions, biting bullets, or paying careful attention to argumentative slipups. The teaching problem, in contrast, is complex and messy: it's difficult to know even where to begin. Perhaps the accounts collected together in this volume offer one such starting point. As we see how award-winning teachers have dealt with the challenges they have faced, we may be inspired to rededicate ourselves to the task of teaching, to try what they have tried, and to develop new strategies and techniques of our own.

•

Our collection begins in Part I: "Teaching Philosophy: A Prologue" with two essays that think about what it means to teach philosophy in the broadest sense. Seung-Kee Lee's convocation speech identifies student learning as the proper goal of teaching—a mark of virtue. Virtuous teachers are able to transform their students, and educated students become happy people. Andrea Tschemplik's piece reflects on how Plato's *Meno* has guided her work in the classroom throughout her career, regardless of institutional setting.

In Part II: "Teaching the Students," we continue on to a group of essays that explore the national shift toward active and student-centered learning. Maureen Eckert presents teaching as the difficult task of serving the middle. David W. Concepción tracks his progression from inexperienced to more mature teacher, from a teacher concerned with how his doctoral advisors and students perceived him to a teacher concerned with the effectiveness of his courses and student care. Paul Hurley recounts how he alters his normative ethics course to meet different student populations and, by way of a rationale, offers a compelling philosophical analysis of the course content. Marie-Eve Morin details the shift in her teaching that had to take place when she was asked to teach large lecture courses: she became a teacher of graduate teaching assistants. James Rocha reflects on his own educational trajectory to understand the value of teaching "a bunch of dead, cis, straight, white, male, privileged, and bigoted philosophers" to students from historically disenfranchised populations. And Courtney Morris considers the special responsibilities involved in teaching ethics to a unique student population: the young people trained and licensed by our government to kill.

From there, in Part III: "Teaching the Course," we take a closer look at a series of individual courses. Mark Piper explains how to enliven and enjoy an introductory critical thinking course. Stephen H. Daniel writes about the intro class he is still actively developing, although he has been teaching the course for more than forty years. Christine Vitrano shares why her gen-ed course on happiness and the meaning of life resonates with students. Paul Woodruff locates the secret to student engagement in a Philanthropy Lab course and later successfully extends this model to an aesthetics course. And Anthony Weston takes us to the Australian Outback, north of Vancouver Island, and beyond for his environmental ethics.

Following this section on the teaching of particular courses, we move on to Part IV: "Teaching beyond the Course" and a group of essays that address the relationship between the academic courses we teach and the broader social-political context in which those courses take place. David Palmer takes seriously his students' objection that there might be more valuable ways to live than the examined one. John F. Whitmire, Jr. designs his courses in light of Sartre's suggestion that academic work is not as valuable as service to the suffering and hears later, from former students, that his community-based learning courses have changed their lives. David C. K. Curry reveals how role-playing games from the Reacting to the Past Consortium can help students learn how to apply philosophical concepts at varying levels of abstraction. Bob Fischer raises the possibility that philosophy, although it can improve society, is often damaging to individuals. And Alexander V. Stehn uses Kierkegaard and Dewey to frame the difference between studying normative ethical theory and becoming an ethical person, after which he uses ethics notebooks to encourage his introductory ethics students to ponder this distinction for themselves.

Finally, in Part V: "Teaching the Teacher," our collection closes with a series of personal reflections on the teaching life. Bertha Alvarez Manninen offers a moving tribute to the mentor who has inspired her to do the same. Elizabeth Jelinek recounts the role that philosophical training played in her grandparents' flight from Nazi Germany. Jane Drexler shares the challenges and frustrations of teaching at a two-year college and the kind of creativity and confidence one must find to make it work. Russell Marcus takes us on a journey through the memories that have emerged as the markers of his career. Nick Smith captures just how we feel when a student passes away. And Martin Benjamin closes our volume with a look at the turn his philosophy career has taken since his retirement. Facing his own mortality, with both the curiosity and straightforwardness of a philosopher, he wonders about the contribution any one of us can make to this grand tradition.

•

Four themes or lessons emerge from this collection. First, rather than aim to leave students with the memory of any particular philosophical doctrine, our best philosophy teachers aim to convey the discipline's spirit. As contributor Stephen H. Daniel puts it in his essay, "Introduction to Philosophy is not a survey of material; it is an invitation to a lifestyle." What characterizes the philosophical life? Philosophers learn not by absorbing the dictates of powerful authority figures, but by participating in open, critical discussions of canonical texts. Philosophers imagine alternative possibilities that force us to justify even our most basic presuppositions and, when such attempts fail, lead us toward new and better ways of thinking. And philosophers tackle valuable questions, questions that matter—about love, beauty, suffering, death, community, power, truth, and life's meaning.

The second theme of the collection raises a perennial concern. Although the value of studying philosophy remains perfectly clear to insiders, even our discipline's very best teachers struggle, along with the rest of us, to convey the importance of our discipline to nonspecialists. Our field's recent interest in public philosophy, active and student-centered learning, experiential and community-based learning, and the diversification of both the canon and its caste of guardians responds in different ways to this challenge. As a third lesson, the essays of this collection make clear that good teaching results from reflective trial and error. Teaching is an experiential, experimental, tinkering practice—not something you can learn propositionally from a book and not something that accrues automatically to a master of philosophical content. Fourth, and last, although pedagogical growth requires classroom experience, experience alone is not sufficient. Good philosophy teachers care deeply about their students and make teaching a professional priority.

The philosophers in this volume are particularly accomplished teachers whose pedagogical expertise has earned them special recognition at their home institutions. But *most* philosophers, we suggest, in virtue of their philosophical training, have the capacity to become excellent teachers. We have all been taught to listen, read, and write carefully; to explain complicated concepts clearly; to remain informed; and to consider the broader social consequences of our work. We like to talk to people (primarily to other philosophers, of course). We have fairly well-developed senses of humor. And we aim to be difference makers: most of us hope that even our most devastating critiques will improve the world in some way. In short, we're sharp, engaged, funny, and progressive—qualities that naturally appeal to students. Despite all of this, not every philosopher is an effective teacher. What transforms a trained philosopher, with the capacity to teach well, into a teacher who is genuinely flourishing is dedication to the task.

Excellent teachers are devoted teachers—teachers who actively look for ways to improve their courses, teachers who unselfishly attend to the needs of individual students, and teachers who keep up in their philosophical subfields, but also in the cognitive science of learning and in the scholarship of teaching and learning. Devoted teachers embrace these responsibilities as uncontroversially valuable, for teaching is the most impactful thing a philosopher can do.

ALEXANDRA BRADNER, Kenyon College; chair, American Philosophical Association Committee on the Teaching of Philosophy; executive director, American Association of Philosophy Teachers.

ANDREW P. MILLS, Otterbein University; president, American Association of Philosophy Teachers.

I. Teaching Philosophy: A Prologue

1

What Is Philosophy? What Is Education?

Seung-Kee Lee
Drew University

SEUNG-KEE LEE has been teaching history of philosophy to undergraduate students for twenty years, first at the Catholic University of America and then at Drew University. Since he arrived at Drew in 2000, philosophy majors at the university have increased by 50 percent and have remained at that level. He received the Drew University President's Award for Distinguished Teaching in 2012. Seung-Kee's most recent publication is "Determination and Dialectic in Kant and Hegel" (*Hegel-Jahrbuch*, 2017). His teaching is driven by his belief that exercising philosophical reason can make your life go better.

Philosophy[1] is often associated with the name Socrates. Socrates is famous for the many things he said and did, and one of these is that he went around asking people specific and, at times, even strange questions—questions like, What is goodness? What is knowledge? What is justice? What is love? What is citizenship? What is beauty? If Socrates were alive today, I think one question that he would ask us American citizens is, What is education?

What I find a bit troubling is not so much that this might be a difficult question to answer as that some are under the impression that there could be more than one answer to this question. We professors are sometimes asked what our "philosophy of teaching" is. And I've heard professors say different things when asked about their philosophy of teaching. For example, some say it is important to make sure that whatever the students do, they have fun doing it; others say students should not only read and think but also learn to put into practice what they read and think; and still others point out

---

1. This chapter is based on the keynote address I delivered as recipient of the Drew University President's Award for Distinguished Teaching at the opening of school ceremony at Drew University in August 2012.

that their job is to provide students with the tools necessary to succeed in the real world.

Now, these may all be valuable in some way as pieces of advice, but there is something odd about asking what one's philosophy of teaching is, just as it would be odd to ask a physician what her philosophy of doctoring is or to ask a physical trainer what his philosophy of exercise is. And this is because doctoring and exercise have their proper goals: the goal of doctoring is healing, and the goal of exercise is health. In the same way, I think teaching has its proper goal, and that is *learning*.

So one's philosophy of teaching, if by that we mean Why do we teach at all? or What should we be striving toward as teachers?, *should* be that students learn. We may succeed in making students happy or joyous, in making students *do* as well as read and think, in providing students with the tools necessary to succeed in the so-called real world, and so on. But if students have failed to learn in doing all this, we have failed as teachers, just as one fails as a doctor when the patient has not been healed or fails as a physical trainer if his clients remain physically out of shape.

Now, if Socrates were listening to all of this, he would probably object at this point and note that if the goal of teaching is learning, we are left with another obvious question, namely, What is learning? To address *this* question, I would like to raise another question that I think is intimately bound up with the question What is learning? and that is What is virtue?

When I first came to this university, I remember seeing for the first time the large sign that was marked "Drew University," which stood beside the main entrance gate right off Madison Avenue. Right beneath the words "Drew University" were the following words: "A Tradition of Excellence." I felt goose bumps when I read these words. The word "excellence" is the translation of the Greek word *arête*, which is more commonly translated as "virtue."

But what *is* virtue? What *is* excellence? The word "virtue" carries multiple meanings, but we should focus on the most general meaning on which philosophers agree: "virtue" is whatever it is, within a human being, that makes that human being good. In other words, it is by virtue of virtue that a person is said to be a good human being.

So the university's motto, "A Tradition of Excellence," indicated to me that it is an institution that supports the long-held belief that teaching, learning, or education occurs when a human being is transformed into a person of excellence or virtue—a good human being—or that a good education is a prerequisite to becoming a person of virtue. How dull my job as a teacher would become if I ceased to believe that my teaching could help students become good human beings.

By far, the most interesting and enjoyable class I teach every semester is the first class of my Introduction to Philosophy course. I begin the class by writing "What is philosophy?" on the blackboard. I then point out that this question is in fact one of the problems of philosophy. A look of puzzlement, a chuckle or two, but mostly curious stares are the result. I pause for a quarter of a minute, during which there is an awkward silence. I then thank the students for not leaving the classroom. "Can you imagine," I explain, "a biology professor telling her students on the very first day of class, 'What is biology? This question is one of the problems of biology.' If you're a student in such a class, you *should* leave the classroom at once." Some laughing ensues, but it soon dawns on the students that they are owed a reason why they should not walk out of *this* classroom.

Instead of offering my students the abstract and abstruse definitions that philosophers have given for philosophy, which I did when I first began teaching undergraduates twenty years ago, I relate a story about the nature of philosophy that captured my imagination as an undergraduate student of ancient philosophy in the mid-1980s. I find it intriguing that the story still strikes a chord with today's millennial students, with whom I'm able to identify less and less as time wears on. It is the story told about Pythagoras, who, upon being asked what a philosopher was, compared three kinds of people who live their lives for three different reasons with three kinds of people who attend the Olympic Games for three different reasons. The vendors and athletes go to the games for "fame and gain," while the spectators go there simply for entertainment. Similarly, in life, some live for money and others for fame, while the best live in search of truth and wisdom.

I point out that probably no student in this classroom is pursuing a college degree as an end in itself. I ask, "Who here plans to retire after obtaining his or her bachelor's degree?" They look around at one another in amusement. So studying in college is a means to attaining a further goal. And what might *that* be? Getting a good job, becoming independent, contributing to society, starting a family, and so on. But aren't these all just means to an end, or *the* end, which is, *happiness*? After a brief pause, most nod in agreement. I then note that Pythagoras' story indicates that there appear to be three possible conceptions of happiness, but he thinks only one of those conceptions is reasonable. A lively discussion and debate ensue: "making money, even lots of it, is not necessarily bad"; "most people think money will make them happy"; "you can be famous and still be a good person"; "why can't you have all three—money, fame, *and* wisdom?"; "the media is all about preaching money, money, money"; and so on.

Ever since early modern philosophers such as Locke and Kant succeeded in driving a wedge between virtue and happiness, to pursue intellectual and moral virtues in the name of happiness is a luxury that few postmodern people can afford. But this is the idea suggested by Pythagoras' story, according to which it is the pursuit of truth and wisdom that not only liberates one from the bondage of living for money and fame but also enables one to attain the qualities that make for a truly happy life. Can learning make us happy? Philosophy 101 students are not quite ready to appreciate the full meaning of that question and its affirmative answer. But even just the thought of the possibility that perhaps their four years of intense academic studies *could* lead, in the end, to their happiness is worthwhile.

"We'll continue this discussion in our next class. Are you glad you registered for a course in philosophy? Are you excited about learning?" I marvel at the genuine smiles and looks of satisfaction on the faces of my millennials as they prepare to leave the classroom.

2

Free to Think

Andrea Tschemplik
American University

ANDREA TSCHEMPLIK has been teaching philosophy for the last thirty years, first as a graduate student at Hunter College while attending CUNY; as a tenure-track faculty member at Upsala College, where she received the Faculty Member of the Year Award in 1994; as a visiting or term faculty member at Drew University and George Washington University; and, finally, as a tenured faculty member at American University, where she has been teaching for the past sixteen years. Her primary teaching responsibilities are an introduction to Western philosophy and courses in the history of philosophy from Ancient Greek to nineteenth-century philosophy.

In most introductory philosophy classes I ask students to spend ten minutes a day thinking. In recent semesters students have looked at me as if I were making an impossible request—"What do you mean 'thinking'"? "Thinking about what?" they ask. And I'd reply, "About your beliefs, your values, or whatever else you would like to think about." I, of course, have no way of checking on whether they are following my recommendation, but on occasions students have come to my office telling me about the power of thinking. One student recently told me that since she started thinking every day, her way of reading had completely changed. Getting students to think and read critically is one of my primary goals in the classroom, and Plato's *Meno* has been my steady guide. Socrates' theory of recollection can teach students that they have the wherewithal to think for themselves and, thus, the opportunity to examine their values and beliefs. Teaching the *Meno* to a varied student population on different campuses over several years has taught me the importance of the mutual trust and respect necessary to foster philosophical thinking.

Teaching the *Meno*

Walking into the classroom with a heightened sense of purpose, I prepare to teach one of my favorite passages in philosophical literature, the theory of recollection from Plato's *Meno*. *Meno* is such a rich dialogue, incorporating themes, images, and arguments, which are often baffling to students. The dialogue begins abruptly. Meno, a wealthy Thessalian visiting Athens, puts to Socrates a direct question: "Can you tell me, Socrates, can virtue be taught? Or is it not teachable but the result of practice, or is it neither of these, but men possess it by nature or in some other way?"[1] Socrates immediately responds that they cannot investigate this question unless they determine what virtue is in the first place. Socrates already displays his characteristic irony, responding, "I myself, Meno, am as poor as my fellow citizens in this matter, and I blame myself for my complete ignorance about virtue" (71b). To this Meno answers that he in fact knows what virtue is because he has heard it defined by Gorgias, the famous sophist, to whom Meno would likely have paid good money to attend a lecture. Parroting his teacher, Meno instructs Socrates that "the virtue of a man . . . consists in being able to manage public affairs . . . [and] the virtue of a woman to . . . manage the home well . . . , and be submissive to her husband . . . ; the virtue of a child . . . is different again, and so is that of an elderly man . . . a free man or a slave" (71e). Doubling down on the irony, Socrates expresses astonishment; having spent a lifetime looking for an Athenian who knew what virtue is, in a single day he has now found two non-Athenians, Meno and Gorgias, who (claimed to) know. And he has encountered a definition, not of a single virtue but of a "swarm of virtues" (72a).

The opening discussion of the *Meno* is an extended exercise in philosophical definition, of virtue and of parallel cases. The section is interesting and very useful for beginning philosophy students, but the scene that really gets students' attention begins at 79e, when Meno vents his frustration and attacks Socrates for constantly undermining his definitions. He compares Socrates to a torpedo fish—ugly with bulging eyes, always stinging and numbing people—and he then asks a question that Socrates labels "eristical": "How will you aim to

---

1. Plato, *Meno*, trans. G. M. A. Grube (Indianapolis: Hackett, 1976), 70a.

search for something you do not know?" (80d). Socrates introduces the theory of recollection in response to Meno's challenge, claiming that it is better and more courageous to inquire into that which one does not know than to remain idle in one's ignorance, or worse, to think one knows when one does not. Imitating Meno, who thinks he knows virtue because he remembers what Gorgias said about it, Socrates claims he heard from wise priests and priestesses that the soul is immortal and knows all things. But unlike Meno, he offers to prove his claim.

On my reading, the importance of the *Meno* comes especially to light when we contrast the way Meno thinks he knows and how Socrates thinks we know. Socrates lays the foundation for the importance of thinking. The first half of the dialogue models different kinds of learning: Meno boasts of all the things he has learned, such as those sophistic "truths," making fun of Socrates for not remembering Gorgias' speech on the topic of virtue. Socrates makes it quite clear that remembering the words of others is not the same as knowing and understanding. Through his elenctic procedure, Socrates demonstrates that Meno does not know what virtue is. When the tyrannical Meno (76b) forces Socrates to define "shape," Socrates offers the mathematical definition of shape, and he earns praise from Meno, who appreciates it. In his first definition, Socrates defined shape as that "which always accompanies color" (75c), which Meno quickly dismisses as a bad definition, because Socrates had not defined color. Socrates then offers shape as "the limit of a solid" (76a), which Meno is willing to accept without questioning what Socrates means by "limit" or "solid." The reason for Meno's assent presumably has to do with his familiarity with this particular definition, having heard some important person propound this mathematical definition of shape. That this is Meno's predilection becomes especially clear when Socrates is forced also to define "color" and provides a bombastic definition in terms of "effluences," in response to which Meno is almost ecstatic. Socrates replies, "It is a theatrical answer so it pleases you" (76e).

I ask students which definitions they like, and I examine with them the extent to which we are all seduced into thinking that someone who uses high-falutin' or technical language is in the know. I identify Meno's style of learning with what Paulo Freire, in his

Pedagogy of the Oppressed, describes as the "banking" style of education, where the sage on the stage makes deposits of knowledge and wisdom into the student's empty mind.[2]

In contrast to the style of learning that relies on remembering what others have said, Socrates introduces his famous theory of recollection, which he then offers to demonstrate by having a slave try to solve the square root of eight geometrically. The students are always eager to prove that Socrates was leading the slave to the correct answer, that recollection does not work. I ask them whether the demonstration constructed by Socrates and the slave is correct and how they know whether it is correct or incorrect. Do they remember it from a previous math class? I then ask them to consider what they make of Socrates' choice of a slave and, particularly, an uneducated slave. The only requirements for the demonstration are that the person speak Greek and can count.

I ask my students how many of them would qualify, if all they needed were the right language and the ability to count. This is the point where many students recognize where we are heading, namely, to the realization that every single person in our room is equipped to do philosophy. Perhaps that's the point of using the slave, I propose, that is, we are all capable of doing philosophy, a universal opportunity rather than an aristocratic privilege. Many students find this message to be a liberating experience, especially those who have experienced prejudice and oppression and those who are confused about how to fit within the norms of society. As Socrates so admirably demonstrated throughout his life, compliance is not a virtue, but thinking may lead to the possibility of living a virtuous life.

The Examined Life and Its Responsibilities

In the college classrooms I have taught—no matter whether in public institutions with first-generation college students or private universities with privileged students—I begin with Socrates' famous assertion in the *Apology* that "the unexamined life is not worth living." Isn't just being alive a worthy thing? What is it that examination adds to life?

---

2. Paulo Freire, *Pedagogy of the Oppressed*, trans. Myra Bergman Ramos (1970; New York: Bloomsbury, 2017).

How does examination produce value? Some of the richest discussions about that question have arisen from my basic skills students, who were amazed at the possibility that they could be a source of value. As the theory of recollection invites us to think for ourselves, Socrates' exhortation to examine our lives reminds us of the responsibility that accompanies our ability to think.

As we wonder about the source of our values, I encourage students to examine whether their values are, in fact, *their* values. We "inherit" a set of values from our family and community, but before embracing those values we need to examine them to see whether they are consistent with one another, whether they contribute to the common good, and whether they provide us with the foundation to lead a good life, the promise of finding happiness. My challenge to my students is to come up with a set of values that make life worth living. Ultimately, my goal is to convince them that they are the authors of their own life stories and that philosophy provides them with the tools to compose those stories. Many students are willing to consider the possibility that they bear ultimate responsibility for their system of values and beliefs, but some are resentful when tasked to give an account of their reasoning for these values and beliefs.

Teaching philosophy is a risky business, because it can irk students to the point of their wanting to lash out at you, to punish you for making them uncomfortable. But having experienced too many positive outcomes, I take it to be a risk worth taking. I am willing to endure the severe rebuke that some students add to their anonymous teaching evaluations, because I know that the ones who benefitted from the course did so in an existential and possibly life-changing way. The most common criticism I receive is that I do not tell students exactly what I want them to do, which confuses them, because in many other classes compliance with the teacher's rule is almost a guarantee of a high grade. The other common complaint I receive is that I make them think too much and don't provide them with clear guidelines about my expectations. But I do. I tell them very explicitly that I expect them to think for themselves. One of my weekly assignments is to write before class discussion a "dialectical" journal that asks students to share their encounter with a passage from the text. Invariably, some student will ask how it will be possible for them to write about something prior to my teaching them the material. This response I take to be another good reason to begin an introductory course with the *Meno*.

Interrogate Everything

I take my teaching evaluations very seriously but, after reading Plato's *Gorgias*, I try to be mindful of the distinction between flattery and teaching. When Socrates examines with Polus how persuasion works, he wonders whether it would be easier for a physician who had prescribed bitter medicine or a pastry baker who offers sweets to persuade a jury of children. I joke with my colleagues that Socrates did not receive a standing ovation for his work, but rather the death penalty. Philosophy is not about pleasing students but making them aware of the responsibility to think for themselves, however painful that might be. I have been known to tell junior colleagues that if everyone in the class loves you, you are probably not doing your job.

In the *Theaetetus*, Socrates characterizes thinking as the soul having a dialogue with itself. Asking questions and attempting to arrive at answers to these queries can be an arduous process, but one that leads to the examined life. I want my students to take the time to think. Instead of accepting the so-called conventional wisdom, interrogate everything. That, I believe, is what a good philosophy class should convey. The importance of the theory of recollection in the *Meno* is a way of teaching students that they have the tools to ask those questions that unsettle our assumptions about "how things are." What gives me hope about the future of a field like philosophy, or the humanities in general, is that human beings seem to have a deep need to come up with new questions. "All human beings by nature desire to know," reads the first sentence of Aristotle's *Metaphysics*. It is the job of a philosophy class to nurture this desire.

I was so convinced that Plato's *Meno* was a powerful dialogue that when I was asked to prepare a mock-teaching class during a job interview years ago, I chose to present Socrates' theory of recollection. To my surprise, my "students" were faculty from various departments, many of whom had never before heard of the *Meno*. I taught them much like I did my previous students, and I could sense some excitement building in the classroom. Before long, they were all participating and debating vociferously the possibility of recollection.

The discussion among my "faculty-students" mirrored the discussion I had with my first-year students.

A Varied Life in Teaching

The colleges at which I have taught over thirty years have been as varied as the student bodies attending them. My first four years were spent as a teaching fellow at Hunter College, one campus in the sprawling City University of New York system. There were students there from every ethnic group and economic status; some students were very well prepared, others less so. For the next four years, I taught at a private college, financially threatened and ultimately closed. Many of those students enjoyed neither economic nor educational privilege, so the college had an extensive and successful basic skills program. After the college sadly shut its doors, I was employed at several universities, each distinguished and interesting in its own way. I taught students who were, for the most part, financially secure and from stronger educational backgrounds, but struggling with other forms of diversity. For each one of these different student populations, I had the pleasure of introducing them to the wonders of the *Meno*. In some cases, reading the *Meno* ultimately led students to add philosophy as a second major or even declare philosophy as their major.

The lessons I learned from my first public college position prepared me for all of my future teaching. Students there taught me that teaching is a collaborative effort, which only bears fruit in a climate of trust. More than other academic disciplines, philosophy requires trust, because we ask our students to examine themselves. Our primary vehicle is the text, but an honest reading of philosophical texts demands that students examine their own opinions and values, most of which they hold dear.

Plato explained in his *Seventh Letter* that he had never written philosophy, because philosophy only happens after intense study of the subject. In conversation with another person, a sudden spark flies and an insight is born in the soul. Something very close to this is what needs to happen in the classroom, and this requires that the classroom become a community where participants can freely engage in inquiry. But it also requires mutual respect—not the kind of respect that students often understand in lessons about "tolerance":

I respect your opinion if you respect my opinion; this is not the kind of respect that leads to the critical examination of ideas and texts. Rather, philosophy requires the kind of respect that follows when an interlocutor comes to view an opinion as the conclusion of a thought process of reason giving. Socrates repeatedly exhorts us to examine our opinions, so that we become aware of them and either defend or discard them, taking on this responsibility. This Kantian form of respect is rooted in an appreciation for human dignity—the ability to view someone else as the author of her own set of principles, each one of which is the upshot of a universally accessible argument.

Teaching at the small liberal arts college was especially satisfying. It was a school with many economically disenfranchised students needing basic skills courses, but also many well-prepared students, American and foreign. I treated the students who needed extra assistance like inquiring minds, rather than leaving them behind. All students enjoy the ability to evaluate arguments critically, to find flaws and bring them to an author's attention. But what was missing from basic skills courses was a way to train students to think critically about their own arguments or, even better, a way to train students to critically evaluate the values and behaviors they adopt. These lacunae were filled by the *Meno*. I developed an informal logic course called "Deception Detection." We studied informal fallacies and then read newspapers to search for political examples of flawed reasoning. The students rose to the occasion, to the point that I needed to warn them not to use their newfound skills at home or with friends. What I learned from my students during those years was the importance of meeting the students at their level rather than talking down to them. I learned that philosophical thinking is a tool that can be deployed on many different levels to meet the different needs of different students.

"License to Think." This motto is written on the back of the T-shirts that my department gives to all new majors and minors. It is a license granted free of charge—an authorization offered to an astonishing variety of people under an astonishing range of circumstances. This "license to think," broader and more flexible than mere vocational training, should be the aim of all education. It is most directly the objective of philosophical paideia.

II. Teaching the Students

3

Competing Visions

Maureen Eckert
University of Massachusetts, Dartmouth

MAUREEN ECKERT is associate professor and cochair of the Philosophy Department at University of Massachusetts, Dartmouth. She works in ancient Greek philosophy, metaphysics, David Foster Wallace studies, and philosophical logic. She is founder and codirector of PIKSI: Logic, a summer institute for diversity in the field of logic. She has won the Chancellor's Award Recognizing Excellence in Service and honorable mention for Innovation in Teaching and Learning with Technology. She has won student-nominated awards, the Walter Cass Recognition Award for Distinguished Service, and the "Breaking the Silence" Rainbow Recognition Award from the UMASS Dartmouth Pride Alliance.

The Perfect Class: A Professor's Perspective

The perfect course would resemble a seamless performance and run of a play: one that transforms the minds of all involved in inestimable ways. My preparation for the course establishes subtle connections between the texts I've chosen to assign and the new, creative assessments of student learning I've developed. I have utilized every resource available, all the latest classroom technology and course website features, yet the quality of the material and its organization shines forth first and foremost on account of these pedagogical tools.

Each lecture and assignment builds upon the former one, the importance of particular details and significance of larger issues in my discipline becoming increasingly clarified as the course progresses. Students are inspired to read the texts and utilize the course website to its maximum. As they work through the material and assignments, they experience personal epiphanies regarding the course material. I come to each class prepared to clarify the reading, and the minute I do so the students are unstoppable. Each and every one of them contributes. Their inspiration overflows into boisterous discussions filled with laughter as well as heated debate, revealing their understanding and appreciation of the material—even bringing to light new perspectives on it for me.

Attendance remains strong throughout the semester, leaving me shocked that it's a full classroom even before holidays. Students approach exams as a means to show off their mastery of the course materials. They are dissatisfied with grades under 90 percent, requesting more work to achieve even higher grades. In the perfect course, students spend time with their writing. Their assignments and papers reflect attentive readings and considerable revisions and editing. It is clear that students have not only read the material, they've reread it and have thought about it and rethought their thoughts. Students in the perfect course go beyond the minimum requirements and delve further to research the issues that matter the most to them. I am deeply supportive of their quests to determine the meaning of the material for themselves, helping them in every way I can. As the course proceeds, a spirit of community between the students and myself develops. We have undergone an intellectual odyssey, one that has covered more ground than any syllabus could accurately describe. When the perfect course is over, each student has delightfully and rightfully earned a grade of A. The perfect course will make me feel really good about everything.

The Perfect Class: A Student's Perspective

The perfect class would be just like watching a show on television that is really interesting and totally exciting every time it's on TV. I'll look forward to it, and I won't mind going to class (if I want to go). Each class will have very funny moments that make us all laugh out loud, with new things happening each time—things I can relate to. There will be lots of cool surprises, but I will always be able to follow what's happening no matter what.

The perfect class will relate to my life, and everything that the teacher says will make sense right away. I will know that I'm learning important things because of how I feel whenever class is over. It will feel like it was worth going to class. We students will get to talk a lot with each other in class, too, which is cool. A whole bunch of my friends will be in the perfect class, and we'll all be together. Being with my friends makes anything better. The teacher will be a cool person who really understands how things are. The perfect teacher will never make anyone feel bad about answering questions, and we will be able to talk normally, like we really do with each other, in the perfect class. The perfect teacher isn't all hung up about things like cell phones and texting.

I will never need to read things for the perfect class. The teacher will tell us everything we need to know that will be on the tests, and I won't even have to study, because just going to class is enough to get a good grade. I hate having to write things, so the perfect class will have writing assignments that I can copy off of websites and the teacher won't care (but, really, there shouldn't be any writing in the perfect class). The class website will be incredibly cool and all the notes for classes will be posted on it so you never even need to take a notebook to the perfect class. The teacher will help me with any problems I have, like, if I had to miss a lot of classes, the teacher will teach me whatever I missed—the teacher of the perfect class doesn't take attendance, anyway—but if I have any problems the perfect teacher totally cares. I really matter to the perfect teacher. When the perfect class is over, I will get an A. The perfect class will make me feel really good about everything.

Compromise and Transformation

Both of these visions are obstacles, and both, importantly, have to do with escaping the truly hard work. My vision of the perfect class requires truly outstanding students, students who don't need much teaching. I guide, mentor, and help them accomplish amazing things. But they arrive to my classroom as careful readers, clear writers, and original thinkers. It's the failing students who need me. When I stopped thinking of the outstanding students as the measure of my pedagogical success, I became a teacher.

I no longer accept either vision of the perfect class. I do the very best I can, teaching to the middles.

4

Learning to Teach

David W. Concepción
Ball State University

DAVID W. CONCEPCIÓN teaches feminist ethics, environmental ethics, and other courses at Ball State University. He uses team-based learning within writing-intensive experiential learning courses. He also uses service-learning, embodied pedagogy, specifications grading, and inclusive pedagogy. He has received all four of BSU's top teaching honors: the Lawhead Teaching Award, the Excellence in Teaching Award, the Outstanding Teaching Award, and the Immersive Learning Award. Additionally, he has earned Ball State's Diversity Advocate Award and Outstanding Service Award. National recognitions include the American Association of Philosophy Teachers' Lenssen Prize for research about the teaching of philosophy, the American Association of Philosophy Teachers' Award of Merit for Outstanding Leadership and Achievements in the Teaching of Philosophy, and the American Philosophical Association's Prize for Excellence and Innovation in Philosophy Programs. He leads workshops around the country to help other philosophy teachers innovate. His current research is focused on inclusive pedagogy.

I couldn't believe how badly he got clobbered. I don't remember his name, but his kick went straight back to the pitcher, who threw him out as he headed for first. That big red kickball hit him so hard that he looked like Charlie Brown when Lucy pulls away the football. But the runner wasn't down for the count. He got up and ran at the pitcher, flailing his arms in repeated botched attempts at throwing a punch. As they rolled around on the concrete, not able to really hurt each other, the teachers jumped in to break it up. It was at that moment in third grade, watching a fight being broken up from third base, that I decided I wanted to be a teacher. I'm no longer sure why this event crystallized into a desire to be a teacher, but I think it was because this incident allowed me to realize that teachers are most centrally people who help kids. I've wanted to be a teacher as long as I've had a thought about being anything, and I want to be good at it. By drawing a few distinctions and telling a few stories, this essay describes some of my attempts so far. Let's begin by distinguishing three partially overlapping types of teaching activities: (1) excellent teaching, (2) scholarly teaching, and (3) the scholarship of teaching and learning (SoTL).[1]

Excellent Teaching

To my way of thinking, an excellent teacher has three things in abundance: (a) teacher virtues, (b) pedagogical knowledge and skills, and (c) content expertise. Presumably, anyone with a Ph.D. has content expertise, so I won't say any more about it. A nonexhaustive list of teacher virtues includes (i) proper love of students, (ii) humility (I am but one voice and I am prone to error), (iii) antinarcissism (teaching is not about me), and (iv) empathy (the ability to see things from students' point of view). Most of what follows is about pedagogical knowledge and skills.

I think the measure of teaching excellence is how much students learn. Students do the learning; as Doyle is famous for saying, "The one who does the work does the learning."[2] As such, excellent teachers are those who design and execute a curriculum, a learning environment, learning activities, and assessment activities that motivate students to learn the maximal amount more than they would have learned in a for-credit setting without a teacher. The best teachers make the biggest difference relative to a context-rich baseline. Excellence is not correlated to the sum of absolute skills and knowledge possessed by students at the end of a course. If it were, then teachers who work with success-ready students would always be better teachers than those who work with students who aren't as success ready, and college teachers would necessarily be better teachers than

---

1. For more about this distinction, see the Society for Teaching and Learning in Higher Education, https://www.stlhe.ca/sotl/what-is-sotl; Kathleen McKinney, ed., *The Scholarship of Teaching and Learning in and across the Disciplines* (Bloomington: Indiana University Press, 2013).

2. Terry Doyle and Todd Zakrajsek, *The New Science of Learning: How to Learn in Harmony with Your Brain* (Sterling, VA: Stylus, 2013), 63.

second-grade teachers. And the truth is, some of our best teachers are working with younger, less success-ready students.

As an Early Teacher

To better midwife student growth, most less-experienced teachers need to enhance their pedagogical knowledge and skills. There is no single, correct combination of these, but without a goodly amount of both, true excellence as a teacher strikes me as out of reach. I tried to acquire pedagogical skills before I started teaching. The week prior to the first day of graduate school, the curriculum department of the university I attended offered a two-credit course (thirty-five contact hours) on instruction for incoming teaching assistants. Given how little I knew about teaching, I learned a lot. But I'm pretty sure a good deal of what happened in these sessions went over my head. During my first year in graduate school, I also visited the class of every faculty member and teaching assistant in my program (approximately thirty people) and spent hours talking with anyone in my department who would talk to me about teaching. While many of my colleagues were fine teachers, I learned more about what I wanted to avoid than what I wanted to do through these visits and conversations. I felt my extra work had well prepared me to teach my first solo class. But I was wrong.

First, my class was badly aligned. A course is aligned when the learning activities and grade-bearing assignments students complete move them in a coherent fashion to the growth that is targeted in the course learning objectives.[3] The learning objectives I consciously had for my students were about improving critical thinking and writing skills, but the learning activities my students performed were almost exclusively reading primary texts and listening to me talk.

---

3. For more on transparent alignment, see David W. Concepción, "Engaging Novices: Transparent Alignment, Flow, and Controlled Failure," in *Philosophy through Teaching*, eds. Emily Esch, Kevin Hermberg, and Rory E. Kraft, Jr. (Charlottesville, VA: Philosophy Documentation Center, 2014), 129–36; and David W. Concepción, "Transparent Alignment and Integrated Course Design," *Essays on Teaching Excellence* 21, no. 2 (2010), http://podnetwork.org/content/uploads/V21-N2-Concepcion.pdf. I learned the notion of transparent alignment from L. Dee Fink, *Creating Significant Learning Experiences: An Integrated Approach to Designing College Courses* (San Francisco: Jossey-Bass, 2003).

I gave multiple-choice and short-answer exams. Since I rarely asked students to evaluate the views in the texts, formulate arguments, or criticize those arguments, they did not intentionally pursue, much less achieve, growth in critical thinking. I hadn't yet realized that if you want someone to get better at something (e.g., critical thinking), that person needs to deliberately practice that thing (e.g., thinking critically). My students quickly figured out that the only thing they needed to do to get good grades was to accurately transcribe what I was saying in class, memorize the right portions of it, and accurately reproduce it at the prescribed time. The learning objective I actually pushed students toward was an improvement in rote memorization and regurgitation skills. Not only did the learning activities I designed not encourage students to achieve the critical thinking goals I espoused, they incentivized the achievement of goals that I consciously did not value.

Even worse and, in retrospect, predictably, early in the semester most students stopped reading. For one thing, I hadn't bothered to show them how to read as a philosopher, so they "got nothing out of the reading." Moreover, they didn't actually need to do the reading. I spent the entirety of most classes telling them what the article said. I didn't ask them to independently evaluate the texts. And I graded them only on accuracy of their reconstructions of discrete ideas. If they came to class and took good notes, there was nothing prudential to be gained by struggling with a text.

Second, I needed to overcome some vices. I had the vice of vanity. I wanted students to think I was cool. I don't mean that I wanted to build good rapport with students that would contribute to a productive learning environment. I wanted them to admire me, principally for social and not academic reasons. (Pathetic, right?) I was also "ruly."[4] Without student input, I constructed class rules that were for my benefit. These rules ensured that I could keep the number of hours I devoted to teaching as low as possible. I scheduled inconvenient office hours so that I would have time to study for the graduate classes I was taking. I created lots of rules and applied them pretty heartlessly. If a student had six absences or more, they

---

4. On the connection between being white and being ruly, see Marilyn Frye, "White Woman Feminist," in *Willful Virgin: Essays in Feminism, 1976–1992* (Freedom, CA: The Crossing Press, 1992), 147–69.

failed the class. One day a student who was hit by a van as he walked down a sidewalk wobbled into class on crutches and narcotics with two thigh-high casts. After missing many days of class because he was in the hospital, he felt he had to attend class to avoid failing. He fell asleep and remained that way for the entire class session. I told myself that justice required uniform and exceptionless application of the rules.

Third, and worst of all, I adopted a self-serving explanation for why my students weren't learning much. I gleefully "bashed" my students with fellow teaching assistants.[5] "These students don't know how to think; they are so lazy; they won't do the reading," we would say, patting ourselves on the back for being better than them. Obviously, student bashing is shameful. But, even worse, it disempowers teachers. If it were true that students "can't or won't do x," teaching would be a waste of time—a fool's errand. Now, when I hear a "my students won't do x" comment in the faculty development seminars I lead, I insist, as gently as I can, that the person who said it repeat after me: "What I mean is, I have not *yet* figured out how to motivate students to do x."[6] The understandable desire to preserve a positive self-concept by locating the cause of a failure in something one believes one cannot change, as when one falsely comes to believe that students' desire to learn is not influenced by teacher actions, needs to be resisted because such indulgent self-protection unacceptably reduces the likelihood of students learning.[7]

Even as an early career teacher, I did some things well. I delivered decent lectures, taught at the right pace, used "real-life" examples and provided clear review sessions and study guides before exams. I

---

5. John H. Gottcent, "On the Time-Honored Practice of Student Bashing," *The National Teaching & Learning Forum* 8, no. 3 (1999), http://onlinelibrary.wiley.com/doi/10.1002/ntlf.1999.8.issue-3/issuetoc.

6. Alternatively, sometimes it turns out "students don't x" is fine because x is not something one is actually trying to teach. In that case, the thing to repeat is "I have self-consciously decided that there are better things for students to learn than x, so I'm going to stop saying that I'm trying to get students to x. I should revise my syllabus."

7. It is also worth remembering that I also didn't have enough content expertise as a second-year graduate student. I couldn't anticipate which bits of information were particularly puzzling to first-year students, and, as such, I didn't develop learning activities to help students work through tough moments.

was humorous, friendly, approachable, enthusiastic, and respectful. But the basic designs of my courses were fundamentally flawed; my actual (as opposed to my espoused) learning objectives—memorization and regurgitation—were shallow, and I didn't offer any "how-to" instruction to help my students improve their critical thinking and writing skills. What's worse, I didn't love my students enough. I was pretty narcissistic, and I had very little empathy.

Developing Teacher Virtues: An Example

To become a better teacher, I needed to habituate into a better person, one who is more loving and empathetic and less narcissistic. An emphasis on virtues does not support the false notion that great teaching is a matter of personality or showmanship. Virtue is a damn sight from showmanship. Nor does it contradict the view that good teaching is something one can learn. It is simply to note the activating power of love and empathy, which are dispositions that one can grow. Servant-leaders who robustly understand and care for those whom they serve are far more likely to have a big impact than those whose service is mostly lip.

Consider an exercise regarding hospitableness that I use when leading faculty development seminars. Imagine that you are in a culture that is far enough from the one you usually occupy that you do not know how to succeed in it. I discourage (but don't prohibit) people from reflecting on an instance of international travel, because I prefer that participants focus on subtler cultural differences that are nearer to, and more permanent in, their lives than the differences experienced on vacation. In this not-home cultural space, you have a host. Write down ten things your host could do with or for you to help you manage and ultimately flourish. (I invite readers to pause here and do this exercise before reading further.)

Participants' answers vary considerably, but there are themes: make sure the guest's basic needs are met (e.g., show them where the bathroom is); introduce the guest to locals; inform the guest about the local customs/rules, especially the idiosyncratic ones; and, finally, don't just tell but show the guest how to do the things they're supposed to do in the setting. Our courses embody arcane folkways, both academic and cultural, with which there is no reason for most of our students to be familiar. We each host our own preferred expression of philosophical culture, a culture that is not the home culture of most students. This thought experiment offers a moment of empathy building—of putting ourselves in our students' shoes.

I think my early journey is instructive, if not typical. I had very little awareness of research-verified best practices or the science of learning. I attempted to innovate via trial and error, schooled by informal conversations with experienced teachers (who also knew nothing about the science of learning). Their wisdom proved useful with regard to teaching basics (e.g., how to write a syllabus) and avoiding disasters. But these modes of improvement didn't generate teaching excellence. I hoped someone would give me a magic class participation policy, one that would make students engage more in class. But what I really needed was a lesson about how to connect preclass preparation with low-stakes, active, in-class tasks. I wanted to know how many pages to assign or which articles to change to so that students would do the reading. But what I really needed was to learn how to show my students how to read philosophy.[8] I didn't need the tips I could get from well-meaning but uninformed colleagues. I needed to study teaching and learning. I needed to learn, among so many things, the science of motivation[9] and how to construct essential questions.[10] My initial improvement strategy—trial and error and informal mentoring from colleagues who had experience but no expertise in teaching and learning—was not getting enough results. I needed to become a scholarly teacher.

---

8. David W. Concepción, "Reading Philosophy with Background Knowledge and Metacognition," *Teaching Philosophy* 27, no. 4 (2004):351–68.

9. Susan Ambrose et al., *How Learning Works* (San Francisco: Jossey-Bass, 2010), especially chap. 3, "What Factors Motivate Students to Learn?"; Paul Green, "How to Motivate Students: A Primer for Learner-Centered Teachers," *AAPT Studies in Pedagogy* 1 (2015):47–60.

10. Jay McTighe and Grant Wiggins, *Essential Questions: Opening Doors to Student Understanding* (Alexandria, VA: Association for Supervision and Curriculum Development, 2013); Jim Sibley, "Seven Mistakes to Avoid When Writing Multiple-Choice Questions," *Faculty Focus*, October 6, 2014, https://www.facultyfocus.com /articles/educational-assessment/seven-mistakes-avoid-writing-multiple-choice -questions; Jeri L. Little, Elizabeth Ligon Bjork, Robert A. Bjork, and Genna Angello, "Multiple-Choice Tests Exonerated, at Least of Some Charges: Fostering Test-Induced Learning and Avoiding Test-Induced Forgetting," *Psychological Science* 23, no. 11 (2012):1337–44.

Scholarly Teaching

Scholarly teachers are people who study research on teaching and learning and deploy what is learned in their courses.[11] All of the great teachers I know are scholarly. The reason for this is obvious enough. Scholarly teachers acquire pedagogical knowledge and skills far more efficiently and effectively than nonscholarly teachers.

My first real foray into scholarly teaching came from the five summers I spent during graduate school teaching at Johns Hopkins University's Center for Talented Youth (CTY) summer program.[12] In CTY, one teaches one three-week course to seventh through eleventh graders who have tested in the top 2 percent on a standardized test. There are seven contact hours per day and five contact days per week. Before I began to design a new bioethics course, my CTY mentor advised: "Don't ever lecture for more than fifteen minutes at a time, and try to not lecture at all. These students will do the reading. Give them something to do that will advance their thinking." I was initially terrified by this edict, and at a loss for what to do with seven hours. I learned that designing and implementing high-impact learning activities is a much more important part of being a good teacher than are the skills associated with cogent lecturing.[13] I came to define "teacher" as a person who uses their content expertise to design experiences that help people grow. I was starting to remember what I knew as a third grader: teachers are people who help "kids." Eventually, this notion evolved into what I now describe as learner-centered teaching. A teacher is learner centered when they ask themselves regularly, What does each student in my class need me to do, to do with them, or to ask them to do, so that they can learn as much as possible today?

As far as I know, there is no science that supports an absolute rule against lecturing for more than fifteen minutes at a time. The amount of new information a person can meaningfully make use of in one sitting is, in part, a function of how expert that person

---

11. Some good places to start growing pedagogical knowledge and skills are https://www.teachphilosophy101.org, http://www.apaonline.org/group/teaching, and https://philosophyteachers.org.

12. http://cty.jhu.edu.

13. For more on high-impact learning activities, see https://www.aacu.org/leap/hips.

is regarding the topic. Whether a talk is dense or sparse matters. Whether the lecture is an initial overview or a march through details matters. However, as a rule of thumb, it is true that long lectures don't maximize learning, especially when listening to lectures is the exclusive or dominant student activity in a course.[14] CTY's insistence that I design activities and not lecture (much) prompted a fundamental change in how I teach. It also was the first time I adjusted my teaching on the basis of what research says. When I returned to the college classroom with a new activity-based course, the increase in student learning compared to my earlier courses was tremendous. Since then I understand the primary teacher role to be learner-centered activity designer. Again, those who do the work do the learning, and the teacher's job is to make sure that students are doing the right work in the right order.

Unfortunately, it would be years before I would acquire a second, paradigm-changing insight. One day midway through graduate school, a well-meaning professor told me that the faculty had just finished their review of the graduate students to determine who would receive teaching assistantships in the upcoming year. Exposing what I take to be a harmful belief that dominated (and still dominates?) graduate programs, he confidentially advised me to do something to *lower* my student evaluations because the faculty interpreted students' satisfaction with my courses as evidence that I wasn't spending enough time on research. I like to tell myself that my reaction was "Finances and future recommendation letters be damned, I'm going to teach as best I can," but that wouldn't be true. While I don't think my teaching got any worse, I did stop trying to get better, and I began a years-long dissembling, talking only about philosophy books when interacting with professors. I hope against hope that current graduate students who aspire to be excellent teachers no longer have to adopt such postures.

After my Ph.D. graduation, I got really lucky. During my first semester on the tenure track, a senior professor pursuing a multiyear, Lumina Foundation–funded project to improve the retention of at-risk students through their sophomore year of college invited me to

---

14. John T. Bruer, *Schools for Thought: A Science for Learning in the Classroom* (Cambridge: MIT Press, 1994).

join his group.[15] I was working with some of my institution's best teachers and was funded during the summers of my first three years to pursue research on teaching at a university that was just updating its promotion and tenure documents to require all review committees to count research on teaching as no less meritorious than traditional subdisciplinary research. I read and discussed a good deal of teaching and learning literature with engaged colleagues.[16] We vetted ideas for pedagogical innovations with each other. I had somehow fallen into a job that was perfect for me.[17]

My teaching changed tremendously during these years. There isn't space here to describe much of what I learned, but here is one example. I redesigned my courses to better serve intermediate learners with interleaved and concurrent assignments. Folks who have more or less no experience with something best acquire initial insights by solving well-defined problems in highly structured sequences of learning activities, where relative mastery of one small thing is acquired before moving on to the next bit of learning.[18] As one gains familiarity with a skill or content domain, "interleaved" experiences often best engender efficient learning.[19] Whereas sequential

---

15. https://www.luminafoundation.org.

16. Among the works that have had an enduring impact on me that are not mentioned in other footnotes are Grant Wiggins and Jay McTighe, *Understanding by Design: Professional Development Workbook* (Alexandria, VA: Association for Supervision and Curriculum Development, 2004); Jeanine Weekes Schroer, "Fighting Imperviousness with Vulnerability: Teaching in a Climate of Conservatism," *Teaching Philosophy* 30, no. 2 (2007):185–200; Uri Treisman, "Studying Students Studying Calculus: A Look at the Lives of Minority Mathematics Students in College," *The College Mathematics Journal* 23, no. 5 (1992):362–72; Maryellen Weimer, *Learner-Centered Teaching: Five Key Changes to Practice* (San Francisco: Jossey-Bass, 2002); James E. Zull, *The Art of Changing the Brain: Enriching the Practice of Teaching by Exploring the Biology of Learning* (Sterling, VA: Stylus, 2002); and everything Craig E. Nelson has ever written about teaching, https://indiana.academia.edu/CraigENelson.

17. Thank you again to my mentor on the Lumina Project, Paul Ranieri, and the department chair and mentor who always supported my career choices, Juli Thorson. I can't imagine what my life would be like had they not helped me.

18. John Bransford et al., *How People Learn* (Washington, DC: National Academy Press, 2000), especially chap. 2, "How Experts Differ from Novices."

19. James Lang, *Small Teaching: Everyday Lessons from the Science of Learning* (San Francisco: Jossey-Bass, 2016), 74–84.

learning "involves practicing one skill at a time before the next (for example, 'skill A' before 'skill B' and so on, forming the pattern 'AAABBBCCC'), in interleaving one mixes, or interleaves, practice on several related skills together (forming, for example, the pattern 'ABCABCABC')."[20] Experts and near-experts learn best when presented with ill-defined problems that require concurrent use of their expertise. Experts do A, B, and C simultaneously to move toward D. For example, beginning swimmers are shown how to get into the water, then how to blow bubbles, and so on. Expert swimmers might be instructed to increase the power from their left leg as they kick while doing all the other things one does to do the breaststroke.

If one knows that interleaving increases the rate of cognitive skill improvement among nonnovices, one will stop demanding complete mastery of a first step before allowing nonnovice students to attempt the second step or even a series of connected steps. At a college with talented students, interleaving work on reading comprehension skills, logical analysis skills, and term paper writing skills at the beginning of an introduction to philosophy course may be best. In schools where the average first-year student is a true novice, some sequential learning is probably best at first. But even in such schools, second-year students should be ready for interleaved learning regimes. Courses with purely blocked and sequential learning activities in later core curriculum courses, and especially in upper-level major courses, should be redesigned.

Two years into the tenure track, I got lucky again. I attended the biennial conference of the American Association of Philosophy Teachers (AAPT) conference. Anyone looking to up their scholarly teaching game could do no better than participate in AAPT events.[21] As great as the sessions were, they weren't the highlight of this conference for me. At some point, I was waiting in a hallway awkwardly and aimlessly shuffling papers, because I knew no one and was sitting in a public place where everyone else seemed to know each other. Apparently noticing my discomfort, a long-time AAPT member introduced herself and invited me to dinner with a bunch of AAPT conference regulars. I cannot overstate how welcoming and

---

20. https://www.scientificamerican.com/article/the-interleaving-effect-mixing-it -up-boosts-learning.

21. For more about AAPT events, see https://philosophyteachers.org.

enthusiastic these people were and are. Finding a professional community that supports teaching enthusiasts was and continues to be crucial to my growth. The larger philosophical community's (implicit, and even sometimes explicit) disdain for matters pedagogical often makes "teaching-first" philosophers feel like outlaws. We need the place of repair that the AAPT provides. But the AAPT goes well beyond repair. The AAPT is inspirational.

Again, I think my journey is instructive if not typical. It wasn't until I discovered and began to pursue scholarly teaching with communities of scholarly teachers that my teaching began to improve at a significant pace. The real reason to become a scholarly teacher is that you will be better able to help the "kids." But let's not forget that students love good teachers. It's a joy to enter a room of happy people who can't wait to interact with you. If you need a prudential reason to become a more scholarly teacher, it is this: your life will have more happiness in it if your teaching is scholarly.

The Scholarship of Teaching and Learning

A scholar of teaching and learning, or SoTL practitioner, is someone who produces their own original research on teaching or learning. Teachers who have spent quite some time developing teaching innovations by studying teaching and learning should share their hard-won insights. The community of philosophy teachers will benefit and the teaching of philosophy will be improved. The process of carefully writing up an important insight is also likely to sharpen one's own understanding of an issue.[22] Finally, a SoTL research agenda can make it easier to secure helpful external funds that might otherwise be out of reach for a philosopher.[23]

---

22. A caution: it may be unwise to spend the time necessary to publish a SoTL article at institutions that will not value such work. It can be imprudent for untenured, tenure-track faculty to pursue SoTL projects when doing so interrupts the development of a coherent and regularly productive non-SoTL research agenda, even at institutions that value SoTL.

23. Among others, the following offer grants for philosophy teaching projects: http://www.teaglefoundation.org/Home, http://squirefoundation.org, https://www.luminafoundation.org, http://www.whiting.org, http://www.bttop.org, https://compact.org, http://lillyendowment.org, https://www.neh.gov, and http://www.spencer.org/what-we-fund.

There are many outlets and many styles of SoTL that are appropriate for philosophers.[24] It is a myth that the SoTL requires the application of social science methodologies. A lack of expertise in deriving p-values from Z, deriving chi square or Pearson (r) values, or even developing Likert scale questions or conducting pre-post comparisons is not a reason to eschew SoTL. What is required for good SoTL is a rigorous and insightful application of a research methodology. Among philosophical methodologies are logical analysis, conceptual clarification, hermeneutical critique, and historical contextualization and repositioning. A quick glance at the journal *Teaching Philosophy* confirms that philosophers can produce high-quality SoTL without becoming or befriending a social scientist.[25] The requirement of an application of a research methodology does mean that a "here's-a-thing-I-do-that-I-think-works" report—that is, a list of teaching tips—is typically not very good SoTL.[26]

I encourage two practices for folks moving toward SoTL publication. First, keep student learning paramount. In most cases, one should move to manuscript preparation regarding a new idea

---

24. Philosophy-specific teaching journals include *AAPT Studies in Pedagogy* (https://aaptstudies.org), *Teaching Ethics* (https://www.pdcnet.org/tej), *APA Newsletter on Teaching Philosophy* (http://www.apaonline.org/?teaching_newsletter), and *Analytic Teaching and Philosophical Praxis* (http://journal.viterbo.edu/index.php/atpp). For a list of general SoTL outlets appropriate for philosophers, see the International Society for the Scholarship of Teaching and Learning, http://www.issotl.com/issotl15/node/21. A few samples of excellent SoTL papers by philosophers who use different methodologies are Daryl Close, "Fair Grades," *Teaching Philosophy* 32, no. 4 (2009):361–98; Matt Whitt, "Other People's Problems: Student Distancing, Epistemic Responsibility, and Injustice," *Studies in Philosophy of Education* 35, no. 5 (2016):427–44; John Rudisill, "The Transition from Studying Philosophy to Doing Philosophy," *Teaching Philosophy* 34, no. 3 (2011):241–71; Ann J. Cahill and Stephen Bloch-Schulman, "Argumentation Step-by-Step: Learning Critical Thinking though Deliberative Practice," *Teaching Philosophy* 35, no. 1 (2012):41–62; Kate Padgett Walsh, Anastasia Prokos, and Sharon R. Bird, "Building a Better Term Paper: Integrating Scaffolded Writing and Peer Review," *Teaching Philosophy* 37, no. 4 (2014):481–97.

25. *Teaching Philosophy*, https://www.pdcnet.org/teachphil. Of course, there are many social scientists worth befriending for other reasons.

26. It is worth noting for folks considering publishing on teaching in non–philosophy-specific journals, nonphilosophers usually really appreciate philosophers' conceptual and definitional clarification abilities.

discovered in part by reading the teaching and learning literature only after refining it through the crucible of multiple implementations in real classes. Second, before asking colleagues to give you comments on a draft, run it by your current students. Review from students is an underused and very valuable resource when developing high-quality SoTL work.

Conclusion

It has been tough to write this essay. It feels self-indulgent, and I feel overexposed. The editors assure me that narratives full of concrete details can be insightful and inspiring. I hope so. In reading about my trajectory, I hope readers are motivated to increase the scholarliness of their teaching. My road to better teaching and SoTL publishing has been nurtured by decades in the classroom, thousands of students, hundreds of interesting journal articles and book chapters, supportive AAPT colleagues, and many teaching-first scholars from outside of philosophy. I hope that many people will share the insights they developed by studying teaching and testing innovations in the classroom. But more than anything, I hope we all continue to grow as learner-centered activities designers who love students. If we do, our service to students will be more than lip and we'll really be helping the kids.

5

Meeting Students Where They Are

Paul Hurley
Claremont McKenna College

PAUL HURLEY taught courses in ethics, political philosophy, and the philosophy of law while working toward his Ph.D. at the University of Pittsburgh in 1988. He then taught for seventeen years at Pomona College and has occupied the Sexton Professorship in Philosophy at Claremont McKenna College (CMC) from 2006 until the present. He was awarded the Apple for the Teacher Award at Pittsburgh, was a three-time winner of the Wig Distinguished Teaching Award at Pomona College, and has been awarded both the Glenn Huntoon Teaching Award and the David Huntoon Senior Teaching award during his time at CMC. He has developed philosophy courses for inclusion in Philosophy, Politics, and Economic (PPE) Programs at both Pomona and CMC. He has overseen the doubling in size of CMC's PPE Program and offers tutorial courses as an integral component of this innovative PPE curriculum.

Undergraduates typically show up at our academic institutions already convinced that study in disciplines such as economics and computer science is important. Although the study of philosophy has comparable importance and enormous practical relevance for their lives, many students arrive profoundly skeptical of such claims, and many are not converted by their first (and often last) encounter with philosophy. To convey the importance and practical relevance of philosophy and motivate students to embrace what it has to offer, I have found it invaluable to craft courses designed to meet them where they are. I will say something shortly to vindicate these claims about the importance and tremendous practical relevance of philosophy for our students, but I will do so by way of reflections about what is involved in meeting them where they are—lessons that I have learned the hard way.

I came to Pomona College straight from the Ph.D. program at Pittsburgh and proceeded to teach ethical theory in what seemed to me to be the obvious way. This was the standard approach at Pitt, an approach that seemed to be effective with students there, and one that I was confident, at the time, was dictated by the material. I first taught normative ethics—consequentialist, contractarian, Kantian, and virtue ethical theories of right and wrong action—then moved to metaethics—theories about what it is to call an action right or wrong, whether there are moral facts, and whether moral claims are relativized to particular groups.

The course was pretty much a catastrophe. The initial material in normative ethics failed to engage a large portion of the class. Many of my Pomona students were not interested in studying theories of right and wrong, because they arrived to my class antecedently convinced that there are no facts (or even quasifacts) about rightness and wrongness. Value is a realm of opinion, not fact. We should each recognize that our opinion is but one among others, and this insight should lead us to tolerance of the opinions of others, which are no more correct or incorrect than our own—merely different. Others held that appeals to value are just rationalizations offered by those in power, and that we are better served dismissing the rationalizations and focusing on the dynamics of power. Still others held that who we are is more or less entirely a function of the society that forms us; hence, what any person values is entirely a function of what her society conditions her to value. There is no objective standpoint from which to coherently ask whether we, or any other group, are right to value what we do.

My point in introducing these metaethical positions is not to criticize them. Each, in the naïve form I have sketched, is pretty clearly implausible, but there are more sophisticated forms that merit serious scrutiny. The point, instead, is that many of my students arrived embracing a metaethics upon which normative ethics is, at worst, confused and a waste of time and, at best, an exercise in making local cultural norms explicit. They could learn the material in normative ethics, but it seemed to many of them pointless and wrongheaded, like being taught phlogiston theory in the twenty-first century. By the time we got to the metaethics, and some of them encountered arguments for taking normative ethics more seriously, the normative ethics ship had sailed, and many were already disengaged from the course. My course failed spectacularly to engage many of these students where they were and, hence, failed to convey the importance and relevance of the material.

My response going forward was two-pronged. First, I flipped the material around, addressing the metaethics first. Second, I took pains to address the particular metaethical commitments with which many of the students entered the course, demonstrating that, in their simplistic forms, such positions, in many cases, were internally incoherent and, in other cases, were difficult to square with competing commitments they held. For example, we worked through arguments by Bernard Williams, David McNaughton, and others[1] challenging the assumption that relegating morality to the realm of opinion dictates tolerance. If intolerant opinions are no more correct or incorrect than my own, why doesn't this bolster the case *against* rather than *for* tolerance? Many of these students came to recognize that they believed that intolerant positions are mistaken, and that holding them can be wrong. Concrete examples often proved invaluable. Pomona had recently adopted a policy banning offensive posters; the criterion for a determination of offensiveness was that someone in the community took offense at what was depicted. This was cited by many students as a demonstration of equal respect for all opinions. But when it was pointed out that homophobes and racists take offense at depictions of men holding hands and of interracial couples, these same students were clear that such opinions should not provide grounds for banning anything—that someone taking offense was not, after all, sufficient ground for a judgment of offensiveness. Something more was necessary, and a role for normative ethics came into view.

Similarly, students who held that there was no objectivity, just power, often held that the absence of objectivity ensured the illegitimacy of the exercise of power by those in power. But they came to realize that if there is no legitimacy to the exercise of power, then any basis for a claim of illegitimate exercise is called into question. If the moral truth that is spoken to those in power is that there is no moral truth, only power, it becomes puzzling why those in power would

---

1. See, for example, Bernard Williams, *Morality* (Cambridge: Cambridge University Press, 1972), 20–25; David McNaughton, *Moral Vision* (Oxford: Blackwell, 1988), 10–13.

have any reason to relinquish or share it, or what kind of claim there could be to compel them to do so. Many of these students became open to the idea that there are ways in which power can be exercised that are more or less legitimate, and that the study of what is and is not a legitimate exercise of power is in fact of great import. Again, a crucial role for normative ethics came into view. A related point can be made concerning the claim that our values are entirely socially situated and, hence, that there is no objective vantage point from which to evaluate our practices. The students in question believed that some ways of socially situating selves, for example, racist, sexist, and radically inegalitarian ways, were simply wrong, and that there are better norms for structuring interactions among persons within such societies, including their own society. Such judgments, however, seem to presuppose precisely the objective value judgments that they were initially inclined to reject as confused or fictitious.[2]

Some of these students responded by further developing their original metaethical views. Others responded to the initial inconsistencies and contradictions in their positions by significantly altering them. Almost all of the students, however, were engaged, and not just with the metaethics, but with the normative ethics that followed. My new approach demonstrated the importance of this inquiry to their beliefs and convictions, revealed deep inconsistencies and internal tensions, and provided them with the tools to develop a more comprehensive, coherent set of commitments with deeper foundations.

These Pomona students often came into my classes steeped in Continental philosophy, so I incorporated into my course philosophers from the Continental tradition, such as Friedrich Nietzsche, Richard Rorty, Michel Foucault, Jurgen Habermas, Jean-Paul Sartre, Catherine MacKinnon, and Alasdair MacIntyre. Approaching the relevant questions in a way that incorporated arguments by authors with whom they were familiar also helped engage these students where they were and, hence, with the central issues of the course.

After seventeen years at Pomona College, I moved to Claremont McKenna College, another elite liberal arts college located a mere 300 yards away. I had taught many CMC students in my Pomona

---

2. Jean Hampton makes this point nicely in her "Feminist Contractarianism," in *A Mind of One's Own*, eds. L. Antony and C. Witt (Boulder, CO: Westview Press, 2002), 227–55.

classes (the two schools are members of a consortium), and took it for granted that the approach I had honed and refined at Pomona would work just as well at an institution similar in so many respects. I was wrong.

The majority of CMC students are economics, government, and organizational psychology majors. Virtually all CMC students take economics and American government during their freshman year. These students tend to be much more focused on the social sciences: economics, public policy, and international affairs. The many CMC students whom I had taught previously, I quickly came to realize, were those drawn toward the very different focus of classes at Pomona. They were not at all representative of the CMC student body. The metaethics-first, Continental, challenges-of-postmodernism-oriented ethical theory course that had engaged Pomona students so effectively fell completely flat with most of my new CMC students. They arrived to my classroom steeped in the theory of rational choice. Rational agents are, or are properly modeled as, self-interested utility maximizers. Egoism is a central challenge for such students. Why should I be moral, particularly when rational choice theory seems to tell me that moral action, whenever it conflicts with self-interest, is irrational? Many allow that morality might be relevant to private interactions among friends and family, but it has no place in the markets in which we spend much of our lives or in the international arena, in which the Hobbesian methodology of political realism is appropriate.

Some CMC students are happy to grant that there is a straightforward answer to what morality requires: just as rational action maximizes our own preferences, moral action maximizes the preferences of everyone overall. But implicit in this approach is the contingency of the grounds for moral action. If what maximizes my preferences does not align with what maximizes overall preference satisfaction, it is irrational to act morally. And because our preferences tend, on the CMC students' view, to be focused upon our own benefit, such an approach appears to suggest that morality and rationality often do not align. In addition, many of these students take the normative problems they recognize to be self-explanatory, and the solutions to be straightforwardly empirical: we don't need philosophy to tell us that poverty is bad and that we have obligations to facilitate the development of the extreme poor. And once we have secured that point, they suggest, the rest is economics. Development is measured by per capita GDP, and the means to fostering development are just the means revealed by social science for raising per capita GDP.

Many of those who do appeal to fundamental moral principles tend to take a more libertarian interpretation of rights, liberties, and duties. For them, morality, including political morality, consists primarily of perfect duties not to violate the claims of others and rights not to have one's own claims violated. You have a duty not to transgress my boundaries, and I have a duty not to transgress yours. Anything more extensive than such minimal duties falls within the realm of the supererogatory—beyond the scope of what's required.

My Pomona ethical theory course failed to engage these students. To many of them, it appealed to outmoded accounts of what reason is and what persons are, accounts that have been superseded by research in economics and organizational psychology. By the point in that first semester that I fully appreciated the magnitude of the problem, it was very difficult to do much about it. Clearly, I had made the same mistake all over again, failing to engage my students where they were, hence failing to demonstrate the importance and relevance of philosophy to them. But at least I knew the appropriate response. I restructured the course, leading off with texts that addressed their widely held convictions. In response to the conviction that rationality is maximization of self-interest, and that self-interested action optimizes interaction in the market, I now introduce arguments by Adam Smith, David Gauthier, or Derek Parfit suggesting that straightforwardly self-interested motivation does not even work within the market sphere; indeed, that it is collectively self-defeating.[3] At the same time, I draw upon work by Simon Blackburn, Amartya Sen, Elizabeth Anderson, and Susan Wolf[4] challenging the plausibility of the identification of reason with self-interest, and exposing certain

---

3. See, for example, Adam Smith, *The Theory of Moral Sentiments* (Mineola, NY: Dover, 2006); David Gauthier, "Bargaining Our Way into Morality: A Do-It-Yourself Primer," *Philosophic Exchange* 2, no. 5 (1979):14–27; Derek Parfit, *On What Matters, Volume One* (Oxford: Oxford University Press, 2011).

4. Simon Blackburn, *Ruling Passions* (Oxford: Clarendon Press, 1998); Amartya Sen, *On Ethics and Economics* (Oxford: Blackwell, 1987); Elizabeth Anderson, "Unstrapping the Straightjacket of Preference," *Economics and Philosophy* 17 (2001):

conflations, for example between maximizing utility and maximizing my utility, that can lend an unwarranted veneer of plausibility to such an identification.

In response to the assumption that our moral goals are obvious and the means to achieve them are a question entirely of empirical inquiry, I draw upon authors such as Sen and Martha Nussbaum,[5] who make explicit what is otherwise merely implicit in the case of development—that it is an essentially normative undertaking of helping to make things better for people. This allows students to see that it is a complex normative question whether achieving some particular empirical goal, for example raising per capita GDP, makes a group of people better. What if the steps involved in increasing per capita GDP also increase the poverty rate, political corruption, and oppression of minority groups? Such an outcome would appear to be regression, not development, and such examples demonstrate that serious normative ethical inquiry is necessary for effective development.

In response to deep-seated convictions that rights and freedom are self-evidently libertarian, I introduce arguments that also appeal centrally to freedom, but take freedom to dictate not only perfect duties not to interfere, but also imperfect duties to help others and obligations to address norms that constrain the choices of groups of individuals. Such alternatives suggest that a young man and a young woman earning the same salary are not equally free, if the former has the option of being safe and having disposable income, while the latter must choose, in a culture rife with violence against women, which one to trade off for the other. They suggest that equal political freedom is lacking if the closest voter registration site for you is two counties away, while mine is around the corner, and if it takes hours on a work day for you to vote in your precinct, but only minutes for me in mine. The point is not to advocate for any particular account of freedom, but to demonstrate that freedom is not a self-interpreting concept and, in particular, that even for a traditional

---

21–38; Susan Wolf, *Meaning in Life* (Princeton, NJ: Princeton University Press, 2010).

5. Amartya Sen, *Development as Freedom* (New York: Anchor, 1999); Martha Nussbaum, *Frontiers of Justice* (Cambridge, MA: Belknap Press of Harvard University Press, 2007).

libertarian, the absence of constraint is not liberty, but license. To see the point of reflecting on what freedom, properly understood, permits and requires is to be motivated to do normative ethics, and to see the practical relevance of doing so for one's life.

In response to views that reason determines what is best for me, while morality determines what is best overall, and that the two often fail to align, I incorporate texts that help make explicit the implicit commitments that many of these students have to the overriding rational authority of moral requirements. These students come to recognize that they both believe that moral requirements are rationally authoritative and presuppose a theoretical framework upon which they seemingly are not. They confront a deep and problematic tension in their commitments and recognize the need to explore this tension through further inquiry.

Again, the point is not to undermine the students' initial views, and many do respond by developing more sophisticated versions of libertarian deontology and of psychological and normative egoism. The point is to confront students with apparent inconsistencies in their own fundamental commitments, to expose normatively loaded commitments that they unreflectively accept as merely empirical and normatively neutral, and to make explicit methodological fissures in their approach to issues of vital importance to them. Confronted with these tensions, they often come to see the importance for their grounds for action and their beliefs of doing normative and meta-ethics, and the importance of bringing the resulting insights to bear in their practical deliberations and decision making.

My previous remarks have focused upon different strategies of engagement appropriate to different student bodies. But another element is engagement with different constituencies within a student body. Half of our students at CMC are women, 35 percent are non-white, approximately 20 percent are from other countries, 30 percent are heterosexual white males, and we have a significant number of LGBT students. Most of our students come from wealthy and highly educated families, but 15 percent are first-generation college students. These differences reflect differences in experiences, interests, and concerns, many of them with profound ethical implications. Courses designed to draw upon the richness of these differing experiences and to make explicit these different concerns engage more students where they are. To this end, my virtue ethics module segues from Aristotle, Alasdair MacIntyre, and John McDowell through Jane Austen to Miranda Fricker's fascinating discussion of the virtue necessary to combat testimonial injustice due to prejudice.[6] My discussion of contractarianism ends with Jean Hampton's ingenious utilization of the contract as a device for identifying relationships in which affection has become a lever for unjust exploitation.[7] My discussion of Lockean property rights in another course is enriched by engagement with Cheryl Harris' powerful essay "Whiteness as Property," and Christopher LeBron's recent work is a superb vehicle for addressing questions of systemic inequity and implicit bias within the framework of political liberalism.[8] Incorporation of such texts and such innovative applications of traditional schools of thought, not only engages more students but facilitates more productive, constructive engagement among students.

By structuring our classes to engage students where they are, we can convey the importance and practical relevance of philosophy in taking them where they need to be. In each of these classes, I taught Aristotle, Mill, Kant, and central contemporary debates in ethics and metaethics, but structuring classes to take students *to* these texts demonstrates the relevance of these ideas to what they care about. If Aristotle's *Nicomachean Ethics* is understood as offering both a sustained, withering critique of attempts to capture all value in the form of external goods such as money, and a powerful alternative to the dismissive understanding of character found in much social psychology, students see what is at stake for them in its arguments. Students who encounter Adam Smith's arguments in *The Theory of Moral Sentiments* that markets cannot function efficiently unless most people, most of the time, manifest the virtue of justice in their interactions with each other, often come to question some of their most fundamental assumptions about markets, rational action, and the nature of the relationship between the public and private spheres. When students come to recognize that although the account of reason that they

6. Miranda Fricker, *Epistemic Injustice* (Oxford: Oxford University Press, 2007).

7. Hampton, "Feminist Contractarianism."

8. Cheryl Harris, "Whiteness as Property," *Harvard Law Review* 106, no. 8 (1993): 1707–91; Christopher Lebron, *The Color of Our Shame* (New York: Oxford University Press, 2013).

inherit from Locke and the founders supports an overriding duty to vote, the rational choice theory that they encounter in introductory economics seems to suggest that voting is irrational, they confront deep tensions within their understanding of reason and rationality, and recognize the need to explore them.

Philosophy, more than any other discipline, provides students with the skills and tools to reflect on their beliefs and commitments. In some cases, they discover fundamental inconsistencies and powerful objections; in others, they discover deeper and more powerful grounds for their commitments, grounds that illuminate and extend their understanding and enhance their ability to both advocate for what they believe and defend their convictions against objections. Along the way, they develop a bigger, richer picture and a sensitivity to difference that facilitates effective engagement across differences. Such inquiry is not only intrinsically interesting, but profoundly important and of tremendous practical relevance. Students crave the tools that philosophy is uniquely positioned to provide them, but they also crave the broader scope intrinsic to philosophical inquiry. We are the discipline of both the "is" and the "ought," the discipline that asks, paraphrasing Wilfrid Sellars,[9] how things, in the broadest sense of the term, hang together. Joe Camp would sometimes put down his pipe at the beginning of his graduate seminars at Pittsburgh, step up to the blackboard in our very small seminar room, and draw a very large pitcher on the board. He would turn to us, point to the board, and say, "Remember that this is what philosophy is about—The Big Pitcher," that is, "The Big Picture." Philosophy is indeed about the "big pitcher." It allows those who engage in it to reflect on their principles, beliefs, and convictions and to come to live a more autonomous life, a life governed by principles and convictions that they reflectively endorse.[10] What could be more important? Structuring our courses to engage students where they are meets them at points of central importance to them and demonstrates the

9. Wilfrid Sellars, "Philosophy and the Scientific Image of Man," in *Frontiers of Science and Philosophy*, ed. Robert G. Colodny (Pittsburgh: University of Pittsburgh Press, 1962), 35.

10. I am here drawing upon Elizabeth Anderson's characterization of autonomy in *Value in Ethics and Economics* (Cambridge, MA: Harvard University Press, 1993), 142.

importance of such reasoned, reflective engagement with core beliefs and commitments.

The skills and tools to develop a bigger, more coherent picture have never been more valuable or necessary for our students than they are now. Our students come to us awash in normative commitments that purport to be normatively neutral, commitments about health, development, consciousness, persons, and rationality. They arrive steeped in methodologies for framing problems that are often profoundly inconsistent with each other, unaware of these inconsistencies. Framing a question within one or the other methodologies—say within rational choice theory versus reason understood as robustly dictating self-evident rights—yields a fundamentally different answer, rendering those unreflectively committed to both ripe for manipulation and susceptible to confusion.

Our students are confronted with the *professed* relativism (i.e., truth and objectivity are myths, misleading vestiges of modernity) and *operant* absolutism of much of the far left, and the *professed* absolutism and *operant* relativism (i.e., relentless attacks on truth, evidence, and the legitimacy empirical inquiry) of much of the far right. Exposing, navigating, and resolving such contradictions and inconsistencies is the philosopher's stock-in-trade. It is a great privilege to be in a position to work with groups of people in a shared project of becoming more reflective, thoughtful, and self-aware about what we believe and what we value—a privilege that brings with it an obligation to do so effectively and responsibly. A commitment to meeting our students where they are is an important part of discharging this obligation.

6

Introducing Philosophy in a Large Classroom

Marie-Eve Morin

University of Alberta

MARIE-EVE MORIN is professor of philosophy at the University of Alberta in Edmonton, Canada. She teaches undergraduate and graduate courses in philosophy, including, since 2010, a large section of an introductory course called "Values and Society." She is the recipient of a Kathleen W. Klawe Prize for Excellence in Teaching Large Classes (2013) and a Faculty of Arts Undergraduate Teaching Award (2016). Prior to her position at the University of Alberta, she was visiting assistant professor at the University of Winnipeg and adjunct instructor at Suffolk County Community College in Riverhead, New York.

As a teacher, I have always found introductory courses most satisfying. There's much to be said about teaching small graduate seminars, where you can delve into the nuances of complex philosophical ideas. But, for me, the most fulfilling experiences come from watching my first-year students discover philosophical thinking. Like many of us, I've always favored the Socratic approach in my introductory courses. I want my students to be puzzled, to think hard about what they're reading, and to challenge the things they've always taken for granted. On my syllabus, I tell them: "My hope and expectation is that you will discover some unexpected insights and new ways of thinking about the world and your place in it." This is hardly a "measurable outcome" by my institution's standards, but it is truly what I strive to achieve. As a result, my role is not so much to teach them about this or that "-ism" but to "make them think." I am there to accompany the movement of their thinking and to challenge them to deepen their capacity for reflection whenever possible. I succeed every time they come up with a new idea or see a problem from a unique perspective. I succeed every time their intellectual horizon expands. In these moments, I can often see the pleasure they get from engaging with ideas and with each other, and I go home reinvigorated.

The Challenges: Dialogue, Interaction, Connection

When I was asked in 2010 to teach the large section of our introductory course—we call it the "supersection," and it normally consists of around 200 students and seven to ten teaching assistants—I was told by many friends and colleagues that I would have to change my approach. I would have to lecture, and this wouldn't leave much room for interacting with my students. Students would see me as a distant authority figure, I was told, and the unidirectional, top-down transmission of knowledge was going to give my course a more "dogmatic" feel. As a result, my teaching evaluations would likely suffer. I was told this was not something I should worry about; it just came with the territory.

Transferring information to students in a large setting is often simpler than engaging them in a Socratic dialogue, and I was well aware that the size of the introductory class would make it difficult to provide my students with the kind of learning experience I wanted them to have. At the same time, I recalled my introductory philosophy course at McGill University. Like so many first-year students, I enrolled in an introductory philosophy course with Professor Storrs McCall. I didn't know it at the time, but Professor McCall had been teaching that course since the early 1980s and would go on to introduce many more generations of students to philosophy after that (more than fifteen years later, one of my undergraduates at the University of Alberta would go on to do his Ph.D. at McGill and become one of Professor McCall's teaching assistants for that very same course).

The course was taking place in one of these large lecture theaters and there must have been 300 or 400 students in it. I remember how Professor McCall would walk into the room, sit on the corner of the desk with his Plato book in hand, and talk to us as if we were having a face-to-face conversation in his office. Sometimes he would get up and write a word or two on the board, or he would ask a question and point at someone to answer. Everything felt natural and simple. He was just sitting there, having a chat with us about Plato. What I learned from this experience is that a class can be big, but it doesn't have to *feel* big. It is this feeling of closeness and accessibility and proximity that I wanted to re-create in my classroom.

Of course, I had to adjust some of my methods. I now use slides instead of the board, because they are easier to read, especially for students sitting at the back. Consequently, my lectures need to be more structured and the material carefully organized. It also means that I have to dim the lights, which can suck the energy out of the students (and myself), especially for a morning class. Even though it's still possible to have some discussion, most of the dialectic now happens between me and myself: I raise a puzzle, propose a solution, point out a flaw, raise a new solution, and so on. I can only hope that my students are actively following the movement of thought I enact for them. I can stop here and there and ask the class for their insights and ideas, but I can rarely take more than a few of the hands that go up. As a result, it's harder to know what students are thinking, what they don't understand, and what they're puzzled about.

Of course, interactive technologies like iClicker and TopHat allow students to answer a question in real time by clicking on their mobile phone, letting you know in real time the percentage of students who know what Hobbes' right of nature is or the number who prefer Rousseau's position over Hobbes'. But sharing opinions anonymously by means of one's mobile phone doesn't necessarily mean that the students are engaging with the issues. It runs the risk of turning philosophical thinking into one of those online polls circulating on social media, and certainly doesn't replace philosophical dialogue.

No matter how well one succeeds in engaging students in a large setting, one thing remains true of large classes: there is very little interaction between the instructor and the students at an individual level. I don't know how well a student did on their first paper, how interesting their argument was on their second one, or how much they improved over the course of the semester. I have no measure of how transformative their first encounter with philosophy has been. Of course, I meet current and former students on campus and about town, now even more often than before. But I don't know their names and often I don't even recognize them; they have to stop me and tell me they are in my class. Some students will come to my office hours, but most of the time it is not to talk philosophy. I will talk to students when they want to contest a grade, when they are not happy with their teaching assistant, when they are suspected of academic misconduct, in short, most of my individual interaction with students happens when there's a problem.

The Opportunities: Numbers, Performance, Mentoring

So why do it? How can this experience still be a positive one? How can it be exciting and rewarding? After I received the Kathleen W. Klawe Award for Excellence in Teaching Large Classes in 2013, I was interviewed by our Arts Pedagogy Research and Innovation Laboratory about my experience with teaching large classes. The interviewer asked me what some of the advantages of teaching large classes were. I was really taken aback by the question. I had spent so much time thinking about the drawbacks of large classes and how to mitigate them that I had never looked at the positive side of the experience. I didn't want the size of the classes to affect my students' experience of philosophy. But I had never thought about what makes large classes especially worthwhile.

First, there is something exhilarating about the numbers. Rather than being amazed by the personal development of a few students, I am now amazed by the sheer number of students who are being introduced into the world of philosophical ideas. I don't know the details of the story of their encounter with philosophy anymore, but I know that behind the numbers there are many stories like the one I used to witness when I was teaching in a smaller setting. On the first day of class, I always take a moment to look at all these young (and also less young) faces eager to learn about philosophy. (At my university, philosophy is only one among many subjects that students can take to satisfy their humanities requirement.) During the lectures, if I pause for a minute, I see hundreds of students mulling over a passage in Plato or Kant. Yes, some of them are inevitably on their phone and I always see one or two yawning here and there—but they are still there, learning. I get the same feeling looking at them in the gymnasium on the day of the final exam, writing down what they have learned throughout the term—all these young people who now know about thinkers and ideas they didn't know existed before.

Of course, not all students will like the course, not all will "get" philosophy, and some will even end up failing the course. And even if they enjoy the course and do well, most of them will not go on to study philosophy any further. But all of them now have encountered difficult, often counterintuitive ideas, and they know there are people out there who think very hard about these ideas. These people are philosophers. A couple of years ago, at the end of the course, a student came to me and said: "This was a really good course, but it just isn't for me. I don't want to think that hard." Though I found the last part disheartening, I appreciated the student's comment. This was not for her, and that's fine. At the same time, I knew that if one day she wanted to "think hard" about some moral or political issues, she could open her philosophy textbook again, or walk into a bookstore and pick a book by a philosopher whose name she would recognize. This is the most important: each year, hundreds of students leave the course knowing what philosophical thinking is. Over a decade, we are talking thousands!

Another feature of large classes that makes it particularly worthwhile for me is the performance aspect of it. Before I decided to go to university to study philosophy, I was studying piano at the Conservatory of Music in Quebec City with aspirations of becoming a classical pianist, maybe not a soloist, but a chamber musician or accompanist. When I decided to change my career path, I knew that the element of classical music I was going to miss most was performing for an audience. Performing is of course stressful. One is acutely aware that it all comes down to that one performance here and now: it doesn't matter how many times one has played this piece perfectly at home, what matters is how well one plays it right now on stage.

It is this aspect of music performance that I have found again in teaching large classes. For fifty minutes at the time, I am onstage and I have to give my students the best performance possible. I have to gather it all together and perform my best explanation of Plato or Descartes on the spot. Of course, in a sense, this is true of any course, even small graduate seminars with ten students. The difference is that smaller settings allow for more flexibility: it is easier to adjust as you go, because it's possible by means of questions and answers, or open discussions, to identify and dispel confusions right away. The lecture in a large classroom feels more like a loosely choreographed dance. Not only must each move between ideas, between slides, between explanations and discussion questions and back be well planned and well timed, but all this must be done while remembering to move to the right, to the left, look to this side, to the back, and then to that side, and so on.

The purpose of this choreography is to occupy all the space of the lecture theater. The importance of occupying space is also something I learned in my experience as a pianist. Even though the musician is confined to a spot on the stage, her musical intention has to travel and reach even the person sitting at the back of the theater. With the nerves, the tendency is to forget the audience, make oneself smaller, and play "inward" so to speak. But a musical performance, and even more so a lecture, is a form of communication and, as such, it must reach each and every one in the audience, no matter where they sit. We cannot assume that the students sitting at the back are not interested, are not following, and have nothing to contribute. By being mindful of the space I have to inhabit, I hope to grab every student's attention, even those sitting at the back, and make sure they don't feel disconnected from what is happening up front.

Finally, the last and probably most rewarding feature of large classes is the mentoring relation I can build with graduate teaching assistants. Friday discussion sections, led by graduate teaching assistants, are an essential part of the course. It is here that students will get to ask questions and truly engage in philosophical thinking. Needless to say, facilitating such discussions can be a daunting challenge for any first-time teacher. In fact, as I always tell my teaching assistants, their job is much harder than mine: I stand there in front of the class and lecture, but they have to find ways of engaging students in philosophical discussions and responding to students' ideas on the spot. They have to think on their feet, often about texts and figures they haven't studied extensively before. For this reason, a lot of my time and energy is focused on supporting the graduate students, so they can be more comfortable in front of the classroom and become effective discussion facilitators.

This goal is greatly facilitated by the training component that is an integral part of teaching assistantships in my department. In addition to leading their discussion sections, teaching assistants are expected to devote significant time to training and preparation. At the beginning of the term, they each receive a teaching assistant guidebook, and we spend a day together discussing expectations for the course and running a mock tutorial discussion. After each Friday session, I will also ask my teaching assistants to complete a short reflection form, where they have to write down what went well, what they did that led to this outcome, what didn't go so well, and what they could have done to prevent the problem. As part of this reflection, they also have an opportunity to formulate a goal for the following week, which can include a skill they want to work on or some new technique they want to try in the classroom. The purpose of this exercise is to keep me apprised of their accomplishments and make them more reflective about their own teaching practice.

Teaching a large class, then, is really a collective endeavor, and it is essential that the teaching assistants be fully integrated into the teaching team. Of course, team teaching is always a challenge: It requires a lot of organization to ensure that each teaching assistant is covering the same material, hitting the same points, following the same grading scheme, applying policies in the same way, and so on. It also requires that I, as primary instructor, let go of some control, in order to allow my teaching assistants to find their own teaching style. To help with both of these challenges, my teaching assistants and I meet every week to discuss activities for the next Friday sessions. This is where the bulk of the training is done. At these meetings, assistants can reflect on their past session, pool their experience by sharing their successes and struggles with others, and seek advice if they encounter any issues in their section. Rather than being left to their own devices and learning by trial and error, the assistants truly can rely on a mentoring and peer support system.

As an instructor in a large class, my primary teaching relationship has shifted from my students toward my teaching assistants. They are the ones whose growth and development I witness over the course of a semester. They are the ones who will come to my office after their tutorial to tell me how well it went or to ask for advice. Through them, I will get to hear about my students: someone made a particularly insightful comment, the person who is normally quiet raised their hand twice today, and so on. This is more than an indirect way of learning how my students are doing. To the satisfaction that comes from hearing that my students are learning and gaining insights is now added that of seeing the teaching assistant's excitement about having been the "midwife," so to speak, of these insights.

Witnessing graduate students who, so far, have enjoyed reading and writing about philosophical ideas discover the excitement that comes with being able to transmit their love of philosophy is one of the most rewarding outcomes I have had the privilege to witness.

7

Teaching Value Theory to the Disenfranchised

James Rocha
California State University, Fresno

JAMES ROCHA grew up off Crenshaw Blvd. in South Central Los Angeles and is currently assistant professor of philosophy at California State University, Fresno. He received his B.A., M.A., and Ph.D. in philosophy at University of California, Los Angeles. James taught as a lecturer at California State Polytechnic University, Pomona and as adjunct faculty at Pierce Community College in Woodland Hills, California. He next served as an assistant professor, associate professor, and head of philosophy at Louisiana State University. To be closer to his family, James moved to Fresno State, where he enjoys teaching students from diverse backgrounds. James has received teaching awards in four different contexts: as a teaching assistant at UCLA, as an adjunct faculty member at Pierce, as an assistant professor of philosophy at LSU, and as an associate professor teaching honors at LSU.

If you were to ask me which philosopher, living or dead, I would like to have dinner with, it would be difficult to answer. It certainly would be hard to turn down a long conversation with Immanuel Kant. While I have studied his works for pretty much my entire adult life, there's one small problem: Kant's a racist,[1] and I'm not white.

Okay, maybe that's not a small problem.

---

1. For discussions on Kant's racism, see Christian Neugebauer, "Hegel and Kant—A Refutation of Their Racism," *Quest Philosophical Discussions: An International African Journal of Philosophy* 5, no. 1 (1991):50–73; Thomas E. Hill, Jr. and Bernard Boxill, "Kant and Race," in *Race and Racism*, ed. Bernard Boxill (Oxford: Oxford University Press, 2003), 448–72; Charles W. Mills, "Kant's *Untermenschen*," in *Race and Racism in Modern Philosophy*, ed. Andrew Valls (Ithaca, NY: Cornell University Press, 2005), 169–93; Gabrielle D. V. White, "Should We Take Kant Literally?: On Alleged Racism in *Observations on the Feeling of the Beautiful and Sublime*," *Philosophy and Literature* 37, no. 2 (2013):542–53.

That might make for a rather uncomfortable dinner conversation. Yet, I still might do it. Even though there are other philosophers with whom I could better enjoy table banter, I still would choose to talk philosophy with Kant—primarily because I believe there's so much I could learn from him.

And there's the rub. I wish to learn from a racist, who, were he alive, might not like me very much. As a half-black, half-Chicano who grew up in South Central Los Angeles, Kant would surely doubt my philosophical abilities—which both philosophy students and professors routinely do. There would certainly be frustrations in engaging with him. I would not feel fully respected by either the man or even some of his philosophical positions. Yet, in spite of it all, I do not doubt his significance as one of the greatest philosophers of all time. Even though his theoretical work contains both embarrassing foibles and outright bigoted beliefs, Kant's works are inherently interesting and often provide plausible groundings for important philosophical positions, especially in moral philosophy. Though I must admit this opinion is biased, as I have already devoted my entire adult life to studying the man, and so clearly I'm hoping there's some valid reason for having done so.

My reasons for teaching Kant (along with other racist, sexist, heterosexist, speciesist, and otherwise bigoted philosophers) to a wide variety of disenfranchised students—whom Kant and those philosophers might ignorantly hate—mirror my reasons for wanting to have dinner with Kant. In my opinion, you can be both a bigoted and good—even great—philosopher. To explain this view, I will use my life story, and then I will share some of my methodologies for working around philosophical bigotry.

As a philosopher, I believe philosophy is incredibly valuable for everyone. Disenfranchised students, in particular, may benefit the most from learning more philosophy. Obviously, I'm biased: I just said that as a philosopher, I think philosophy is incredibly valuable. Duh. To be more precise, though, I believe that the kind of philosophy that is important even for disenfranchised persons often is the very kind that honestly does not *overtly* apply to their lives. Even while it is essential to teach feminist theory, philosophy of race, queer theory, and other topics and theories that apply directly to real lives, what I'm interested in here is why it is so important to also teach topics that lack such clear connections.

From Ghetto Dreams to Cartesian Love

There are a good number of reasons that disenfranchised persons are underrepresented as philosophy majors, philosophy graduate students, and professional philosophers. I will address three. To start, the field contains a significant amount of bigotry. We teach a ton of dead white men, and their concerns often do not relate to the lives of disenfranchised persons. There's little I can do in this chapter to help with this first problem, but, hopefully, my life story will encourage thought about the other two.

My life starts pretty much as far from the academic setting as one can get. I was born and raised in South Central Los Angeles—where I learned to rush out of the living room when gunshots went off on our block or to try to get sleep in spite of the sounds of police helicopters and sirens ringing throughout the neighborhood. One of my earliest childhood memories is of the blood of a grocery worker, with whom my father regularly chatted, running down the aisle—the store still in full operation, even before the blood was cleaned up. Nowhere in Kant's otherwise diverse and sizeable opus does he discuss the ethical issues that revolve around a shopkeeper wishing to do good business, right after one of their employees has been murdered.

Prior to my siblings attending college, no one in my family had done so—neither a distant aunt, an uncle I never met, nor a cousin several times removed had a college degree. My sister majored in psychology, and my brother majored in computer science. But I was the first person in my family to take a philosophy class, and I would be the first to take on an allegedly impractical major. My father read a good bit of philosophy, especially Asian philosophy, on his own. During my childhood, we would often drive around town with philosophy books on tape playing on the car radio—and I hated every moment of it.

In spite of that childhood reaction, as soon as I started my first year at UCLA, I was desperate to learn Nietzsche, Sartre, Camus, and other philosophers who I thought would express the existential dread that I felt at a young age growing up in the ghetto—a deadly trap from which I was not confident that I would ever escape. But, of course, this was UCLA—one of the most analytic of analytic departments—and there were not a lot of classes on existential dread. Instead, I began with Philosophy 1: "Beginnings of Western Philosophy." Instead of pondering the meaning of God's death or the precise date on which Meursault's mother died, I would be learning the theory of the forms and hylomorphism. I was fairly certain that neither topic would connect to the many hours I spent listening to the police scanner, pondering the various ways in which I was surrounded by needless death.

Yet, in spite of the fact that my philosophical interests have always been grounded in my life experiences, I thoroughly enjoyed the class. And I really fell in love with philosophy in my second class, Philosophy 21: "Skepticism & Rationality." We spent a lot of time on Descartes, but also covered the British empiricists. And, to be honest, we spent a lot of time on whether I was dreaming, evil demons, and the problem of induction, but, of course, no time at all on the doubts we might raise about the mainstream view that we should blame personal choices for racial inequity. That is to say, I was a poor black/Latino kid from South Central loving philosophy even while acknowledging that it had no clear relevance to life in the ghetto— or at least none that I could see. But, at the same time, I wanted to learn more about the construction of rationality and the nature of knowledge. I didn't see how these topics were relevant, but I loved metaphysics, epistemology, mind, and so on.

While we must recognize that my life provides only anecdotal evidence, it is important to note the danger in thinking that students from disenfranchised backgrounds will not be able to appreciate purely abstract philosophy—the kind of philosophy that has no clear relevance to real life. Even well-meaning stereotypes miss the mark a large percentage of the time: the assumption that students who have experienced oppression will wish to use philosophy to study oppression may often be true, but will not apply to all such students. Given the power and influence of the professorial role, we must take active steps to ensure that our passive presumptions do not place artificial limits on our students. While earning my undergraduate degree, I was most interested in working in metaphysics, mind, and epistemology. Those were the topics that excited me—the topics I wanted to spend my life pursuing. I chose philosophy as a career while studying the epistemology of Descartes and Hume. That's what hooked me, and could likewise hook others like me.

During my graduate work, however, I again felt the pull of relevance. While I wanted—and continue to want—to spend my life learning about Descartes, Hume, metaphysics, and epistemology, I felt that I needed to write on topics that were a little more relevant to the problems I had experienced in the real world. So, I turned to ethics and political philosophy, with an eye toward future work in philosophy of race. My first idea for a dissertation project was to figure out why Kant believed the state owed welfare payments to the poor. I felt this project was relevant, historically significant, personally interesting, and philosophically rich.

Yet, it quickly became clear that, in order to complete this more relevant project, I first would have to acquire a much deeper understanding of the foundational issues and concepts. Thus, I wrote a dissertation on the concepts of autonomy and coercion, and the relation between them, asking whether it was possible for someone, such as the state, to coerce an autonomous agent into doing what they ought to do. My topic was now a few steps removed from real-life issues. The point of the new project, to me, was clear: philosophically, we are better positioned to grapple with the questions we truly care about once we have tackled the more fundamental, historical, and often abstract issues that structure our contemporary debates. Although this certainly is not the only way to engage in philosophy, it is an approach that I remain grateful for having learned. I resolved to prepare my students in this way, as I began to teach value theory.

From Socratic Methods to Malcolm's Bullets

Thus, in graduate school, I developed an appreciation for learning abstract fundamentals from dead white guys, with the hope to utilize this knowledge in later, more practical pursuits. I'm neither saying this is the only proper foundation for socially relevant philosophy, nor that we cannot prepare to study contemporary social issues by looking to philosophers who are not dead white men. What I do want to emphasize is the utility that I have gained, and wish to impart to my students, from the careful study of certain dead white men. Thus, I will share some of my pedagogical techniques that make use of dead white men, many of whom are bigoted dead white men, but also damn good philosophers. I will show how I incorporate activist voices; engage students in applied discussions, through questions about the reading; and provide sufficient room for students to follow their own interests when writing term papers.

Our field has already promoted the inclusion of philosophers into our courses who are not cis, straight, white men. We should be wary of a syllabus that contains only cis, straight, white men. Significantly, I add to this impulse by attempting to incorporate the voices of social justice activists, which demonstrates how the abstract theories we discuss can be used to bolster more practical and activist arguments.

For example, suppose I want to teach human rights theory, which can be a largely abstract and conceptual enterprise. To avoid the feeling that abstract political philosophy may be irrelevant to students' lives, I start with Malcolm X's "The Ballot or the Bullet." Clearly, this speech is controversial. The point of teaching it is not to get students to agree with it, but to see how a historically significant figure attempted to use human rights discourse to argue for political change. Malcolm X believed that there was a practical need to expand from arguing for civil rights, to arguing for human rights—specifically because the latter allowed oppressed persons to challenge the United States on an international level, for example, through filing complaints with the United Nations.[2] Thus, the utility of introducing Malcolm X's speech is that it establishes how politically active people utilize human rights discourse. Whether or not you agree with Malcolm X's controversial stances, students recognize how he employed a philosophically abstract concept, human rights, to fight for his political causes. This instructional strategy begins with something concrete and socially relevant, which later motivates a transition to the more purely conceptual discussion of human rights, in particular, and political philosophy, in general.

Another technique I use to keep students involved is graded daily participation. I begin every class by asking random students questions about the readings. There are a few purposes for this graded, verbal assignment. First, it encourages students to do the reading, as

---

2. Malcolm X, "The Ballot or the Bullet," in *Malcolm X Speeches*, ed. James Lite (Amazon Digital Services, LLC, 2012) Kindle Edition.

they will be publicly questioned. Yet, since the questions are fairly easy and randomly assigned, there is less pressure than there would be with pop quizzes. Second, I use this method to determine what the students learned from the readings and what puzzled them. One of the most important questions I ask is "What questions did you have about the reading?" This tells me, before I start to lecture, what in the reading puzzled and challenged my students. Moreover, it is a hard question to guess at, if they did not do the reading at all. Third, and most relevant here, the question-and-answer period allows us to find the practical relevance of our abstract readings together.

Because I will often ask students how their readings might be relevant to contemporary issues and/or their lives, students come to class having thought about why these abstract and conceptual issues, often written by dead white men, are relevant to both practical concerns and events from their own lives. In this fashion, it is not entirely up to me to determine how our philosophical issues connect to real life—and it should not be. While I hail from tough beginnings, my experiences are necessarily personal, anecdotal, and limited. Yet, I do not believe that philosophical concepts, issues, and questions are similarly limited. While Kant's bigotry is unquestionably real and problematic, the formula of humanity remains philosophically interesting and applicable to a plethora of real-life issues for a diverse population struggling to make it in the world. Asking the students to examine the relevance of an abstract, philosophical issue to their lives and to their social/political concerns adds perspective to and enriches our classroom discussions.

In this way, our classroom is jointly owned, as our discussion is cooperatively produced. While reading a particular dead, white, bigoted man, our understanding of that philosopher's work is produced by compiling the ideas of a diverse and often disenfranchised audience. While Kant did not believe in same-sex marriage, I have had numerous LGBTQ students who have used Kantian ethics to enrich arguments for LGBTQ rights and activism. My courses regularly move back and forth from purely abstract discussions to students finding and conveying their own real-life applications.

Finally, following along this track, I try to provide students the largest available latitude for their term papers. While a term paper has to demonstrate learning from the course texts, I encourage my students to apply our course materials to their interests—including, if they wish of course, their real lives and politically motivated applications. Even if the course is about the ethical theories of Aristotle, Kant, and Mill, I encourage students to apply those ethical theories in their term papers to topics that most interest them. While I may encourage students interested in graduate school to consider more abstract questions, I leave the choice in their hands. I let them know that they can do good philosophy while pursuing their interests— including their political or activist interests—while also grounding their work in philosophical history and abstract theory.

Based on my own experiences, I understand both the overwhelming desire to make philosophy relevant to one's own life experiences and the importance of keeping even applied philosophical work theoretically and historically grounded. Since many of my students, especially as I now work in the California State University system in Fresno, come from similar disenfranchised backgrounds, I understand that they may struggle to find the value in philosophy. Yet, I believe that I can reach many of these students by selecting significant historical figures and connecting their philosophies to students' backgrounds; encouraging discussion about the practical applications of more abstract theories through graded questions and answers; and assigning open-ended term paper topics.

From Kant's Formulaic Bigotry to Empowered Students

The primary reason that all of this work to make philosophy more welcoming and inclusive matters is specifically because philosophy really is good for the students. It is of the utmost importance that philosophy is shared among disenfranchised persons, because philosophy is one of our great social resources. The fact that philosophy is not more equally shared among various social groups is a significant, but largely overlooked, problem for distributive justice. And, no, I do not at all feel that I'm exaggerating.

I have probably given roughly a hundred speeches recruiting students to major in philosophy. To a large extent, recruiting philosophy majors is a Herculean task—as students, by and large, do not arrive at college interested in our major. At the same time, the major almost sells itself, once you can convey to students some basic information: empirical evidence, from test scores to midcareer earnings, shows that philosophy majors excel at a wide variety of tasks. We philosophy teachers know that the reason for these positive results is that we are teaching our students incomparable skills. There's little more important in life, whatever your career, than being a good speaker, writer, and thinker. Regardless of whether students later remember how Hume and Kant differed on the power of reasoning, philosophy teachers provide students with *the power of reasoning*. In brief, we are making our students into better people: better thinkers, better writers, better speakers, and hopefully better moral agents.

This raises a significant problem of distributional justice, for philosophy is provided to members of oppressor groups at a much higher rate than it is to oppressed persons. If students gain so many essential life skills from a philosophy education, then educators should ensure that all students have equal access to that education. While philosophers show great concern for other distributional injustices, unequal access to philosophical education is largely overlooked. Yet, ironically, as philosophy teachers, this injustice is closest to our lives and, thus, the one we might most easily rectify.

Ultimately, I am working to draw connections between my early life experiences in South Central to my current teaching at Fresno State, in order to increase access to philosophy. Though I would like to bring more philosophers from disenfranchised beginnings into our professional academic community, that is not my primary goal. Instead, my main hope is to teach philosophical skills to disenfranchised students, so that they can use those skills to improve their lives, no matter what career they might choose. So, I teach my students a bunch of dead, cis, straight, white, male, privileged, and bigoted philosophers. I also assign philosophers from backgrounds similar to those of my students, and I teach nonphilosophers who use philosophical tools to fight for social justice and other political causes. Finally, in every class, I encourage students to find their own ways of applying philosophy to their lives. This call for engagement culminates in the students writing a term paper on a topic of their choosing—which allows them to follow their own interests and to find their own motivations for using their new and hard-won philosophical skills in social application.

In the end, maybe Kant would not be happy with so many students of color, women, and LGBTQ students learning and then using his philosophy to pursue ends with which his anachronistic writings did not agree. But who cares? Kant was a bigot. And maybe the best way to teach him a lesson is to have all of these disenfranchised young people employing his theories to empower themselves.

8

Imagine Yourself in the Bird: Teaching Philosophy at the U.S. Military Academy

Courtney Morris
U.S. Military Academy

COURTNEY MORRIS is an assistant professor of philosophy at the U.S. Military Academy, West Point. Her interests include Kant's theoretical philosophy, early modern philosophy, and nineteenth-century philosophy. She received her Ph.D. from the University of California, Riverside, where she won four teaching awards for her work as a teaching assistant. She was recently a finalist for the Dean's Teaching Award for Junior Faculty at West Point. In the classroom, she aims to get the students engaged and invested in participating in philosophical dialogue, not only with their peers and instructors, but with the great thinkers of the past and, most importantly, with themselves.

Sometimes, as I walk through the campus where I teach—"Post" as they call it—I imagine a snapshot of me and my surrounding area. Groups of students walk toward me, not marching, but very orderly. They are donned in their ACUs (active combat uniforms) and greet me with a friendly nod and a "How are you, Ma'am?" Because I am a civilian, they do not salute me, but "Ma'am," like "Sir," is a deferential term reserved for your superiors. The armed MPs stand guard and the academic buildings—former military forts—loom over us. The Hudson River creeps below us, and the historic West Point chapel peeks through the green trees above us. I imagine sending that snapshot, without explanation or context, to my twenty-year-old self—a peacenik, antiestablishment, college student toting a dog-eared copy of Emerson's essays. College for me was liberating: no one mandated my schedule, oversaw my appearance, or outlined my future—quite different from the place where I now teach.

The Department of English and Philosophy at the U.S. Military Academy was not where I expected to end up. But my maxim on the job market (I'm a Kant scholar) was to send an application to every opening for which I was qualified. I was surprised when USMA contacted me for an interview—*What would the military want with me?*—but I followed through with the process. During my in-person interview, I was struck by the intelligence, open-mindedness, and collegiality of the officers and civilians. But it was not until I taught a class of cadets that my initial skepticism transformed into the hope that I would be offered the job. It was not just that the cadets came to class prepared. ("They were ordered to!" I joked.) It was that they genuinely cared about examining their own beliefs. It seems unfair now, but back then this open-mindedness surprised me.

I knew the cadets would be smart. USMA is a highly ranked liberal arts school. But like many self-proclaimed pacifists who have no direct experience with members of the military, I harbored a vague mistrust of it. Many civilians, I've found, have the same type of uneasiness. "They teach *philosophy* at West Point?" people sometimes ask. "Yeah, it's a thing," I say, repeating a line from the philosophy majors here. The curriculum covers the ethics of war and related issues, but it also covers Descartes, Hegel, Russell, Rawls, Quine, and the like. We converse about Gettier cases, feminism, and whether there is a teleological suspension of the ethical. (The cadets have surprisingly passionate views about Kierkegaard.) Most of the time, my initial impression of the cadets proves correct, and they are the ideal students. Other times, they are the more typical. They fall soundly asleep during class.

The Academy imposes on them a regimented schedule that runs from 0630 to 2230. That schedule is easy to blame for their consistent sleep deprivation, but they also deal with the problems of other young adults: they are figuring out who they are, getting dumped, feeling homesick, and having fights with their parents. They watch *Game of Thrones* when they should be reading Plato. Some struggle with their sexual identity or religious beliefs. Some deal with even more difficult problems like unplanned pregnancies, a parent's death, or major health problems. They are, in so many respects, just like college students anywhere.

"Two Hundred Years of Tradition . . ."

In important respects, of course, they are not. Their uniforms distinguish them from their civilian counterparts. A uniform simultaneously erases any appearance of individuality and differentiates each student by communicating how and whether one should be addressed, where one stands in the military's hierarchy, and what one has or has not accomplished. The only part of the uniform the students remove for class is their "cover" (their hat), which I have come to think of as the completion of their military identity. Their uniform signals that they attend an institution that is much more than scholarly. It instructs them in combat and target practice. It requires them to play sports, or as MacArthur said, compete on the "fields of friendly strife." It demands obedience. It trains killers.

To say, then, that a military education comes without tensions would be disingenuous. Order and regimen rule the cadets' actions. They, like officers and enlisted soldiers, are disciplined and held to ordinances that can seem trivial and arbitrary to an outsider, the strict enforcement of which can seem harsh. They get "corrected" for not having shined shoes, having hair that is too long, not shaving, going to formation late, not having their shirts folded in the right way during a room inspection, not having their hangers evenly spaced, being out of their room after taps, not having their lights off at 2330, and sitting on the same horizontal surface as the opposite sex (the last was reported to me by an old graduate, but is apparently no longer enforced).

Some punishments work to my benefit, like those they receive for skipping or being (even one second) late to class. They include "hours," in which a cadet must walk, with gear on, up and down the central area; rank removal; demotion; and room restrictions. A graduate tells me her husband had so many room restrictions while he was a cadet that he learned to knit. This is not to mention the punishments that come from breaking the cadet honor code ("A cadet will not lie, cheat, steal, or tolerate those who do"), which can include getting kicked out and paying back what would be the price of tuition. (Education here is free, if you don't count the mandatory five years of service in the military after graduation.) The goal is for the cadets to learn to follow rules and orders without hesitation.

Simultaneously, the cadets are gaining a liberal education, the main goal of which, especially in the philosophy classes, is to teach students how to think critically. The Academy takes this mission—and it genuinely conceives of its academic activities as a "mission"—seriously. The core philosophy course, required for every cadet, addresses this tension directly. The first half covers the usual topics of an introductory philosophy course, while the last half covers Just War Theory, which assumes, contra Pacifism, that war is at least sometimes morally permissible. As future officers, every cadet recognizes the seriousness and applicability of studying the morality of war.

I've found, though, that the benefits of studying philosophy often emerge when we are not explicitly discussing war. Plato's *Euthyphro*, for example, ostensibly about divine commands, provides rich ground for us to discuss the nature of following orders. Socrates urges Euthyphro to not blindly accept the permissibility of any action—especially one that might be controversial, like prosecuting your own father for murder—*because someone says so*, and to instead look for independent reasons to justify such an action. "What about commands from a superior officer?" I recently began to ask. Is an action right because your commander says so? Should you do something *just because you are told*?

Cadets will sometimes point out to me that the officer's oath, unlike an enlisted soldier's, does not include the promise to follow orders. Instead, officers vow to "support and defend the Constitution from all enemies, foreign and domestic." (Civilians here take a similar oath.) This is true, but misses the point: oath or no oath, they are at an institution that depends on each member following orders, even if they themselves will, more often than not, be the ones giving those orders. The cadets then point out that soldiers are not obliged to follow all orders, only ones that are "lawful."[1] Indeed, they have a positive obligation to *disobey* unlawful orders. Unfortunately, the judgment that an order is unlawful is one a soldier makes at his or her own peril: the plea "I was just following orders" has almost never been a successful defense in an American or international war crime trial, and a soldier can be (and has been) dishonorably discharged for

---

1. And indeed, this is what the Uniform Code of Military Justice states (Articles 90 and 92).

not following an order he or she deems unlawful, if a superior officer or military jury disagrees.[2]

Thus, students at the Military Academy, just like the officers they aspire to be, must cultivate the habit of following orders automatically, while simultaneously morally evaluating those commands. I hope, and imagine, that most of the time those commands align perfectly with what is morally permissible or even with what is morally praiseworthy. But I also hope that no one with great power in wartime rests easy on the assumption that the two will always coincide. Cadets, as officers in training, must be wide awake, morally speaking, so they can recognize when the two are in tension. That moral alertness requires what I have come to think of as a double consciousness: one that is more or less secure in following routine and one that is constantly *insecure* with that routine.

Of course—and here my Kantian tendencies reveal themselves—this describes all of us. We all must ethically deliberate in the face of pressures from external authorities, whether they be the expectations, beliefs, and practices of our peers or the internal pressures of what Kant would call the "dear self." If the cadets are different then, it is because their external authority has much more power over their everyday actions, their careers, and their very survival than the powers that govern the lives of civilians. Moreover, when commissioned, they will *wield* more power than the rest of us: some of my students will have the legal power to kill and the permission to grant that power to others. So this "double consciousness" is for them, I imagine (I hope), more pronounced, especially when they are deployed.

---

2. The defense that a soldier was "just following orders" was rejected at the Nuremberg trials after World War II; the court-martial for Second Lieutenant William Calley, who was prosecuted for war crimes during the Vietnam War; and the court-martial for Staff Sergeant Ivan Frederick, who was accused and convicted of torturing prisoners at Abu Ghraib prison. At the same time, however, deeming an order "unlawful" can put a soldier at risk, as shown in the case of Captain Dan Quinn, who was relieved of his duty in Afghanistan after disobeying an order to ignore the Afghani practice of using boys as sex slaves. Although Quinn left the Army voluntarily, the Army planned to dishonorably discharge Sergeant First Class Charles Martland, who, with Captain Quinn, intervened in such a case on behalf of an Afghani boy who had been shackled to the bed of an Afghani commander. The Army later reversed that decision.

"That I Ought Not to Kill My Good Son Is Quite Certain . . ."

Kant, of course, understood the tension I describe. In his essay "What Is Enlightenment?" he distinguishes between the "private" and "public" use of reason.[3] An example of the latter is when a soldier argues, perhaps in an academic article, that the 2003 American invasion of Iraq was unjust. An example of the former is when that same soldier follows all the lawful orders she receives while serving on the ground there. As is frequently the case with Kant, it would have been nice if he had further developed his distinction. What if a private command requires one to break the moral law? Undoubtedly, Kant would say that no one has the authority to command such a thing, not even God. This reading is indicated by Kant's discussion of Abraham and Isaac's story, in which Kant claims that Abraham can be certain that killing his son would violate the moral law and thus that it is not God who commands him to do so.[4] But that point makes scant difference when faced with the matter-of-fact authority of an actual superior. Recognizing an immoral command, whether one is expected to follow or give it, requires a robustly developed sense of moral reasoning, as Kant would surely agree, but also requires the courage and motivation to act *against* an actual, if not moral, authority.

The cadets, and perhaps most civilians, tend to believe that it is obvious when an order is immoral. Many examples from history confirm their suspicion. I discuss with the cadets the gruesome details of the My Lai massacre during the Vietnam war, in which American soldiers killed, and sometimes raped and tortured, an estimated 500 unarmed civilians. William Calley, who at the time held the rank of a newly commissioned cadet, reportedly gathered many such civilians and killed them execution-style. He claimed in his court-martial defense that he was following orders. Indeed, Calley's superior, Captain Ernest Medina, testified that he relayed an order granting his

---

3. Immanuel Kant, "An Answer to the Question: What Is Enlightenment," in *Practical Philosophy*, trans. and ed. Mary J. Gregor (New York: Cambridge University Press, 1996), 15–22.

4. Immanuel Kant, *The Conflict of the Faculties*, trans. Mary J. Gregor and Robert Anchor, in *Religion and Rational Theology*, trans. and eds. Allen W. Wood and George Di Giovanni (New York: Cambridge University Press, 1996), 233–327, 7:63fn.

men "permission to destroy the village, to burn down the houses, to destroy the food crop that belonged to the Vietcong, and to kill their livestock."[5] The assumption was that only members of the Viet Cong were there.[6] But when the company arrived, they were met only with unsuspecting women, children, and old men, cooking breakfast outside their hutches. It is at this point, obviously, that the American soldiers should have disobeyed any order to kill. Warrant Officer Hugh Thompson was reportedly the only soldier to recognize this. After landing in a helicopter and surveying the scene, he alone ordered the soldiers to stand down, threatening to shoot them if they did not obey.[7]

Discussion of this history serves many purposes, not the least of which is to educate the cadets about the history of the institution to which they belong. Moreover, it provides a case study for the possible tension between orders and morality. But I fear that this case, along with other examples we discuss, such as the abuses at Abu Ghraib prison, make it seem as if situations that call for good ethical judgment are both obvious and rare. A similar problem plagues typical thought experiments in philosophy: "There is a runaway trolley. . . ." These scenarios are designed to isolate readers' intuitions. But, in order to be effective, in that regard, the remaining details of the scenario must be so extreme that the scenario becomes unrelatable. "They're idiots for being on the tracks!" students often say and, in response to the My Lai massacre case: "Of course we would never shoot up civilians!" An education at USMA, if it has accomplished its mission, has transformed a cadet into a "leader of character." The cadets are not the William Calley's, they insist, but the Hugh Thompson's. And I believe them.

But not all cases are so clear. One of our most important class discussions centers on a video clip, released by Chelsea Manning, of a 2007 firefight in Iraq. In the clip, a group of American soldiers in a helicopter (a "bird") hover high above a Baghdad neighborhood

5. See *Investigation of the Mai Lai Incident, Hearings of the Armed Services Investigating Subcommittee of the Committee of Armed Services, House of Representatives, Ninety-First Congress, Second Session*, pp. 57–58 and 61 (https://www.loc.gov/rr/frd /Military_Law/pdf/MyLaiHearings.pdf).

6. Ibid., 57.

7. As reported in Seymour M. Hersh, "Coverup-1," *New Yorker*, January 22, 1972.

where a group of people congregate. The video, taken from the vantage point of the helicopter, is grainy, but the soldiers' dialogue is
mostly audible. One soldier in the bird reports that he sees "five to
six individuals with AK47s." The actual video footage shows nothing
so clear, although, at one point, we can see what one of the soldiers
believes to be an RPG (a rocket-propelled grenade), perhaps reasonably so. After receiving permission to engage (a most misleading
word), the soldiers open fire. The people on the ground run for cover,
but there is nowhere to hide. Most die. When a van arrives, seemingly to pick up the bodies and tend to the wounded, the soldiers
fire another round of shots. As we find out, several of the victims
were innocent civilians. And indeed, whether any of the victims were
insurgents is disputed, although it is probably true that at least two
were indeed armed.[8] Two victims worked for Reuters, one a photo-
journalist, who held an object that could be mistaken for an RPG:
his camera. Two children were in the van, including a girl who was
injured and rushed to a subpar Iraqi hospital.

The cadets are sober and serious after watching the video. Some
are quick to condemn the soldiers and say that they were too trig-
ger happy. Some agree with Ethan McCord, the soldier who pulled
the injured children from the van, who said, "Personally, I believe
the first attack on the group standing by the wall was appropriate,
was warranted by the rules of engagement. They did have weapons
there. However, I don't feel that the attack on the [rescue] van was
necessary."[9] Other cadets hesitate to morally criticize either engagement. "Imagine yourself in the bird!" a cadet once said. In fact, this
is easy for them to imagine. They can relate to the soldiers there in
a way they cannot relate to William Calley. Some express sympathy
with these soldiers that they would never grant to Calley. Of course,
I want them also to imagine themselves on the *ground*. But the cadet's
plea deserves attention. Go ahead and imagine it yourself: you are in
a helicopter, having previously waged battles in which your friends
have died. You are in the middle of a war in which the measure of
success is vague. You are charged with fighting an enemy who wears

8. See Elisabeth Bumiller, "Video Shows US Killing of Reuters Employees," *New
York Times*, April 5, 2010.

9. See Kim Zetter, "US Soldier on 2007 Apache Attack: What I Saw," *Wired*, April
20, 2010.

no uniform, does not announce itself, follows no rules of war. Your imperative to fight is not the one your grandfather had in Germany or Japan. The nation you represent is divided over its support for the current missions of the military. Yet here you are, in the bird.

Reasoning in the Bird

So often ethical dilemmas and their solutions only exist in our austere imagination, where the messiness and actuality of life does not interfere. This sometimes makes ethical deliberation, especially about war, appear easy. But a soldier does not have the benefit of ignoring all the details an ethicist might deem as morally irrelevant. And those details, like the phrase "the fog of war" suggests, can make it hard to see clearly: there is strategy to consider, missions, orders, and survival. There are emotions: moral ones, like resentment and indignation, but also rage, fear, and anger. Soldiers morally deliberate under a pressure that most of us will never experience.

The lack of context—and some questionable editing of the video courtesy of Wikileaks—makes it difficult to judge what the soldiers in this bird should have done. I ask my students, instead, what the soldiers should be *thinking*. What ethical principles should guide them, as they request or give permission to kill? We discuss the principle of noncombatant immunity, which states that noncombatants should be immune from the harms of war. We discuss the principle stating that a soldier should exercise due care in discriminating legitimate and illegitimate targets, and that he or she should engage only in harm that is necessary to win a battle or war. We discuss the doctrine of double effect, which instructs soldiers as to when it is okay to harm an innocent person. We discuss the attitude soldiers should adopt toward those they kill, and whether the language of the soldiers in the video—crass and flippant—reflects that. Finally, we discuss how to keep all these principles clear and prioritized in the face of other loud truths, including the fact that dehumanizing the enemy makes it psychologically easier to kill.

It is easy to start talking in clichés when speaking of soldiers, their ethical duties, and war—particularly for someone like myself, who has never, and probably never will, experience war firsthand. What strikes me as true, though, trite or not, is that soldiers carry a moral burden that most civilians don't, especially during wartime. It is not that soldiers are morally unlucky; their entry into the military is voluntary. But they are more morally vulnerable, more liable to moral injury, more likely to face ethical dilemmas, and more likely to be moral heroes.

I have learned much about the nature of perseverance, commitment, and hard work from my cadets. I watch their everyday actions—waking up early after little sleep, sitting through long briefs they do not find interesting, studying for long hours, preparing for their meticulous room inspections—all with a smile I cannot imagine my college-aged self mustering. I hear about them failing a lot—they are presented with so many chances to fail. But I hear about them trying and trying and trying again, confident and steady in the knowledge that hard work and persistence eventually win the battle. I've become close to a few cadets who have overcome remarkable personal obstacles to remain at West Point. I cannot share with you their stories, but I hope someday that they will share their own. There are days that the military, with its red tape and formality, irritates me. ("Two hundred years of tradition unhindered by progress" they love to joke.) For each of those days, however, there is another when a cadet inspires me, makes me laugh out loud, makes me rethink a philosophical position, or reminds me that waking up early allows you to accomplish quite a lot. I think often, especially when I am teaching ethics, of that one cadet's warning not to gloss over the messy details of real-life ethical deliberation.

Often, after class, a cadet comes to my office to continue a philosophical discussion—how we might apply ethical principles to obscure historical battles, to express concern about the moral permissibility of the atomic bomb, or, more commonly, to further explore a text or idea I am teaching: Plato's *Republic*, Kant's transcendental unity of apperception, or a passage from Schopenhauer. These conversations are the highlights of my days, and they all end the same way. I tell the cadet to have a good day. She says, "Yes, Ma'am," and prepares to reapply her cover.

The views expressed in this paper do not necessarily represent those of the U.S. Military Academy, the Department of the Army, or the Department of Defense.

III. Teaching the Course

9

Critical Thinking and Empowerment

Mark Piper
James Madison University

MARK PIPER has been teaching ethics and critical thinking since the fall of 2000, first at St. Louis University and now at James Madison University. His writings on education and pedagogy have appeared in the *Journal of Philosophy of Education* and the *International Journal of Ethics Education*. He is the recipient of three major teaching awards at James Madison University. In 2015 he was awarded the Carl Harter Distinguished Teaching Award for the College of Arts and Letters, in 2016 he received a School of Liberal Arts Alumni Legacy Fund Award for excellence in teaching and research, and in 2016 he was the recipient of one of four inaugural Madison Vision Teaching Awards, which are administered and determined entirely by students. Mark is keen to make his teaching as relevant and useful for his students as possible, and to that end he focuses on teaching the development of philosophical skills that have broad utility.

"The essence of the independent mind lies not in *what* it thinks, but in *how* it thinks."
—Christopher Hitchens[1]

"Words have power, you dumb piece of shit."
—Demetri Martin[2]

Although much has changed since I started teaching, there have been some constants. For example, I can usually count on a significant number of my introductory students having little notion of philosophy other than believing that, whatever it is, it is almost certainly a waste of time. In a similarly contradictory vein, I can

---

1. Christopher Hitchens, *Letters to a Young Contrarian* (New York: Basic Books, 2005), 3.
2. Demetri Martin, *This Is a Book* (New York: Grand Central Publishing, 2011), 191.

usually count on many of my introductory students having little idea about critical thinking other than believing that, whatever might be involved in it, they're already pretty good at it. My critical thinking course is focused, in part, on helping my students appreciate the error in these judgments.

As this chapter is primarily focused on my experience of teaching critical thinking, I won't say much about how I address the myth that philosophy is a waste of time, other than to say the following. Typically, I can get students to see that (1) they have fundamental theoretical and practical beliefs that are very important to them, (2) it is important for them to know the truth about these matters, (3) empirical science cannot provide answers to many of these questions, and (4) where empirical science is silent, philosophy uses reason to address matters of fundamental theoretical and practical belief. Students who appreciate these points tend to view philosophy more favorably.

As I construe it, critical thinking most broadly refers to the study of persuasion, both rational and nonrational, with a focus on teaching students how best (a) to recognize and employ rational forms of persuasion and (b) to avoid and not be fooled by nonrational forms of persuasion. I begin the course with a study of the basics of philosophy and then move to critical thinking proper, including an examination of what counts as an argument, different types of argument, what makes for a good argument, improving credibility assessments, and ending with a study of rhetorical tricks and fallacies. Based upon student feedback, the study of rhetorical tricks and fallacies is the most important and useful part of the course, and it's certainly the part of the course I most enjoy teaching.

Welcome to Class

As I mentioned above, most of my students consider themselves fairly accomplished independent thinkers before the course begins. This is an advantage and a disadvantage. On the positive side, students are typically already committed to the importance of critical thinking, so there are preexisting motivational hooks onto which I can latch if I do my job well. On the negative side, this positive self-assessment often gives introductory students false confidence in their existing critical thinking skills, which can discourage them from taking seriously the notion that they need further instruction. Although this is a kind of hubris, I certainly don't hold it against them. Most of us were the same way. And the rise of a culture of self-promotion in the form of exponentially expanding social media opportunities and demands has, in my view, unfortunately caused many people to confuse *feeling* distinctive with having authentic independence of mind.

One of my most important tasks when teaching critical thinking is to replace this common, usually unfounded, and unfortunately sophomoric self-assessment (and actual paucity of critical thinking skills) with both (1) a greater awareness of our proneness to error in matters of persuasion and (2) the skills required to separate good argumentation from fallacious reasoning and rhetorical trickery.

I do not pull any punches when it comes to sharing some rather bleak news at the beginning of the course. I inform my students that, in all likelihood, most of us are far worse critical thinkers than we think we are and that we are all far more prone to being deceived and manipulated than we would care to think. I stress that although it is common to hear people *say* that they think for themselves and determine their own belief systems and preferences and the like, in fact, real independence of mind is rather rare, largely because it requires a set of skills that many do not possess or even realize that they need to possess in order to be a truly independent thinker.

It is very interesting for me to see that, semester after semester and year after year, this rather dismal assessment of general critical thinking ability elicits little to no resistance or resentment from students. Perhaps this is partly because I treat my students kindly, or because I do not exclude myself from these negative judgments. Perhaps students tend to succumb to a better than average bias and consider themselves the exceptions to the rule. Some students likely welcome the idea of a challenge. Yet another factor in play, I think, is that students are intrigued by the prospect of a special kind of personal advancement: if what I am saying is true, and if these problems are in fact quite common, and if a course in critical thinking can help to overcome these problems, then perhaps the outcome will be a form of empowerment that will render them exceptional in an important way. I do not shy away from using this as a motivator. On the contrary, I am very explicit in telling them that perhaps the most compelling reason for them to give a damn about the course is that it will *empower* them; that they will be on the giving and receiving end of persuasion their entire lives; that they will benefit from the ability to tell good arguments from bullshit; and that greater critical thinking skills are crucial to becoming an individual in the deeper sense that almost everyone wants.

So I don't pull certain punches. But I also want to enjoy teaching the course, and for me this involves getting on well with my students. Although I have often thought that some students would make the greatest strides if I were more of a taskmaster, I couldn't sustain that approach and enjoy teaching at the same time. I have found the work to be more pleasant for all involved if an atmosphere of mutual respect and unity can be established. Self-effacement helps with the former, and humor helps tremendously with the latter, so I use these as often as I can without allowing the instruction to suffer. Cursing from time to time also helps. It gets their goddamn attention—and often gets a laugh, too.

Relevance and Student Motivation

One factor that makes teaching critical thinking enjoyable is its obvious relevance outside of the classroom. Persuasion is everywhere. This holds, of course, for broader life decisions: large purchases, elections, relationships, jobs, forks in life's road, and the like. But in between these events, we all still move in an unceasing, all-permeating, and unavoidable pollen cloud of persuasion. I often remind students that they likely won't get five minutes out of class before someone or something attempts to persuade them of something. The practical upshot of this ubiquity is clear to students: if they lack critical thinking skills, then they will be systematically vulnerable to others' attempts to influence their beliefs and actions with nonrational or marginally rational methods. And, what to many is even worse, they won't even be *aware* that they have been so influenced. They'll be suckers, taking others' belief cargoes onboard without anything like proper examination, blithely ignorant of the fact that there aren't good reasons to do so, all the while falsely thinking that they alone are steering their ships, when in fact their ships are being steered largely by others.

But it is one thing to make promises about the personal empowerment potential of a critical thinking course and another thing to fulfill those promises. This typically happens when we start talking about rhetorical tricks and fallacies. One route I like to take in this regard at the very outset is to say a few words about how rhetorical devices can lead us to believe things without providing anything like an argument in sight, and then to interrupt myself, before proceeding with the lesson, to tell them quickly about the situation in Sri Lanka: "A terrible civil war has been taking place there between the constitutionally elected government and a terrorist group known as the Tamil Tigers. The fighting has raged for decades, with the constitutional government and the terrorists locked in a bitter contest that has brought much suffering to the people." I then stop and ask: "Who are the good guys and the bad guys in Sri Lanka?" Student answers are just what you would expect them to be. "And did I give you any explicit *reasons* to think that way?" Significant silence followed by slow shaking of heads. "Not at all. But if class had suddenly ended after I gave you that description and you later talked with others about the situation in Sri Lanka, chances are you would view the Sri Lankan government favorably and the Tamil Tigers unfavorably. What happened there? I just infiltrated your belief system and made you believe what I want you to believe, and I did it without any real evidence or argument. Just a couple of words."

I try to let the moment sink in for a bit. Humor helps to bind a class, but sober moments have a more lasting impact. "Think about how easy it was for me to get inside your head and organize the furniture without giving you any good reasons why. This happens constantly. Constantly." This is a solemn moment for many students. Whatever they want to be, they don't want to be dragged along unknowingly by the nose. Doing precisely that a few times and showing them afterward that and how I did it can be a powerful motivator.

I like to use proof surrogates in this way. I tell them that "studies show" this or that, and later I ask them to remind me, in a moment of embarrassing forgetfulness, what studies have shown. They respond dutifully, at which point I ask them if they have actually been given any explicit reasons to accept the studies or even any detailed mention of the studies to which I have referred. Students get the point. Slapping a justificatory I.O.U. on a claim might be psychologically effective in relation to persuasion and associated actions, but from a rational point of view it shouldn't be.

Students can be motivated to study critical thinking by a desire to avoid embarrassment. Students also are motivated, I must admit, by the alluring prospect of winning debates. They hope to master the study of rhetorical tricks and fallacies well in order to get what they want more effectively. Of course I can't deny that this is possible; I won't lie to them. I am quite clear in telling them that rhetorical tricks are especially psychologically effective, which is why they are used so often by advertisers, politicians, and professors, among others. Yet I try to focus students' intentions in two ways: (1) I stress that the most important use for this knowledge is defensive—to prevent being duped by poor forms of persuasion, and (2) I stress that, if students care about *learning* or *finding the truth*, then rhetorical tricks and fallacies should be avoided at all costs.

Methods and My Motivation

It is a special pleasure to teach critical thinking during the run-up to presidential elections. It is a powerful opportunity to teach students the relevance of critical thinking skills in relation to an event of obvious social significance. And it certainly doesn't hurt, when it comes to fostering student motivation, that students feel significantly empowered by learning how to see through the rhetorical and fallacious smoke that politicians on both sides of the aisle generate so frequently. Few student exclamations are as satisfying to hear as when they catch a politician committing a rhetorical trick or fallacy.

I love to engineer "eureka" moments like this, both inside and outside class, and it is easy to do so in a way that hooks into popular culture. I don't know of any more powerful way to get students to see the relevance of critical thinking skills. My students study advertisements, tweets, op-eds, comment blogs, TV shows, and debates; they observe their peers' persuasive acts and report on them, and they monitor their own persuasive habits. If I can get a student to see a rhetorical trick or fallacy in action in one of these areas, then I am typically nine-tenths of the way toward showing them that the class has something valuable and useful for them. This is one of my most important goals: to show them that what we're studying *matters*.

Students tend to respond very favorably to these methods, and I would be lying if I didn't admit that I derive satisfaction from student acclaim. In my experience, teachers who profess to be motivated *purely* by altruism or by a commitment to abstract principles of learning tend to be good people who are overly concerned that taking pleasure in praise smacks of shabby and inglorious motives. But it is only human, I think, to enjoy commendation, and it can be a very effective vehicle for improvement.

I would be lying if I didn't admit that part of my enjoyment of teaching comes from the fact that I like to be onstage, at least to some extent. I like to be a storyteller and an explainer, to weave narratives and grab my students' attention and hold it, building suspense, lowering it again, raising it again, eliciting an unexpected laugh, growing serious when warranted, and leaving them wanting more. I have more than a little bit of the showman in me. Perhaps some might think that I should be ashamed of enjoying teaching for reasons that are self-serving, but it seems to me, rather, that some, albeit certainly not all, of the better teachers are people who teach because they like the activities involved in teaching, just as some, albeit certainly not all, of the better parents are people who have children because they enjoy parenting. So I try not to judge myself too harshly for enjoying the spotlight. I think it improves my performance.

Finally, I derive a great deal of satisfaction from seeing my students' critical thinking skills improve, even if they don't show gratitude, give praise, look interested, or acknowledge my existence. Perhaps this is, in part, because I enjoy the thought of having been an effective influence on them, but this can't be the whole story. I could have a much larger influence on them, I am sure, if I were to indoctrinate them directly by employing the very rhetorical tricks and fallacies I warn them against. The other part of the story, I think, is that I take satisfaction in teaching critical thinking because I think it makes for a better society. I don't mean to suggest that I am motivated by the utopian vision of a society whose members are all paragons of responsible civic engagement, although that is certainly a pleasant vision to contemplate. I'm referring to taking satisfaction in the thought that I am contributing to peppering society, even if just a bit, with people who tend to avoid unthinking conformity, bullheaded dogmatism, shallow consumerism, and knee-jerk partisanship, while tending to embrace and promote civil dialogue, logical acumen, open-mindedness, healthy skepticism, and individual awareness. I must admit to being very partial toward such people; I think they typically make the best voters, interlocutors, consumers, learners, friends, partners, and parents.

Lastly

These days, the Academy tends to reserve its most significant praise for advanced scholarly publications. I certainly see value in scholarly work, and I especially admire scholars whose writings are powerful and accessible enough to have a broad impact within the wider public. Thus far, my own publications fall far short of that, which isn't to say, of course, that I am not proud of them. But my most important professional work, the work that is the most impactful, is my teaching. And it is equally undeniable that, of all my teaching, my most broadly impactful class is critical thinking. It is humbling to think that I may have a part to play in empowering young people by helping them to gain the skills and habits necessary to think for themselves, to appreciate the power of words, to appreciate good reasoning, and to avoid the lure of rhetorical manipulation and persuasive gibberish.

It is even more humbling to think that, for some of my students, these habits and skills will become essential parts of who they are as people.

Paradoxically, being humbled in this way can also be very empowering for *me*. I may not be one of the great philosophers, *but, as a professor, I have the inestimable honor of having influenced and improved the lives of generations of students.*

10

Getting It Right:
Forty Years of Intro to Philosophy

Stephen H. Daniel
Texas A&M University

STEPHEN H. DANIEL is a Texas A&M University Presidential Professor for Teaching Excellence (2007). Before coming to Texas A&M in 1983, he taught at Spring Hill College (Mobile, AL) and Mount St. Mary's College (Los Angeles). From 2007 to 2012, he was the Fasken Chair in Distinguished Teaching and received university-level distinguished teaching awards in 1992 and 2005 and college-level distinguished teaching awards in 1987 and 2004. In addition to teaching awards from the A&M Center for Teaching Excellence, honors program, and student government, he has received grants to mentor new faculty, develop new courses, and incorporate technology into instruction. A specialist in seventeenth- and eighteenth-century philosophy, he has written or edited eight books and sixty articles and given seventy-five conference presentations, including articles and talks on teaching, testing, and writing research papers.

Before I came to Texas A&M University in 1983, I taught as many as five classes a semester (with four preparations) at a small liberal arts college in Mobile, Alabama. There I learned something that has characterized my teaching ever since: you don't teach material; you teach students. I have found that unless students are interested in the issues or questions raised in a discipline, they will not try to understand a problem or its complexities. Instead, they simply memorize facts or do what is necessary to get a grade. So before I begin a course, before I make an exam or assignment, before I meet with a class on any day, I ask myself the following:

• Why should my students care about what we are discussing?
• How can I interest each student by simplifying and clarifying the issues we address?

- What skills or information do I want my students to develop and retain from this activity?

These guiding questions require that I acknowledge that different students learn in different ways and that I draw on a wide range of teaching strategies in my courses. Graduate students want to show their mastery of topics in depth; upper-division undergraduate majors thrive on connecting issues; and nonmajors in small (15-student) as well as large (325-student) introduction to philosophy courses enjoy the excitement of evaluating different views (including their own). All of them revel in tackling questions they find intriguing, so I pique their interests initially with simplified answers, then challenge their positions, and finally provide lots of feedback. The trick is to make them always want more.

Here I will focus on teaching Intro to Philosophy, a course I have taught for almost forty years. I am most interested in what I need to do to make that first college-level contact with philosophy an experience that students will want to continue. I have discovered that with each semester I want my students to experience the same curiosity and passion for philosophy that I originally had and, to this day, continue to have. That means that I introduce new topics every semester into my course and have invoked well-known figures in ways that make them pop off the page for their novel views. In pursuit of different pedagogical objectives, I have shifted from the "teaching paradigm" to the "learning paradigm," gone through clickers and PowerPoint presentations, and explored the unique dynamics of small classes and 300+ student lecture halls. In that process, I have discovered that, regardless of the environment, students can get turned on to the prospect of engaging philosophy, as long as they see a point to it.

Over the past decade and a half, I have drawn insights about teaching from Maryellen Weimer's *Learner-Centered Teaching*,[1] Ken Bain's *What the Best College Teachers Do*,[2] Parker Palmer's *The Courage*

---

1. Maryellen Weimer, *Learner-Centered Teaching: Five Key Changes to Practice*, 2nd ed. (San Francisco: Jossey-Bass, 2013).

2. Ken Bain, *What the Best College Teachers Do* (Cambridge, MA: Harvard University Press, 2004).

to Teach,[3] James Lang's *On Course*,[4] and Weimer's *Inspired College Teaching*.[5] From these teachers and others, I have learned that our classrooms are places where students demonstrate their reflective abilities if they are allowed to pursue answers to questions they find intriguing. So my task is to show them that philosophy can be intriguing, puzzling, even bothersome—and for more reasons than simply a bad grade.

In my "learning-centered" model of teaching, I do not assume that all Intro students are initially able to think philosophically, or even know what philosophy is, or once they begin to find out what it is, are inclined to do more of it. I see it as my task to get them hooked. From day one—and that is the excitement of teaching an "introduction" to philosophy: it always seems like day one—the course is an opportunity to get students to care about something that they have most likely only thought about from afar. They think they are in it for the content, but having taught the course over and over, I see it for what it really is: an opportunity (finally) for them to identify themselves as the *doubter*, the *knower*, the *condemned*, the *agent*, the *believer*, the *citizen*, the (ultimate) *loser*. They need to know that it's about them personally, in that it reveals how well they think (or at least, about how well they can pretend to think). Indeed, if they can pretend long and well enough, it might just take hold, and they can find themselves slipping unawares into really thinking, despite their efforts to avoid it.

So I do all the things that teachers are supposed to do: pick textbooks that capture students' interests from the beginning and explain why our topics—knowledge, freedom, identity, mind-body metaphysics, God, ethics, political obligation—are arranged in that order. I indicate to them (on the first day and intermittently during the semester) why I chose a textbook that introduces the philosophical subfields in that order. I avoid anthologies, because they are disjointed and assume different levels of expertise. The same goes

---

3. Parker J. Palmer, *The Courage to Teach: Exploring the Inner Landscape of a Teacher's Life*, 20th anniversary ed. (San Francisco: Jossey-Bass, 2017).

4. James M. Lang, *On Course: A Week-by-Week Guide to Your First Semester of College Teaching* (Cambridge, MA: Harvard University Press, 2008).

5. Maryellen Weimer, *Inspired College Teaching: A Career-Long Resource for Professional Growth* (San Francisco: Jossey-Bass, 2010).

for historical introductions. Despite efforts to make Plato sound appealing, he and the other early Greek thinkers are some of the most puzzling and remote thinkers a beginning philosophy student can face. Even selecting a few sources (e.g., Plato's *Apology* or *Republic*, Descartes' *Meditations*, Nietzsche's *Gay Science*) assumes students are already interested in what those authors have to say—which is a *big* (and often unjustified) assumption.

For four decades, I have bounced from textbook to textbook, looking for that perfect combination of coverage, accessibility, and cost. For now, my textbook in Intro is *Ultimate Questions* by Nils Rauhut,[6] a relatively short and inexpensive overview that I supplement with readings from the following authors: Huemer (on skepticism), Berkeley and Kant (on knowledge), Strawson and Sartre (on freedom), Jackson (on qualia), Hume and Kierkegaard (on religion), Mill, Kant, Nietzsche (on ethics), Rawls and Nozick (on justice), Nagel (on the absurdity of life), and Sally Haslanger, Rosemarie Tong, Lucius Outlaw, and other women and minority writers (on exclusionary practices). Thankfully, there are more exhaustive and accessible Intro texts currently in press that should be available in the next year or two.

Teaching classes of Intro that are large and small, honors and regular, has made me appreciate the opportunities provided by each, and I have tried to adapt what I have learned from each to what I do in the others. For example, in large classes it is important to focus on a few basic points, and it is amazing what benefits follow in teaching small honors classes from using that approach. In small classes, it is important to have individuals speak up on some aspect of the topic of the day. But I have learned that I can generate interactive discussion even in a larger auditorium. This requires calling on students from day one and expecting some students to be underprepared. But that is where my Socratic training kicks in, focusing the class on the issue we are discussing, rather than on any one student's lack of preparation. In a large class, it is important to get students thinking that they are as responsible for contributing in a class of 325 students as they are in a class of 20, even if that means simply keeping up with

---

6. Nils Rauhut, *Ultimate Questions: Thinking about Philosophy*, 3rd ed. (Upper Saddle River, NJ: Prentice-Hall, 2011).

the reading. When they don't complete the homework reading, I use the opportunity to ask background questions that any student can answer, regardless of their before-class preparation.

Some teachers worry that a course with more than 300 students cannot possibly engage students in a way that captures the spirit of Socratic exchange. My response to this is to think outside the box, imagining how to play out, in students' minds, the kinds of exchange they would have had in a more intimate setting. Because I have engaged in those exchanges for decades, I can anticipate just about every puzzle, response, or objection students might have. But, every so often, a student will say something that I have not expected; and that is when things get interesting.

Before the semester begins, I try to contact all of my students by email to tell them how to get copies of the textbook online at a cost cheaper than they would pay at a local bookstore. I create a website for the course, and on those website pages I provide:

- information about the course
- links to amazon.com and elsewhere where they can get books cheaper
- the syllabus listing each day's assignment
- links to the PowerPoint slides that I will be using in any particular day's lecture
- tips on how to study for the tests and do well in the course
- links to the more than 1,300 objective-format (true/false, multiple choice) questions I have created for quizzes and classroom exams
- information about how to contact me by both email and personal phone

In the mega-sized course, I begin each class with a three-minute clip from a popular film dealing with our topic (e.g., the existence of God, freedom, artificial intelligence, morality). When the lights come back up, I am on the stage ready to start class. (That way I avoid the three wasted minutes when students end phone calls or conversations or put their books away.) I anticipate what I would have written on a chalkboard and clearly identify major concepts on PowerPoint slides. I usually create only three slides for a class (thirty-six-point font minimum) because I do not want the slides to get in the way of our exchange of ideas in class. I want the slides to complement and provide a framework for those ideas. As in my smaller courses, students earn extra points by answering a few multiple-choice, true-false questions on the assigned reading during class (either online or on paper). That way, I get a sense of whether they are getting the point we are discussing *and* I have a record of who was there.

Even though these points by themselves can amount, at most, to a change of only one letter grade, the practice gets students into the classroom and gets them thinking about the issues we discuss. This improves the quality of our time together, even in the intimidating context of the auditorium environment. On Fridays, smaller groups of twenty-five students meet with one of my teaching assistants to go over the material in a more intimate setting. In the last ten minutes of the Friday sessions, students are given a few more multiple-choice, true-false questions to discuss and answer with one another. Over the years, I have posted more than 1,300 questions for quizzes and classroom exams, and I post all of them (along with notes for my class) on my course websites.[7] These sites are now accessed by teachers and students from around the world through links on scores of other sites dealing with philosophy on the Internet. I mention these aspects of my classes because I believe that successful teaching depends not only on commitment but on attention to detail.

In my relatively small Intro classes, I am "old school" when it comes to technology: in class, a chalk or dry board is all I need. In my mega-sized classes, though, I want to communicate my enthusiasm for philosophy and to make sure that my 300 students are clear about the issues we discuss. So I use PowerPoint, not because it is fashionable, but because it fulfills my aims of clarifying what we read and allowing students 150 feet away to see what we are talking about.

Of course, I would love to have the luxury of always interacting with students in small groups of less than twenty-five—that, after all, was what attracted me to teaching in the first place. In those classes, students may receive their ideas by listening to an instructor or reading a text, but they *learn* the material when they teach it to

---

7. See, for example, people.tamu.edu/~sdaniel/quests1.html or people.tamu.edu /~sdaniel/quests4.html.

one another. That is why I free up time in my classroom for students to formulate positions based on their reading and to answer questions I pose to the class. On occasion, I will highlight a topic in an assignment so that students know beforehand the issues on which I would like them to focus. But they know that such targeted discussions always occur within a broader framework, and that that framework will be the focus of the questions on midsemester or final exams, or will become the topics of one of the three or four 500-word essays they will have to submit online over the weekend.

Because students often lead hectic lives, I think of assignments in my Intro to Philosophy class as opportunities not to make those lives more challenging, but for students to develop insights about philosophical concepts in application. That's why the questions I assign always have some practical relationship to students' daily routines. That might sound a bit artificial, until we realize that philosophy ultimately is supposed to be mundane. That is, as much as we might think that philosophy is concerned with extraordinary concerns, we need to make philosophy (especially in Intro classes) something that engages students where they live.

A discussion about functionalism or the ontological argument or Kantian ethics can sound like a bunch of claptrap to someone for whom physicalism, a proof for God's existence, or universal moral obligation is essentially beside the point. But that is where I come in. It is my responsibility in the classroom—or at least, I take it as my responsibility—to show students that what we philosophy teachers do can make a difference. Though my Intro courses ask students to study a long list of philosophical approaches—utilitarianism, deontology, empiricism, rationalism, and so on—it is not this list that will remain with my students after they complete the course, but the vexing philosophical problems that generate the list. The difference we make, as teachers of philosophy, lies in the many ways in which we encourage new students to ask themselves new questions.

That is why I find that I am always "on," always the guy who wonders about things such as truth or meaning or right. I show my appreciation for my students' efforts simply by being available, by taking every opportunity to chat with them in the hallway after class, and by inviting them to my house so that they can sit on our porch, go fish or canoe in our pond, or just visit with one another in the country, before heading back to finish up exams and papers. Some have told me that, looking back, they think of our study sessions before exams and visits to my house as markers of what they imagined a college education would be like (one that was not replicated in other courses). Those are the students whose lives I think I have touched.

Bottom line: Introduction to Philosophy is not a survey of material; it is an invitation to a lifestyle. Some students will be intimidated by the prospect of being hoodwinked into thinking that it contains solutions to our problems—indeed, to their problems. But as a teacher, my job is to show students how philosophers have always cautioned against such a facile view of their calling. When we are being honest with ourselves, we acknowledge that we really don't believe we have the answers or the truth. We know only that we are engaged in a series of exercises that prompt us to wonder about the point of what we do. We can try to make that sound more important than it is by saying that it underlies all other endeavors, but we would be fooling ourselves if we did. That is why it is so important for me to keep going back every semester to my Intro class—not to see if I can get it right this time, but to remind myself, through my discussions with philosophy's newest students, why we are called to pursue philosophical questions in the first place.

11

On Teaching "Happiness and the Meaning of Life"

Christine Vitrano
Brooklyn College

CHRISTINE VITRANO is an associate professor of philosophy at Brooklyn College, CUNY. Her areas of expertise are happiness, well-being, and value theory. She regularly teaches courses in normative and applied ethics, including a course on happiness and the meaning of life. Her monograph *The Nature and Value of Happiness* was published in 2014. She has also coedited an anthology, *Happiness: Classic and Contemporary Readings in Philosophy*, with Steven M. Cahn. Her latest book, *Happiness and Goodness: Philosophical Reflections on Living Well*, was cowritten with Steven M. Cahn, and it examines philosophical theories of well-being and the good life. In 2009, she was the recipient of the Mrs. Giles Whiting Foundation Fellowship for Outstanding Teaching in the Humanities at Brooklyn College.

I'd like to share my experience with a course that is not only my favorite to teach, but is consistently rated by students as one of the best they have ever taken. Happiness and the Meaning of Life tends to attract students from all over the college, many of whom have never before taken a philosophy course. Part of the success of this course probably can be attributed to the subject matter, happiness, which students (and frankly most people) tend to find intrinsically fascinating. However, I suspect another reason students rate this course so highly is that the material is immediately applicable to their lives. They are able, in a very commonsensical way, to critically evaluate these philosophical theories by reflecting on their own experiences. By the end of the course, even those with no prior background in philosophy can critically engage with challenging texts.

As a comparison, in my Introduction to Philosophy course, I try to get the students excited about some of my favorite topics, such as epistemic skepticism, mind/body dualism, the problem of personal identity, and free will. While I loved all of these issues as a student, I majored in philosophy and would go on to do this for the rest of my life. I can't say the same for many of my students, who often take this introductory course in order to fill college requirements. While I hope my enthusiasm and creativity in presenting the material hooks some of them, for many, these issues are simply too abstract or far removed from their lives to be of consequence. I find this to be especially true of students who are majoring in business and the sciences. They want to know why these issues matter, and it is often hard to give them a satisfying answer, other than, "Well, some of us find these questions fascinating."

When I teach Happiness and the Meaning of Life, however, none of these problems emerge, because we all care about happiness and whether our lives are worth living. Regardless of whether one continues to study philosophy, biology, or marketing, we all want to live happy lives, and we all want them to be meaningful. So this course tends to hook students immediately, especially those students who are otherwise skeptical of philosophical pursuits.

Given that we are living at a time when the value of the humanities in general, and philosophy in particular, is being questioned—both by the administrators, who view us as superfluous, and by the students themselves, who are under increasing pressure to pursue more directly vocational courses of study—I think philosophy departments could benefit tremendously from offering a course like this, which is sure to attract new students and boost enrollments.

In what follows, I'd like to offer some background on how I developed this course, my teaching style, and the kinds of students it typically attracts. Then I will discuss some of the topics we cover and why I think this course works so well. I'll present two versions of the course—one that relies on anthologized readings and the other that uses my own monograph—and I'll explain why each is effective, depending upon the student population.

First, some background. My interest in happiness began in graduate school, where I wrote my dissertation on contemporary theories of happiness. Steven Cahn and I put together an anthology of classic and contemporary readings on happiness, which was published by Oxford University Press. I developed the very first iteration of this course for City College, where I was a visiting professor. For that class, I only used our anthology, focusing on both the classics (Plato, Aristotle, Epicurus, Epictetus) and on contemporary scholars writing about happiness. The class, which filled immediately, was a huge hit. The students loved talking about happiness, comparing the different views, and critically examining how the concept has changed from ancient times to today. It was not difficult to spend the entire semester just focused on happiness—and from what I recall, we didn't even get through all of the contemporary readings on the syllabus.

When I started at Brooklyn College, our chair encouraged us to develop new courses in our research areas. When I told her about the course I did at City College, she suggested including another topic besides happiness, just to keep the course interesting. I agreed with her, for although the course was very popular at City College, I found, by the end of the semester, that the theories became a bit repetitive. I was aware of the literature on the meaning of life (I had written a paper criticizing Susan Wolf's view), so I thought it might be interesting to combine the two topics in one class. The meaning of life literature parallels the happiness literature, in that there is a debate between people who think the concept is subjective (or wholly determined by the subject's own feelings about her life) and those who think there are also objective requirements (such as performing worthy activities or pursuing valuable projects). Combining these two topics—starting with happiness and then switching to questions about meaning—worked well. By the time I get to the meaning of life part of the course, the debates are somewhat familiar, and the students have an easier time working through the arguments.

We started offering my happiness class at Brooklyn College once per year, though the first time, we offered it as a special honors seminar (which mainly attracted philosophy majors). Once approved by the college curriculum committee, we were able to offer the course as a general elective, with no prerequisites. This dramatically changed the dynamic of the class, because it started attracting large numbers of students from across the college, many of whom had never before taken a real philosophy course. In response to this change, I had to adjust the way I presented some of the content, and I developed the second version of the course, which I will describe later.

The great thing about this course is that it is so adaptable: using the exact same readings, one can teach this course to either beginning or more advanced philosophy students, simply by changing how extensively and how deeply the material is covered. With beginners, I spend more time just familiarizing them with the issues, such as the ancient moralists' fixation on the superiority of the intellect over the pursuit of brute pleasures. If I am starting with students who have some background in philosophy, I raise deeper questions about human nature and whether these theories accurately characterize the good life for humans. I find the more advanced students are also better at coming up with objections to these theories. The beginning students often agree with just about everything they read, so I often have to raise objections for them. But, either way, the students engage in critical analysis—first, by exploring the premises of the different theories of happiness and meaning and then by questioning whether these theories are plausible.

My teaching style hasn't changed that much over the years. I tend to favor lectures (without PowerPoint slides), but I always incorporate a lot of class discussion, which is often the best part of the class. In the other philosophy classes I teach, getting students to talk—either to answer questions or comment on the readings—can be challenging, especially when the readings are abstract or not directly connected with real life. The wonderful thing about this course is that all of the students can feel confident about offering their views, because happiness is something we all know (and care) about. Even the most shy students will participate in this class, unlike in others, where I have to work much harder to elicit student participation.

I tend to begin each lecture by carefully going through the arguments from the readings—writing key premises on the board and then asking the students questions about whether they agree with the arguments. Often, just trying to understand the main thesis can take up almost an entire class. But I always make sure to engage in some critical analysis, asking them whether they think this is the right approach to happiness (or living meaningfully) and then encouraging them to think about what's wrong with this view.

As I noted earlier, the beginning students tend to find everything convincing, so I have to do a bit more work to get them to see what's wrong with these views. In more advanced classes, students will initiate the objections, and I find it is more useful to play "devil's advocate" by defending the view under attack (or at least by explaining how I think the author would respond to their objections). Class discussion is a vital part of any philosophy course, but especially in one on a topic like happiness, where most people have some kind of opinion to offer.

I suspect part of the popularity of this course is due to the fact that it addresses topics people who aren't familiar with philosophy expect philosophers to talk about. I remember when I took my first philosophy course, I expected to learn about the meaning of life or what makes life worth living. I find many of the students in my introductory class have the same expectations and are somewhat disappointed when I begin with metaphysics and epistemology. I think many students have questions about why they are here and what they can do to be happy, yet few courses allow them to explore these issues rigorously, without devolving into a glorified therapy session. This course addresses their concerns, but also engages their critical reasoning skills and challenges them to read difficult texts. They make the effort to read through these texts, because they understand how these readings are directly connected with their own struggles.

The great thing about many of the readings (especially in the classic portion on happiness) is that although they were written thousands of years ago, the problems they address and the suggestions they offer are just as applicable today as they were back then. My students are quick to realize this and are often amazed by how little we have changed as humans, despite our technological advancements.

Next, I'd like to explain the progression of the course, including a brief discussion of the first two lectures. Of the two topics, happiness and the meaning of life, I find happiness to be the topic about which students are really curious, so I tend to spend more time on the happiness readings, roughly two-thirds of the semester, with the final one-third devoted to the meaning of life readings. Over the years, I've varied the readings I cover in the meaning of life portion of the course, most recently adding in readings on death, immortality, and the afterlife, because so many of the theories of meaning tread over the same territory. (How many times can we discuss the Myth of Sisyphus?) But I've continued to use the same anthology, which offers plenty of options. I tend to do in-class, short essay–style, noncumulative exams, so the first two exams cover the happiness readings, while the final exam is devoted to the topics connected with the meaning of life.

As I mentioned earlier, I have done this course two different ways, and I've had success with both. The first way is to have the students do all the primary readings from our anthology on happiness.[1] For the meaning of life readings, I use another anthology, *The Meaning of Life*, edited by Klemke and Cahn and also published by Oxford.[2] I think this version works best with students who are more advanced or who have some background in philosophy. Some of the readings are certainly challenging, and those new to philosophy will have a harder time engaging with them.

The second version of the course uses my book on happiness[3] instead of the anthology, and I discuss a different theory of happiness in each chapter. For instance, one chapter focuses on the identification of happiness with pleasure, another on virtue, and several focus on satisfaction views. For each theory, I discuss the arguments in favor of the view and then raise objections. I defend a life satisfaction view of happiness and then defend it against possible objections. I also discuss the connection between happiness and morality and evaluate various strategies for achieving happiness. This book works very well with beginner students, who have no prior experience with philosophy, because I explain all the different theories carefully, and I offer a lot of illustrative examples. I've found the students really like using this book, but I do think if you have more advanced students, it is better to use the anthology and have them read primary texts.

In the past, I have left the meaning of life portion the same in both versions—though, as I noted earlier, I have changed the topics to keep the course fresh. However, I would like to offer one more variation that I have not used personally but intend to try in the future. For the meaning of life portion, I would like to try using our

1. Steven M. Cahn and Christine Vitrano, eds., *Happiness: Classic and Contemporary Readings in Philosophy* (New York: Oxford University Press, 2008).

2. E. D. Klemke and Steven M. Cahn, eds., *The Meaning of Life: A Reader*, 4th ed. (New York: Oxford University Press, 2017).

3. Christine Vitrano, *The Nature and Value of Happiness* (Boulder, CO: Westview Press, 2014).

new book *Happiness and Goodness: Philosophical Reflections on Living Well*.[4] This book could replace the Klemke/Cahn reader or could be used as a supplement. The book raises questions about morality, meaning, futility, and death, all relevant issues to this part of the course. The book presents these theories in a clear, concise manner, using a lot of examples to illustrate and raise objections to the different views. The readings in the Klemke/Cahn anthology are definitely more challenging, so if students are just beginners, this book might be more approachable for them. With more advanced students, one could use both readers—choosing some primary readings from the Klemke/Cahn anthology and using our book to supplement the discussion.

I always begin the first day (after we've gone over the syllabus) with a free association on happiness. I encourage students to say anything that comes to mind when they think of happiness—what they think it is (or isn't). The basic idea is to encourage them to talk and not be afraid to offer their views, even if they're unsure. I also like to ask them why they are taking the course and what they hope to get out of it. This usually creates a friendly atmosphere right away, so they will feel comfortable participating in the class discussions.

For homework, I have them read the introduction to the anthology, in which the psychologist Daniel Nettle discusses three different senses of happiness, and an article from the *New York Times Magazine*, "The Futile Pursuit of Happiness," in which Jon Gertner interviews several psychologists about their findings on happiness.

The second lecture starts out with a brief discussion of "necessary and sufficient conditions" (and I use the old standby example "bachelor" to illustrate). I do this because I want to show students how one can raise objections to a definition simply by reflecting on one's own experience and knowledge of a concept. I then explain Nettle's three senses of happiness—pleasure, satisfaction, and virtue—using necessary and sufficient conditions. Hedonists view pleasure as both necessary and sufficient for happiness. Satisfaction theorists view pleasure as necessary (one could not be satisfied with a life devoid of all pleasure) but not sufficient for happiness, because some pleasures

---

4. Steven M. Cahn and Christine Vitrano, *Happiness and Goodness: Philosophical Reflections on Living Well* (New York: Columbia University Press, 2015).

fail to promote satisfaction. Finally, virtue theorists view satisfaction as necessary (one can't be happy with a life with which one is entirely dissatisfied) but not sufficient for happiness, because, on their view, one's satisfaction must be derived from living a virtuous life or doing objectively praiseworthy activities. These three views dominate the literature, so it is worthwhile to spend a bit of time explaining each view and how they differ. At the end (if there's time), I discuss the article from the *New York Times Magazine*, asking students what they got out of it, what surprised them, what they agreed with, and so on.

In the subsequent lectures, I try to go through all the classic views first (Plato, Aristotle, Epicurus, the stoics) before moving on to the more contemporary satisfaction views (which often refer to the classic views). I like to end the happiness section with the topic of happiness and morality and the question of whether morality is necessary (or sufficient) for living a happy life. The happiness portion of the course ends with their second exam, and then we move on to the meaning of life. I used to spend more time considering different replies to the question of whether life is meaningful, such as theistic, nontheistic, and existential nihilist replies. But recently, I've cut some of that material out to include a discussion of death, immortality, and the afterlife. I think these are all interesting topics on their own, and they tend to generate good discussions, but they also provide the opportunity for rigorous philosophical analysis. (Fischer's article[5], for instance, which responds to Williams' Makropulos case, models for students how to dissect an argument and challenge its premises.)

I hope this overview of my course Happiness and the Meaning of Life has been helpful. This is one of the best courses I've ever taught, and judging by my students' responses on their end-of-term evaluations, they seem to find it very rewarding as well. I still get emails from students who took this course years ago, telling me how they remember what they learned and how the material has stayed with them. I don't get that same feedback from the other courses I teach. The happiness course seems to mean a lot to students, which, honestly, makes teaching the course that much more rewarding.

---

5. John Martin Fischer, "Why Immortality Is Not So Bad," in *Life, Death and Meaning*, 2nd ed., ed. David Benatar (Lanham, MD: Rowman and Littlefield, 2010).

12

Learning to Not Teach

Paul Woodruff
University of Texas at Austin

PAUL WOODRUFF has taught philosophy and classics at the University of Texas for over forty years. Before that, he served with the U.S. Army in the American War in Vietnam and won a teaching award at the Special Warfare School. At Texas, he has won five teaching awards and been admitted to the Academy of Distinguished Teachers. For fifteen years, he directed the Plan II Honors Program and was made inaugural dean of the School of Undergraduate Studies. In that role, he brought in a new core curriculum for all undergraduates at the university. His publications include a number of translations from ancient Greek that are designed for student use (and published by Hackett). His latest book, *The Garden of Leaders*, will be released in October 2018. It recommends a curriculum rich in the humanities, offered by teaching methods that call for independence and leadership on the part of students.

From the start I was uncomfortable taking a role as a teacher of philosophy. I had raced through the Ph.D. program at Princeton far too quickly, and I felt that I knew barely enough to teach a single class on the subject. Understand me: I was not nervous about teaching itself or about addressing large groups of people. I had taught for six months at the Army's Special Warfare School in Fort Bragg, where I had lectured for classes of up to two hundred officers, sometimes of higher rank than mine, and I had won a teaching award there. After a year's service in Vietnam, I thought I knew a lot about the subject I had been assigned to teach by the Army. I was confident I could tell my students things that might save their lives and help them prosecute the war effectively. In retrospect, I now believe I was wrong on all counts. In teaching those classes, I was implicated in an especially inhuman aspect of a war that would succeed only in devastation. Still, by doing so, I learned that I could teach effectively, even if what I was teaching was detestable. I knew the basics of teaching. What I did not know was philosophy.

I still don't know much philosophy. But I know more now, and most of what I have learned in the last forty-five years I have learned by teaching. From the first day, I loved interacting with my students, and I was delighted to find that I learned more teaching a course than I had ever learned taking one. I felt selfish, banking a salary from students who were paying to learn, while I was the one learning, and they (I surmised) would soon forget whatever I told them.

Speaking with alumni and alumnae, I started asking them what they remembered from philosophy courses in the past and discovered they remembered hardly anything. If they did remember something from a course, it was usually about how the professor had treated them. So I began to suspect that what I said did not matter as much as how I interacted with the students—what kind of example I set. This point is not specific to philosophy: anyone who teaches anything is teaching, by example, how a person with authority may behave; in other words, any teacher teaches ethics and leadership. And many of us do it badly, as the graduates assured me.

Changing Shape

I have been in one classroom or another, in the role of teacher, for forty-five years, and in that time I have shifted away from my earlier goals. At first I wanted to be a good teacher. Now I try to put teaching aside and let the learning happen, as much as possible, through student interaction. I have been fortunate in being assigned seminars for first-year students in a lovely honors program, the Plan II Honors Program. This is an interdisciplinary arts and sciences major, for which I have conducted seminars in literature and philosophy as well as lecture courses in philosophy. More recently, I have taught in a first-year seminar program open to all students—one I helped to organize when I was a dean.

The first time I conducted such a seminar, I found that the students interacted only with me, and this, I soon learned, was inevitable in view of the shape of the classroom and its table. The table was a long rectangle, placing students in such a form that they could all see me, but not each other. The very shape of things defeated my goal of inducing the students to practice learning from each other. Did I tell you my hobbies include furniture building? I had designed and made small tables before; now I resolved to design an enormous one. It would have to seat twenty people, with no straight lines, so that everyone could make eye contact with everyone. I also wanted the table to have no legs that would interfere with seating arrangements.

The table was sixteen feet long by eight feet wide and rested on a trestle with no legs around the edge. Its shape was a perfect ellipse— no straight lines. An ellipse has two centers (foci, to be exact), which make a nice symbol for an arts and sciences program, and, as my wife Lucia pointed out to me, a perfect symbol of an ideal marriage. Building it was a huge task, in which students helped me. We finally finished and installed the table in a seminar classroom in the middle of a fall semester. I was pleased to see that the atmosphere of the class I had been conducting improved markedly from the day we moved to the new table. Since then I have fought hard against being forced to use a table with straight sides.

A recent observer in a seminar of mine was pleased to notice that the students were listening to each other, responding to each other, and actually teaching each other quite a lot. When a student spoke, she had a beanbag in her hand, which, after speaking, she threw to the person of her choice, who would now catch not only the beanbag but also the thought she had put on the table. I did not need to say anything to keep the discussion moving.

Changing the shape of the table helped me change the conception of my role in the classroom. Before, I had thought of each hour in the room as mine to fill by doing or saying things; around the new table we all saw that same hour as a time for the students to do things—so much so, that students recently complained about the minilectures I was giving in such a room during a MWF course on Mondays, when I thought they might not feel like doing much themselves, but listening. I was wrong. They wanted to participate.

A Course Totally Redesigned

I have experimented over the years with various ways of engaging students with each other, and I am currently having some success with setting teams of students in competition with each other. A few years ago, I had good experiences with classes that I divided into competitive teams. For example, a Philanthropy Lab Course[1] I taught some years ago went very well. The class was provided with $100,000 to give away to reputable causes (other than the university) at the end of the semester. These were real dollars provided by the Once Upon a Time Foundation. The foundation's goal was to make every dollar work twice—once in the education of the students, and once again in the good causes to which the students gave the money.

My class—all first-year students—divided itself into teams representing such causes as the arts, education, poverty, health research, and human rights. They were required to do extensive research as individuals in the causes that interested them and present their results to their teams. Each team then chose one student's cause to support and prepared to debate the other teams. All this left me little time for lecturing or conducting the usual class discussions, but the students were learning like wildfire—how to use library databases, how to evaluate charitable causes, how to write up strong papers about them, how to make the case orally for their causes. Along the way, they were also learning to work better in groups. There were no laggards, because the dollars were real, and they all cared where those dollars would go.

More recently, I had to design a course from zero in short order. I had planned to offer a graduate seminar on Thucydides in classics, requiring knowledge of Greek, but hardly anyone took a nibble at it. So it was canceled at the last minute, and I had to invent a new course on a topic guaranteed to attract undergraduate students—philosophy of art. There's no swelling passion for philosophy of art in Texas, but our university has a requirement in the fine arts, and this course satisfies it. I had taught the subject in my early years when I still thought of myself as a teacher. The texts I had used were bulky anthologies with only about one item in ten that I would want to use again. I had no time to create my own text, though this is easier now than it was. A proposal I made for an aesthetics textbook in the 1980s went nowhere and no longer appealed to me. So I decided to try something totally different.

---

1. The Philanthropy Lab Courses are sponsored at a number of universities around the country by the Once Upon a Time Foundation, which donates funds for students to distribute. In recent years, universities have been raising additional funds to support the courses.

Could I transfer the Philanthropy Lab model to a course on the arts? "Why not?" I thought. I did not have real dollars, but I could imagine a fund that my class could give away to the most worthy art project that a team proposed. At the end of the semester, they would constitute a foundation and award grants to realistic projects developed by the teams. Rather than impose my artistic taste on the class, I invited them to state their interests, and I then formed them into teams around those interests. Guess what? Rap music loomed large. Very well, not my cup of tea (I play cello in chamber music), but there must be an aesthetics of rap, and my students would explain it to me. They did.

The six art forms around which the teams coalesced were architecture, modern dance, film, fiction, rap music, and popular music other than rap. I would conduct the class for the first six weeks; after that, each team would take a week to present its art form, using a format I would give them. Then at the end of the semester the teams would present projects for funding and the class would decide how to spend the $100,000. Winning teams would earn not only the esteem of their peers but also bonus points toward their grades.

In the early weeks of the class, we read a few basic texts, such as Aristotle's *Poetics*. I derived a format from Aristotle and asked each group to use its teaching week to develop a poetics of its art form: a definition, an enumeration of elements, a theory about what makes the art good (when it is good), and an account of its value for performers and audiences. I gave an example myself, presenting one of my favorite art forms to the class and providing a poetics for it. The form was chamber music—totally new to all, but one, in the class and so a good example for what my students would have to do for each other. They would have to define the art form, give clear examples, and answer specific questions about the aesthetics of that art form—for example, when a piece is good what makes it good?

In the middle six weeks of the course, we learned from the students about each art form and came to some understanding of what a poetics for that form would look like. The oral presentations (for which I had given them guidance as to content, delivery, and timing) went well, and we all felt we had learned something about the arts. Modern dance was new to all but its team members, architecture was little better known, and film was quite unknown as an art form. Rap was familiar to the whole class, but its aesthetics were not.

The teams chose readings for the class, in consultation with me, and also proposed exam questions for the final exam—knowing that they would have to answer the questions posed by other teams. So I gave my students the full experience of teaching—choosing material, thinking it through, and devising ways to assess student learning. They seemed to relish this and learn from it. Meanwhile, students were writing papers presenting the material they would bring before the class, each student taking one part of the poetics of the team's choice. They were also beginning to develop—and do research for— their grant proposals. As with the Philanthropy Lab, each team would choose a student's project and work together to promote it in the debate section that ended the course.

The teams were set up with rotating leadership, and leaders were required to submit reports on team activity under their leadership. I have taught courses on leadership in other programs, and I was doing so now, but surreptitiously. At the end of the semester, I would ask students to write up what they had learned about leadership from the experience. It turned out that most of them learned a lot by observing each other's successes and failures, and writing that up seemed to cement what they had learned.

At the very end, we had a very positive sort of debate, with teams competing in pairs and passing through elimination rounds. Teams were invited to look for weaknesses in their opponents' proposals, but these were not knockdown adversary debates. A ballot committee with a member from each team chose the voting method and devised the ballot. In the end, the architecture team won over the class with an elegant proposal for the design of a green wall on a particularly brutal brutalist building on our campus.

My main interests in the arts—painting, poetry, classical music, and theater—did not appeal to my students, and I would not have been able to reach them through the arts that they cared about most, which were beyond my range. So this course design allowed each team to learn philosophy of the art forms that actually meant something to them. Nevertheless, every student's horizons in the arts were expanded—not by me but by their peers, people whose taste they trusted. Modern dance, for example, was a great success. We all had our eyes opened.

As with the Philanthropy Lab, this course design left me little time for traditional teaching, but it gave the students unusual opportunities for learning. I could have *taught* them more philosophy in a traditional course, but I doubt they would have *learned* much of what I could have presented in lectures. They would, simply, have safely knocked off a requirement. As it was, what they did learn in this course I think would stick with them—especially about the art forms they loved. What exactly did they learn? That is hard to assess. The final exams showed that they had learned enough to write good essays on the art forms they had presented, while giving accurate answers to test questions on the readings chosen by other teams. They also thought they had learned something about leadership, and I agreed. They had adjusted to work together in teams, and they had taught the class effectively with little guidance from me.

Besides learning some new things, the students had good practice writing, doing research, and speaking about topics they cared about. The skills involved are useful in any line of work, I believe, since they are easy to transfer from the arts to other subjects.

I graded students individually on their presentations and on the formal papers that grew out of them. This is essential for an academic team-based course; students rightly insist that instructors grade them on the merits of their own work, which reveals what they have individually learned. Nonacademic teamwork, such as for military operations, is rightly evaluated on a team basis; if one member fails on a military team, all of them might die, and so the members need to learn by experience that individual achievement, by itself, is irrelevant in such situations. But not in my classroom. I would like to find a way to assess and grade leadership on the teams, but I have not found a method that I am willing to use. The military model, a 360-degree peer evaluation, is unpopular with students. It can be devastating, when you are very young, to find that your peers all dislike you. It's far better, I think, to ask students to evaluate their own learning about leadership. A self-evaluation should be graded pass-fail, and could be built around questions like these: What have you learned about how to chair a meeting effectively? What would you do differently as a leader next time?

Student evaluations of the course were quite positive, with a number of students (including graduating seniors) writing that this was the best classroom experience they had ever had. I fished for negative comments, however, and these were informative. Some students pointed out that my lectures were better than the student ones (no surprise, but gratifying). And some complained that the readings were not well chosen. I have done better in subsequent applications of this style of course. If students are to engage in teaching, I need to do more work—not less—to prepare them for doing so.

Influence

After many years teaching in the same place, I frequently encounter former students, some of whom are now gray-haired grandparents. I have wonderful friends whom I met in my classroom when we were all young together. The children of former students sometimes enroll in my classes. One would think that by now I would know what kind of influence I have had on the thousands of people who have coursed through my classrooms. At most, I have a crude idea about what my classes have meant to the very few people who have told me what they wanted me to hear. I know this much at least: I am not a good influence on students aiming at an academic career. The way I approach philosophy is alien to the approach of most highly rated graduate schools. My work has always been interdisciplinary, which can be a hard sell in many departments, and, since receiving the gift of tenure, I have spent a lot of time on translations and on topics in ethics for a general audience—neither of which would earn points for a young scholar. The result is that my former students are often disappointed if they go on in philosophy. Surviving graduate school, finding a job, and getting tenure are all harder than they ought to be for them.

But because I love what I do, I never discourage a student from trying out the academic route. I warn students, however, about what they will have to do to succeed—and about all the luck they will need in addition to hard work, talent, and a capacity for jumping through hoops. They will have to do well at some tasks that they do not like, and would not set for themselves, in order to earn the freedom to write as they wish and try to change the field to suit them better. Looking back, I think I have had more influence through what I have been, than through what I have said, in the classroom. This is impossible to assess, however. Teachers pass gifts along to a stream of students who are being swept toward careers and family obligations. Along the way, most of them will drop what we have given them over the side, to lighten their burdens. We will never know how often they will catch a glimpse of some small idea we gave them rising again to the surface, or what it will mean to them when they do.

13

Moments of Grace

Anthony Weston
Elon University

ANTHONY WESTON has taught Philosophy and Environmental Studies at Elon University since 1993, where he has been honored both as Teacher of the Year (Daniels-Danieley Award, 2002) and Scholar of the Year (Distinguished Scholar Award, 2007). He is author of over a dozen books, half of them textbooks that attempt to reimagine some field of philosophy by modeling a different way of teaching it, including the widely used *A Rulebook for Arguments* (Hackett, 5th ed., 2018) and *A 21st Century Ethical Toolbox* (Oxford, 4th ed., 2018). His forthcoming *Teaching as the Art of Staging* (Stylus, 2018) proposes a model of the teacher as an "Impresario with a Scenario" sharply alternative to both the familiar "Sage on the Stage" and "Guide on the Side." He has taught abroad in western Canada, Costa Rica, and Australia, "under the open skies" as much as possible, and is a founding member of Hart's Mill Ecovillage, which is his current main form of philosophy in action.

In memory of Jim Cheney

In 2004, Patsy Hallen, Australian teacher-activist-writer-dreamer, invited me to co-teach that year's version of her eco-philosophy course out of Perth's Murdoch University, which she organized around two long backpack trips into the outback. Thus my fiftieth year found me quite literally all the way around the world from my Carolina home, traipsing overland with adult students—master's level, mostly, in their twenties and thirties, from all over the world—through the red desert and along the shores of the tumultuous Southern Ocean, sleeping under the shimmering unfamiliar stars, and later car-camping with my family up and down the west coast and among the great monadnocks of the Red Centre and the rainforests of the Northern Territory.

Something is going on out there. This group felt it especially strongly at the awakening of the Earth at dawn in the bush. The fast-shifting clouds, the countless purposeful insects, the lilting birds, the last full exhale of the soils' pores before the coming heat of the day, the quizzical but poised rocks—there is something immense and powerful in that land, seemingly just out of reach, even a hint of numinous more-than-human fellow travelers. Not for nothing do Australian Aboriginal peoples speak of Dreamtimes. With permission, we followed Aboriginal paths through the land, winding our way between billabongs, meeting together for talk or sometimes more or less silent wonder under the wide-open skies, joined by sea eagles and kangaroos on occasion, our nights filigreed by vivid and unprecedented dreams, our days sustaining the ongoing multiple human dialogues that also wove through our walkabouts.

People who take long wilderness trips usually take many days to feel the beginnings of a real shift in their perceptions—to awaken into the larger world, to the winds and weather and the great rhythm of light and dark, to the creatures and the powers of the place. The din of machinery and the buzz of electronics have to subside first, and the senses reawaken. But they do. Even then, there are no guarantees—it takes some spiritual preparation, though I don't necessarily put it to students that way, and it takes some pedagogical strategy, such as eliminating electronics (no phone, no cameras—which makes for useful discussions as well). Still, even three or four days in, the effect is marked.

Perhaps a certain receptivity is built into the rhythm of such experiences. Nature on the whole moves slowly: think evolution, or tectonic drift, which utterly transform everything, repeatedly, but over vast time spans. The power of such experiences then may derive partly from our own shift of tempo, shutting down the near-instantaneous and interruptive modality of the cellphone for the cosmic and the chthonic near-timelessness of the glittering stars at night or the contemplation of the backstory of grains of sand on a beach. That shift, at least, that openness, is the precondition from our side. The world, for its part, imperturbable and sublime as always, just welcomes us back. "I thought the earth remembered me / she took me back so tenderly. . . . / I slept as never before, a stone on the river bed / nothing between me and the white fire of the stars."[1]

---

1. Mary Oliver, "Sleeping in the Forest," in *New and Selected Poems* (Boston: Beacon Press, 1993).

Tricky Rocks

Teaching like this—or more accurately, fellow traveling with students—out on the edge of hyper-anthropocen*trized*[2] modernity is actually to come to the very *center* of the world if one looks at things from a larger-than-human perspective. Thus a 2006 and 2007 summer class out of Royal Roads University in Victoria, British Columbia, part of a master's-level curriculum in Environmental Education and Communication overseen by Professor Rick Kool, took Rick and me and twenty students, mostly Canadian environmental organizers or teachers themselves, up Vancouver Island to Tofino in vans, then onto a small boat that services mostly logging operations up that roadless, precipitous, primeval coast and its islands, to drop us at a site called Cougar Annie's Garden—once the homestead of a legendary though problematic local figure (that's "Annie"), now being restored as a residential study facility on temperate rainforests as well as a historical site, part of Hesquiaht First Nation traditional land. There we lived for a week in small cabins up the mountainsides, no electricity, no contact with the outside world, just the forest and the bay, grizzlies foraging by day and the dance of the nebulae at night.

We took turns doing meals and between sessions hiked for miles along logging roads and Hesquiaht trails, as well as cedar plankways, passing occasional shrines or other structures, being built onsite as a labor of love by the current owner and main resident, winding between 800-year-old trees and, incongruously, hothouse-type flowers from bulbs that the eponymous Annie used to grow for sale. Hobbitty little outhouses invited us to help fertilize semiwild gardens right below us down the steep mountain slopes, while we gazed through ornately crafted windows dozens of miles across the bay. We swam in a small and spectacularly frigid lake behind the site with a mysterious "Whale Rock" in the middle—in Native lore, a site of great power—that showed itself, with exquisite delicacy, to only a few of us, just as the ancient stories, credited by none of us at first, told us it would.

Again we were living and learning—no real distinction—in the very midst of a vastly larger world: the whole numinous Pacific

---

2. Anthony Weston, "Non-anthropocentrism in a Thoroughly Anthropocentrized World," *The Trumpeter* 8, no. 3 (1991):108–12.

Northwest surround, its fjords and tumbling waters of the west coast of Vancouver Island, at the edge of a familiar world but at the very center of another. Not "remote" at all—quite the contrary. Once again the grand scenario was an immersive, continuously unfolding encounter in an uncompromisingly larger-than-human frame.

Classes and small study groups met constantly on the decks, in a small, half-open chapel near the lake, or in the gardens. Students worked on a signposting project for one of Rick's classes. (How do you present such a site diplomatically, informatively, provocatively, honestly?) For mine, the theme was storied modes of inhabitation or co-presence, as I called them—one mode of "environmental communication," or what my late friend and wilderness companion Jim Cheney called "ethics as bioregional narrative."[3] Out loud as well as outside, we read the works of the Haida-Gwaii storyteller Skaay of the Qquuna Qiighawaay (John Sky), a long Sapsucker narrative in particular, while at the same time we could savor the voice of this very land under its own open sky and surging waters, the mewling and drumming sapsuckers themselves all around us.

I invited the students to take the next step too. One of the main projects for my class that week was for each participant to find (or be found *by*) what I called a *Storied Token* of the place: some natural being or object or specific process, emblematic of the place, around which both their own human and the place's more-than-human stories might crystallize. Of course, the Token had to show itself in the first place. Tokens and their stories may come to each of you in specific ways, I said: your task is chiefly to be open to them. This is "environmental communication" too, but in a far more ancient and mysterious mode than we have learned to expect.

Students responded with immense heartfulness and variety. Days were spent preparing, feeling their ways back into the natural world, attending to the solicitations, as David Abram puts it, of specific more-than-human Others right around us.[4] We finally spoke of them together on our last long late-summer afternoon before heading back to "civilization." Some Tokens were small pieces of wood,

---

3. Jim Cheney, "Postmodern Environmental Ethics: Ethics as Bioregional Narrative," *Environmental Ethics* 11 (1989):117–34.

4. David Abram, *The Spell of the Sensuous: Language and Perception in a More Than Human World* (New York: Pantheon, 1996).

invoking the tree elders, scraps maybe from the boardwalks whose rough waviness brought out a certain quirky and fleeting magic in the place at the same time, counterpoint to the gravity and immensity of the trees. One Lebanese woman linked the massive ancient cedars of this faraway temperate rainforest to the legendary cedars of her homeland—now reduced by millennia of depredations to a few small plots, slowly regenerating in the hearts of the people as well as tenaciously on the eroded hillsides.

Another participant brought us a set of nested crab shells and spoke of molting—shell-shifting—as life-story, both literally and as metaphor. When she finished, her friends in the class, knowing her own life-story, spontaneously stood up and honored her as doing the same thing. She's beaming and sobbing at the same time. Another brought a miniversion of the Whale Rock. She had not seen it in the lake herself, she tells us. In fact she was seriously irritated that the old-goat story apparently was true—it really was going to hide from all the women. But then she resolved to take it that the rock was actually manifesting itself to her in another way, as something she could carry with her and warm with her own body's warmth. We contemplated this.

In a similar spirit, I brought my own Storied Token, a little totem that came to me on a previous kayak trip in this region: an oyster shell that welded itself to a small rock, the ensemble, if held at the right angle, irresistibly bringing to mind the wing of the Winged Victory, the famed though still mysterious Samothracean (fragment of a) monument now in the Louvre. A winged rock, then, quite literally: it flew home with me from my previous trip and flew back for this one. More allegorically, it is a symbol, to me, of how the whole spirit of the place, literally the fusion of life and rock, itself can "take flight" in our own imaginations and, yes, "environmental communication." The oldest stories tell us that rocks themselves are alive—they just move at a different tempo, but they do indeed move: all over the surface (by water, by ice, by us . . .) and by plate (think tectonics), up and down, into crust and mantle, and even through space. This one . . . flies.

All Our Relations

Why care about nature? Really, why? Like most moderns, my environmental ethics students can produce a whole range of decent reasons. Because of its beauty. Because of its antiquity. Because of some special kind of intrinsic value that philosophers haven't been able to persuasively articulate just yet, but will soon, we promise. Because God created it and actually did *not* sign it over to us to ravage as we please, despite what the first pages of Genesis seem to say. Because, if nothing else, human well-being and indeed sheer survival depends on it. We study all of these sorts of arguments—the usual themes of environmental ethics—and my course, like many others, seems to be moderately successful at enabling students to develop and claim voice to them.

Behind and alongside these reasons is another sort of reason, though, and a reason at once so simple, so central, and so overwhelming that it hardly seems like a "reason" at all. It even seems embarrassing to state it, especially baldly, and somehow sentimental to embrace or celebrate. This is simply that we are related to everything, and everything to us. Native people speak simply of awareness of "All Our Relations." Australian philosopher Freya Mathews puts it in a more contemporary philosophical idiom when she writes that for Aboriginal peoples, human subjectivity is not the primal frame within which everything else emerges, but rather is itself "emergent with a larger subjectivity, always already an emanation of land, of country, of world."[5] And for Mathews too, this awareness is also vastly illuminating, heartening, grounding. It does not just "ground" a formal ethic, but literally constitutes an entire way of life.

I do not propose here to even begin to argue for such a worldview—as if it even *is* a "view" for which one might argue in the first place, which already puts it into a distinctively modern/subjectivist/disconnected frame. These are very large issues. It does pose a major pedagogical challenge, though, which is more in line with the themes of the present collection. Even those teachers who may have little sympathy or less understanding of the "Old Way," as the poet Gary Snyder and others call it, would likely agree that this encompassing

5. Freya Mathews, *Reinhabiting Reality: Toward a Recovery of Culture* (Albany: SUNY Press, 2005), 103.

feeling for the natural world at least needs to be taught as part of an environmental ethics class in the name of inclusiveness and "coverage." Their aim, as mine, is in part to help students——especially environmental studies majors——become conversant with the broad range of existing approaches to environmental values, and hence able to interact constructively with a wide range of constituencies in the real environmental debates they will soon join.

Yet "All Our Relations" cannot be left a merely curious verbal formula when our students are going to be dealing with people for whom it is an orison to the encompassing animate world. Besides, who knows if it might not speak to our students' souls (even . . . our own?) in ways that the usual forms and formulae of environmental ethics do not? In any case, students need to have some sense of how it *feels*, how the world manifests when attended to in this way. But how can we teach such a thing? How do we offer students even the barest glimpse of what such a world is like, and of the profound ethical reorientation that arises out of it, when it is so far from anything that they (or we, mostly, either) are likely to have experienced or even considered before?

For multiple reasons, school per se is a profoundly unwelcoming or simply impossible setting for such a learning.[6] Students are systematically separated from worlds of mystery and magic and indeed any larger world but for the classroom; few learn how to *listen*, certainly not with the heart; and the slow and patient nurturing of wisdom through actual experience in the widest world is certainly not on the agenda. Most of us know better than to bring up the Old Way in serious academic company, at least as anything other than an anthropological curiosity: we would be quickly and patronizingly dismissed as credulous, soft headed, prone to talking to birds or the Thunder. In school, more than almost anywhere, consensus reality rules, and reproduces itself.

---

6. Lucy Wren et al., "What Is a Good Way to Teach Children and Young Adults to Respect the Land?" In *Proceedings of the Yukon College Symposium on Ethics, Environment, and Education*, ed. Bob Jickling (Whitehorse, Y.T.: Yukon College, 1996). See also my piece "Instead of Environmental Education" in the same volume, along with my "What If Teaching Went Wild?" in *Philosophy of Education 2002*, ed. Scott Fletcher (Urbana, IL: Philosophy of Education Society, 2003), 40–52.

Yet I have found that it is possible, after all, at least sometimes, in partial and ambiguous ways to be sure, to enable students to glimpse the natural world in another guise. Or rather, more precisely—for to be precise here is actually a demanding etiquette[7]—I have found that it is possible to create certain conditions for the emergence into experience, at least fleetingly, of that vastly encompassing animate and responsive world from which, in an Aboriginal view according to Mathews, our own subjectivities and indeed our very beings themselves emanate. I hasten to add, in the spirit of the same etiquette, that I certainly do not claim credit for this, let alone any specific technique or method to somehow "produce" such experiences. They won't be produced on cue, anyway. The spirits tend to be shy, as a shaman might explain, and often very particular. Thus, while I realize that the present volume is supposed to be more like a volume of success stories—celebrations of teaching—and while no one could be more appreciative of and committed to active teaching than me, what I aim to share here is something quite different: very partial and barely replicable "successes" at best. Just moments, and a way of thinking that accommodates and enables them. Just moments—but what moments!

Thunder Speaks After All

In my Environmental Visions class and sometimes in others, I ask my students to consider the animals or places or forces of nature with which they identify and whose power or presence they feel they may share in some way. Many name specific animals: Cat or Dog, Dragonfly, Elephant, Stingray, Deer. A runner may be Cheetah. Some pick favorite places, places that speak to them, like Beach, or specific beaches. Some are waves, there is the occasional tree, sometimes Wind or Rain or Lightning or Sun. One African American student at heavily white Elon declared herself Chameleon. A partly Native American student was a Buffalo: in his dreams he becomes a buffalo, runs with his fellows, and can ask them to take him other places or into other identities in turn. And unlike most students,

---

7. Jim Cheney and Anthony Weston, "Environmental Ethics as Environmental Etiquette: Toward an Ethics-Based Epistemology in Environmental Philosophy," *Environmental Ethics* 21 (1999):115–34.

he did not choose this Affinity Being: it was given from birth, his clan animal.

Actually, I say, no one should think that they are doing all the choosing. As with the Storied Tokens, there is more of a dance here. It is at least as true that other beings/powers choose *you*. Are there animals, I ask, that regularly come to you, in dreams or awake? Perhaps you have even had specific encounters, numinous or electrifying, that stay with you?

Of course, it is possible to pick an Affinity Being in a superficial way. Nonetheless, there turns out to be immense power in opening this door even a crack. I have found repeatedly that the beings with whom my students embrace affinities show up in unprecedented numbers and in striking ways—across our paths, on the web, in our dreams. I had not seen rabbits for years on campus until one of my first-years declared herself Rabbit one spring. Within days we were stumbling over them. Another in the same class was Shark, partly on account of a diving encounter, face-to-face. Long after the class was over I was still sending him links to shark films that would not stop turning up on my listservs. Yet another was Dragonfly, and what followed was the summer of, yes, dragonflies.

Of course, it may be said that Dragonflies and Rabbits and Wind and all the rest are always around anyway, and we just notice them more when we or someone else identifies (with) them. And it is true: they are always there. But why is this itself not the magic? Maybe the greater task is to learn receptivity and to welcome more such beings more of the time. But it is also arguable that this kind of welcome may in turn have consequences in the world. Why wouldn't creatures and other spirits be more apt to come to those who long and look for them? Part of the lesson is that others beyond the human can be at least as unpredictable, surprising, provocative, and enigmatic as we ourselves. To expect otherwise is another way of missing the point.

Usually my classes invoke our other-than-human affinities outside, around a fire if possible—Fire being a presence too, of course—or in some other ceremonial space. The effects are often uncanny. After the last Fire Circle, my co-teacher Frances Bottenberg wrote a striking note:

I actually had an eerie sense that [students'] faces and postures took on something of their animal (or plant or elemental)
alter-egos when they began to speak about their connections to
their totems. . . . Bear had a growl in his voice I hadn't noticed
before. . . . Cat seemed calmly twitchy like cats are, ready to spring
or lounge at the drop of a hat. . . . The way Otter moved her hands
as she talked reminded me of the way otters play with objects
in the water, turning them over and over. . . . Cloud was always
glancing up, maybe taking all this lightly, as if from above. . . .
Shark's teeth glinted, especially when she said she "always follows
the blood"! Oh, and of course there was kindly but stern Owl, so
owl-awkward trying to read his poem with one eye, and then the
other. . . . I could list more.[8]

One first-year class met for our Council at dusk around an off-
campus fire pit. Storms were predicted—a major front was coming
through—and the evening skies were gray, but we gathered outside
anyway, stoked up the fire, and began to speak. Each offered gifts as
well as warnings to the others. Turtle offered his patience, deliber-
ateness: precisely the ability to go slow. Shark offered the reminder
that the world's most self-congratulatory animal (guess who) needs to
seriously temper his arrogance in the waters. Sun offered eternal light.

Between the circle speakers, the crickets and the frogs spoke up.
We gave them their turns too, waiting until they paused for Owl
(that was me, in my owl-head mask and academic gown: my personal Affinity Being is Daddy Longlegs, but philosophy's disciplinary
totem is the Owl) to sound the drum for the next student speaker.

We made it all the way around. At the end, Owl made a toast
to the class. It was our final meeting, and the last class of the year
for most of the students, the very end of their first year of college. I
offered them best wishes for the summer. As I raised my paper cup
at the end, just after my last word, there was the first peal of Thunder. A startling grace note, perfectly timed. A Thunderous Amen.

The students drank their sparkling cider. Now it really was time
to say goodbye. Shedding mask, I invited them to fill their cups in
their imagination with whatever they wanted to leave behind from
this first year of college, as well as whatever part of their Affinity
Being they now wanted to give back to the world—and then to

---

8. Frances Bottenberg, private communication, 2013.

throw their "full cups" into the fire. In they went—more than a few students visibly holding back tears.

The flames leapt up one last time. But by now the lightning was close and leaping too. The winds were lifting and we could hear the rain not so far off. Rushed embraces. Have a great summer. Then they sprinted across the woods for their cars. Or jumped or galloped or crawled or flew, only half returned to human—in the next flash of lightning I had the distinct apparition of an animal stampede. Thunder followed on top of it. Then, within half a minute, it was pouring, the start of a solid day of desperately needed hard rain.

Lakota philosopher Vine Deloria writes about how Europeans consistently misunderstand Native peoples' rain dances as means of manipulating or producing rain. Observers turned cynical when they realized that the shamans only begin rain dances when it appears that rain was in the offing anyway. But of course, replies Deloria. The function of the rain dance is not to produce rain but, as he puts it, to "participate in the emerging event."[9] Wedding dances don't produce weddings, do they? That is why you only dance when the rain is practically upon you. So this, so to say, was our Thunder dance. This class certainly "participated" in a remarkably thunderous "emerging event"—as close to speaking, I suspect, as Thunder cares to get.

The Heron

Sometimes the Visions course meets at the lodge, a nearby former church camp with a lake, a few shelters, a building with a fireplace for when it is too cold to meet outside, large grassy areas where we can sit in the sun on blankets in a circle. The Fire Circle is here too. Most of all, it offers relative quiet, the chance to be outside without distraction, with alert senses for once, in good company: with the winds that are always active; the turkey vultures wafting about and checking us out, along with the occasional hawk and chittery kingfisher; sun and the falling leaves; and, at the start of one especially memorable fall term, lots of rain and thunderstorms as a succession of hurricanes brushed by. We spent most of our first few weeks meeting in the shelters.

---

9. Vine Deloria, *Spirit and Reason: The Vine Deloria, Jr. Reader* (Golden, CO: Fulcrum, 1999), 50.

That fall we declared our affinities around a smoky bonfire on a cool afternoon. Windy, too, with low clouds scudding by: the smoke blew everywhere, and there was a lot of it, so we all went to our next classes smelling like we'd been camping all week. That year it turned out I had Rain, Dolphin, Jaguar (a Mexican woman with Huichol roots, whose distant shamanic ancestors might well have been jaguars too), Salmon, Bear, and many others.

We also had Great Blue Heron. As it happened, we had seen a Great Blue here at the lake below the lodge, once, early in the term. But she'd never been back, though one end of the lake seems like fine heron feeding ground. Still, the heron's appearance that day was part of the reason D chose it for her Affinity Being, I think. The other part was some kind of quiet grace, a body that could be ungainly but in fact had an unmatched elegance; and a quickness too. Long periods of utter stillness, punctuated by the lightning strike of the beak. Imagine the inner life.

Then came the day that D who was also Great Blue Heron was to present her term project on animal-animal, cross-species communication. We'd spoken, often, of human-animal communication, but she wanted to go several steps further, to look at a bigger picture. Usually she'd been very quiet and did not say much, though she was a perceptive and animated person when she got going. Now she had just begun to speak, a sentence or two, already with that same animation and self-possession. Everyone sat up a bit straighter, smiled.

D was sitting with her back to the lake. But now just as quickly our eyes were drawn up and behind her. Suddenly a shadow was floating by to her right, then spiraled down toward the water. Today of all days, this exact moment of all moments, Great Blue came back.

She floated down to the brilliantly sunlit end of the lake, in full view, the deeper part where feeding is (I'd think) not so good, landed in the most graceful way, right in the brightest sun. There she stood for a minute, looking us over and showing herself just enough, and then just as elegantly took back off, skimmed the water down to the other end of the lake, landed and proceeded to hunt up the stream and out of sight.

We were stunned into silence. No missing the magic here. I seriously wanted to end class right there, despite just having begun. What could you say or do after that? It was D's day, though, and she had a lot to say. So, after a time, we collected ourselves and began to speak again, haltingly and unwillingly as it was. For in a certain way everything had already been said, or (more accurately) done. We came back to that Visit in every reflection on the class for the rest of the term. No one who experienced that moment could have any doubts that animals "communicate," indeed in a far deeper way than any one of us, even D herself, had yet named or even imagined. Great Blue's return was something primal, a brief upwelling of a communicative flow far more powerful than language itself, a flash of something for which our only available word may once again be "magic," but that hints at far deeper receptivities and harmonies possible in the larger world.[10]

Like the Daddy Longlegs that keep turning up in my tents and on my shoulders, herons actually keep coming to my classes—always, strikingly, in the mode of punctuation or emphasis, opening or closing some process, though never again in so crystallized a way as on D's day. Of course, as Deloria says, you have to be open to them in that way. And for starters, obviously, you have to be outside. Again, again, again: the natural world is not some kind of stage scenery or piece of clockwork—not if we "participate in the process." Here there can also be gifts out of pure generosity, hints of pervasive unseen flows. At moments like these, every teacherly self-consciousness gives way before awe.

---

10. Anthony Weston, "Working the Dark Edges," *Canadian Journal of Environmental Education* 19 (2014):70–79.

IV. Teaching beyond the Course

14

Is the Unexamined Life Worth Living?

David Palmer
University of Tennessee

DAVID PALMER is an assistant professor of philosophy at the University of Tennessee. He enjoys introducing philosophy to beginning students as well as helping more advanced students develop their own views. David has won the White Undergraduate Teaching Award in 2012 and 2016 (every year for which he has been eligible) and, in 2012, the Chancellor's Excellence in Teaching Award, the main university-wide teaching award at UT. David's guiding aim in the classroom is to present philosophy as a conversation.

"Does he *really* think that?"

The student, a business major, is asking the question. He seems sincere, but genuinely shocked that someone would think this. I look around the classroom. Some students have their heads in laptops, a few are texting. A dozen, however, are looking right at me, waiting for an answer. They can't believe it either. *Yes*, I can see them thinking, *Does he really think that?*

I turn and see the keywords chalked on the board: "Plato," "Socrates," "*Apology*," "defense," "trial." There are a few circles and other abstract markings that I tend to make when teaching. The topic, of course, is Plato's *Apology*. The setting is the second week of my Introduction to Philosophy class. A foggy Tuesday morning. I've just spent the last thirty minutes running through an outline of the *Apology*: the charges brought against Socrates, the oracle at Delphi, Socrates' subsequent mission. And now we've come to its most famous line—perhaps philosophy's most famous line. I write it on the board:

"The unexamined life is not worth living." I pause for a moment. The student's question is hanging.

"What do you think?" I ask.

"Well it sounds like he believes it."

"I think so too."

"But how can he? Does he really think that if people don't examine their lives, then their lives aren't worth living? That's just ridiculous. It's so arrogant."

I see other students nodding in agreement.

"I mean, I get it. *He* lives an examined life, and he thinks that's valuable. But why does that mean everyone else has to do that too? It's just elitist. Completely arrogant. Why does he think that everyone has to do philosophy if they want to have a worthwhile life?"

"Yes!" another student begins. "What's wrong with just living in the moment? Why does Socrates say you have to examine everything? I don't want to spend all my time examining every single thing I think or every decision I make. It would be exhausting."

"Exactly," says the business student. "Aren't there lots of different lives that are worth living? If you want to question things all the time, and that brings you happiness, then good for you. Do that. But what's wrong with the person who just does stuff? He knows what he likes and just does it. That's a perfectly meaningful life, right?"

"We can't all be philosophers," the other student says, "constantly questioning everything. And surely those of us who aren't philosophers have lives that are worth living. My mom and dad have never studied any philosophy at all and they have great lives. What's wrong with that?"

All the students in the class are looking at me now, wondering how I'll respond. I slowly sit in my chair and scan the room. This is the part of my Introduction to Philosophy course that I used to dread. I always assign the *Apology*. It's part of the sequence that opens the semester: *Euthyphro, Apology, Crito*. It's important to me to have beginning students read classic works. But I used to dread this part of the course because I feel the students' frustrations. I understand where they are coming from. Perhaps philosophy's most famous slogan is also its Achilles' heel. As the student said: If philosophers really do think that the unexamined life is not worth living, then isn't this just arrogant, pretentious, and out of touch? Or, as another student once told me, "It sounds like philosophers are just trying to justify their own existence."

Clarifying the Issue

I've always struggled to address these issues, and my difficulties have long bothered me. I've felt like a poor teacher at times. Part of the problem here is that a lot of what the students are saying seems right to me. Maybe living a life of self-examination is *one* way to live well. But why think that it's the *only* way? Surely, there are *many* kinds of lives that are worth living—including some that involve little, or perhaps even no, self-examination at all. Are we really supposed to think that those people—perhaps the majority of people—who don't regularly engage in the kind of self-reflection and examination that, according to Socrates, embodies philosophy are thereby living lives that are, in some significant sense, not worth living or, in some important way, lacking value or worth? In what follows, I want to take this opportunity to clarify these issues as they occur in the class-room and explore how best to respond to them. As I'll explain, I've changed the way I now reply to these kinds of questions, and this is due (I think) to understanding more clearly what's at the root of the concerns the students are expressing. As I've now come to appreci-ate, being a good teacher isn't just a matter of answering a student's question correctly; it also involves understanding *why* a student is raising the question in the first place.

When I consider this student skepticism about Socrates' claim, I'm reminded of some remarks that the contemporary American poet August Kleinzahler makes in a now infamous book review in *Poetry* magazine of *Good Poems*, a collection of poetry edited by Garrison Keillor.[1] *Good Poems* is inspired by Keillor's long-running NPR radio segment "The Writer's Almanac," in which Keillor read poems on air. Kleinzahler chides Keillor for selecting poems that make absolutely "no demands on his audiences, none whatsoever."[2] He hypothesizes that Keillor does this because Keillor seems to think that poetry should be available to everyone, no matter what their background or level of appreciative talent. And this is important, in Keillor's vision, because, no matter who they are, people's lives are

---

1. August Kleinzahler, "No Antonin Artaud with the Flapjacks, Please," *Poetry* 184, no. 1 (2004):50–56.

2. Ibid., 51.

better—enriched—from reading or listening to poetry. In contrast to this sentiment, however, Kleinzahler writes:

> Ninety percent of adult Americans can pass through this life tolerably well, if not content, eating, defecating, copulating, shopping, working, catching the latest Disney blockbuster, without having a poem read to them by Garrison Keillor or anyone else. Nor will their lives be diminished by not standing in front of a Cézanne at the art museum or listening to a Beethoven piano sonata. Most people have neither the sensitivity, inclination, or training to look or listen meaningfully, nor has the culture encouraged them to, except with the abstract suggestion that such things are good for you. Multivitamins are good for you. Exercise, fresh air, and sex are good for you. Fruit and vegetables are good for you. Poetry is not.[3]

Is the same true of philosophy? After all, the vast majority of people will pass through life perfectly content without being exposed to philosophy in any serious way. Surely their lives are not diminished by this lack?

Kleinzahler goes on to say:

> Are we not adult enough yet as a culture to acknowledge that the arts are not for everyone . . . and that good or bad, art's exclusive function is to entertain, not to improve or nourish or console.[4]

Should we think that philosophy isn't for everyone—that whatever philosophy's purpose (if, indeed, it has one), it isn't to improve, nourish, or console?

One way to respond to these questions—at least in the context of the *Apology*—is to bring to light some of the background assumptions that Socrates makes, as well as some of his other philosophical beliefs, in an effort to explain *why* he thinks that the unexamined life is not worth living. In fact, this is how I used to proceed when discussing the *Apology*. I used to answer the students' questions by highlighting the earlier parts of the *Apology* in which Socrates says that the gods sent him to Athens to implore people to "care for their souls" rather than pursue wealth, power, or honors.[5] I'd then emphasize that caring for one's soul, through rigorous self-examination, is

---

3. Ibid., 52.

4. Ibid., 54.

5. Socrates, *Apology*, 29d–30b.

important on the Socratic picture because it's by this kind of self-examination that knowledge of the good is revealed.

Moreover, knowledge of the good is crucial for Socrates, for he holds that such knowledge is all that's needed to live well: knowledge is necessary and sufficient for virtue. (According to his "intellectualism," if a person knows what is the right thing to do, then she will do it; correspondingly, all wrongdoing, on his view, is explained by ignorance.) Therefore, there's a direct link on the Socratic view, I'd suggest, between an "examined life"—since it's by carefully examining ourselves that knowledge of the good is revealed—and a life that's truly "worth living"—since this knowledge is necessary and sufficient for virtue.

But this infuriated students further. They were frustrated with my answer for two reasons. First, they doubted the assumptions on which it was based. (A common refrain was "Does Socrates really think that whenever I do something wrong, this is only because I didn't know any better?!" Another was "I often know what I should do, but I still don't do it.") But second—and more importantly—my reply didn't really speak to the concerns that they were expressing. When students, like the business major, are asking whether Socrates really believes that the unexamined life is not worth living, they're not asking a specific question about how Socrates' claim about the unexamined life fits in with the other parts of his philosophical system. (In fact, for them, these extra details can make Socrates' overall picture of how human beings work seem even more incredible.) Instead, they're using this quote as an opportunity to ask a much broader question about the nature of philosophy—namely, what, exactly, is the "point" of philosophy? Why study it at all? What value does it have? What is its use?

There's something curious about these questions. On the one hand, these classroom issues about philosophy's point are important, and as philosophy teachers we have to confront them. But there's a puzzle here. Do students in introductory classes in *other* academic subjects—physics, engineering, history, religious studies, and so on—typically question the very point or purpose of studying those subjects at all? Would students in these classes routinely ask their professor why they are learning about force, momentum, or gravitational pull? Would they ask what use there is in studying past wars, presidents, and kings, or what value there is in learning about the roots of Christianity? My sense is that they would not. Of course, students might not find these subjects *interesting*; they might find the classes dull. But my anecdotal experience is that, at least typically, this isn't because they are questioning the very point or value of these subjects. Rather, although they acknowledge the importance of physics, history, or religious studies, these subjects just don't particularly resonate with them.

Why, then, are matters different in the philosophy classroom? Why are beginning students quite happy—indeed, why do they often feel *compelled*—to question the very grounds or justification of philosophy in a way in which such questioning does not occur with the same frequency in the classrooms of other academic subjects?[6] Surely, much of the answer—as we've seen from Socrates—is that philosophers like to position philosophy as something that's essential to a well-lived life, in a way in which physicists and historians don't frame the significance of their subjects (even though they, of course, think that their subjects are important). Moreover, students pick up on the way in which we, as instructors, raise doubts about the utility of our own discipline.

Of course, the view that a life without examination is less valuable or worthwhile than one containing it (or perhaps not even worth living at all) isn't just held by Socrates or by those who share his view about the relationship between knowledge and virtue. It's something that appears throughout the history of philosophy. To give another example of this view at work, consider Bertrand Russell's description, in *The Problems of Philosophy*, of a person who has no exposure to philosophy at all. Russell says:

> [Such a person] goes through life imprisoned in the prejudices derived from common sense, from the habitual beliefs of his age or his nation, and from convictions which have grown up in his mind without the co-operation or consent of his deliberate reason. To such a man the world tends to become definite, finite, obvious; common objects rouse no questions, and unfamiliar possibilities are contemptuously rejected.[7]

---

6. Of course, the point of these other academic subjects can be—and sometimes is— questioned, but not nearly as frequently as the utility of philosophy is challenged.

7. Bertrand Russell, *The Problems of Philosophy* (Indianapolis: Hackett, 1990), 157.

Are we really supposed to think that someone who doesn't practice philosophy is "imprisoned" in her commonsense beliefs and habits—as if being guided by commonsense and habits is something that should be looked down upon and condemned? Of course, commonsense at times leads us down the wrong path, but *many* things lead us astray. Following commonsense and habit doesn't seem especially noteworthy in this regard. Moreover, isn't it *more* desirable to live in a world that is "definite, finite, and obvious" than one that is uncertain and unstable? Who wants to live in uncertainty?

Russell continues:

> The life of the instinctive [i.e., nonphilosophical] man is shut up within the circle of his private interests: family and friends may be included, but the outer world is not regarded except as it may help or hinder what comes within the circle of instinctive wishes. In such a life there is something feverish and confined, in comparison with which the philosophic life is calm and free. . . . Unless we can so enlarge our interests as to include the whole outer world, we remain like a garrison in a beleaguered fortress, knowing that the enemy prevents escape and that ultimate surrender is inevitable. In such a life there is no peace, but a constant strife between the insistence of desire and the powerlessness of will. In one way or another, if our life is to be great and free, we must escape this prison and this strife.[8]

Noble sentiments, to be sure. But these remarks—just as much as Socrates'—embody the elitism that many students feel characterizes the way that philosophers think about the importance of their subject. I can hear the business student asking me: "Does Russell really think that a person who dedicates himself to his family and friends—and doesn't spend his time doing philosophy, wondering about the 'outside world'—is living a 'confined' life in a 'beleaguered fortress'? That just sounds ridiculous." How, then, should we understand the importance of philosophy? What exactly is its value? More specifically, how should we understand it in the context in which most people seem to live perfectly meaningful, worthwhile lives without ever having engaged in philosophy in any serious way?

---

8. Ibid., 157–58.

Responding to These Concerns

In the context of the *Apology*, I now respond to these student concerns differently. Rather than attempt to situate Socrates' claim in the context of his other beliefs, I approach the issue in an alternative way. The claim that many people live worthwhile lives without ever having engaged with any philosophy rests, I suggest, on an unduly narrow view of what philosophy is. If we understand engaging in philosophy as requiring the study of Plato, Descartes, Hume, and so on, then—of course—the claim is correct. Most people live worthwhile, meaningful lives without ever having read Plato or any other philosopher. But we needn't look at philosophy in this way. If we view philosophy in *broader* terms—as, for instance, the activity of identifying and evaluating the principles that underlie our beliefs and choices, with the aim of making better choices and forming more defensible beliefs—then, I suggest, the claim is far less plausible. For surely everyone engages in philosophy, understood in this broad sense, from time to time.

Sometimes this occurs in overtly practical contexts. For instance, a person might not be sure about which political candidate to vote for, so she "steps back" mentally and considers, more generally, what's important to her—a candidate who prioritizes lowering taxes, one who focuses on expanding healthcare, and so on. In the light of this, she makes her choice. But she might be challenged in discussions with friends to explain and defend her choice, and might, therefore, be called upon to defend the more general principles that, at least implicitly, guided her decision making. Alternatively, a person at a restaurant might order a meat dish and be asked by her vegetarian companion why she thinks that it is okay to eat animals. After all, the vegetarian might say most animals are raised in factory farm conditions, and even those that have room to roam are raised purely for us to eat them, simply as a means to our own pleasure. Thus, the meat eater is being asked to reflect on her own moral principles about whose interests in the animal kingdom count most and why, and to what degree it is morally permissible for humans to use other animals for their own benefit.

Other times, the activity of philosophy occurs in more abstract contexts. For instance, when a close family member or friend dies—especially if the death is sudden, early, or tragic—people are often led to wonder about "what happens to you when you die" or whether there really is a God overseeing things. A person who believes wholeheartedly in God might now wonder how an all-knowing, all-powerful, all-good God could let such a death happen. For others, belief in God might be reinforced. Perhaps a sudden death is best explained as being part of a "greater plan," albeit one that is currently unknown to us. Such events also lead to reflection about the nature of our own selves. Is there a part of us—a soul—that survives bodily death? Or are we simply very complex physical systems, our minds being nothing more than our brains, and so once our bodies die, we die too? Taking time to think about these issues is, of course, to think philosophically about one's place in the world and about the larger forces that shape it.

Finally, as I emphasize to students, viewing philosophy in these broader terms—as an activity (i.e., the activity of identifying and evaluating the principles underlying our beliefs and choices) that has a certain aim (i.e., the aim of making better choices and forming more defensible beliefs)—also helps to reveal its value. For whether the choices or beliefs at issue are practical (e.g., who to vote for or what food to eat) or abstract (e.g., what happens to us when we die), surely everyone, I suggest, wants to make better choices and form more defensible beliefs. Moreover, viewing philosophy as an activity with a certain aim helps to explain why studying philosophy in the classroom is valuable. For, like many goal-directed activities, philosophy is a *skillful* activity, one that can be honed and improved with practice. The more practice people get at this activity, the better they'll likely be at it—and, therefore, the more likely they'll be to achieve its goal. That is, the more likely they'll be to (in fact) *make* better choices and *form* more defensible beliefs. And—to return to Socrates' dictum—what could be more valuable, in a worthwhile life, than doing that?[9]

---

9. I'd like to thank Yuanyuan Liu, Anna Samreth, and Clerk Shaw for many helpful discussions.

15

A Slow Apprenticeship with the Real

John F. Whitmire, Jr.
Western Carolina University

JOHN F. WHITMIRE, JR. is associate professor at Western Carolina University, where he has taught courses in European Continental philosophy and history of philosophy, as well as interdisciplinary courses in philosophy, religion, and literature since 2005. He taught previously at Villanova University, where he received his Ph.D., and at Haverford College. At WCU, he has won the University's Excellence in Teaching Liberal Studies award (2011), the College of Arts and Sciences' teaching award (2016), the Honors College's award for mentoring undergraduate research (2008), and the Center for Service Learning's award for excellence in teaching a service-learning course (2011 and 2013). He chaired the Philosophy and Religion Department at WCU for five years and has served as president of the North Carolina Philosophical Society. Whitmire's scholarship, on Kierkegaard, Nietzsche, Sartre, and Derrida, has focused on the ways philosophical anthropologies are broadened, deepened, or problematized by an author's autobiographical writings and literature. His teaching aims to help students find or create meaning for themselves, in dialogue with texts that speak to their minds and hearts, and to then encourage students to act concretely on those values and beliefs.

> "I've served a slow apprenticeship with the real. I've seen children dying of hunger. Over against a dying child, *Nausea* cannot stand as a counterweight."
> —Jean-Paul Sartre[1]

---

1. Jean-Paul Sartre, interview by Jacqueline Piatier. Originally published in *Le Monde*, April 18, 1964, my translation. The original interview is available in French via the online archives of *Le Monde*, without pagination. Unless otherwise noted, for the remainder of this essay I refer to the translation of the interview by Anthony Hartley, "A Long, Bitter, Sweet Madness," *Encounter* (June 1964): 61–63.

What does "living existentialism" mean? As a philosopher trained primarily in the nineteenth- and twentieth-century traditions of European Continental philosophy, and particularly existential phenomenology, this question—initially raised by a roundtable and Festschrift in honor of one of my mentors, Thomas Busch—means primarily coming to terms with human suffering. What I'm concerned with in this essay is what it means *to live* the later Sartrean insight that we have to come to confront suffering directly and concretely, and how that confrontation might allow us to productively reshape our teaching—and our lives.

In 1964, Jean-Paul Sartre published what was at that point supposed to be the first volume of his autobiography, titled simply *Les Mots* (*The Words*).[2] After its publication, there was some understandable confusion about the text, given that Sartre wrote an initial draft of the work (tentatively titled *Jean sans terre*) in the early to mid-1950s, and then put this manuscript aside, returning to revise it several years later.[3] Sartre addresses some of those difficulties in an interview he gave to Jacqueline Piatier of *Le Monde* in April 1964. In that discussion, he describes the evolution of his own positions—including his views on literature and politics—from his earlier work, through his Marxist "conversion" of the early 1950s and consequent attempt to abandon literature in favor of political action, to the position he stakes out in the 1964 interview, that "despite an apparent contradiction there is no difference between service to an entire community and the requirements of literature" (62).

I first came upon this interview by way of Sartre's justly famous and much commented-upon line there, that *Nausea*—published in 1938, when Sartre was just thirty-three, and described by him in *Words* as "the masterstroke of writing" (251)—"cannot act as a counterweight" when placed "over against a dying child" (62). In my own earlier teaching and writing, I didn't fully appreciate the force of this comment, and I didn't even track down the full interview to

---

2. Jean-Paul Sartre, *Les Mots* (Paris: Éditions Gallimard, 1964). In this essay, I utilize Jean-Paul Sartre, *The Words*, trans. Bernard Frechtman (New York: George Braziller, 1964).

3. For a much fuller exposition of the philosophically performative position of *Les Mots*, see my "The Double Writing of *Les Mots*: Sartre's *Words* as Performative Philosophy," *Sartre Studies International* 12, no. 2 (2006):61–82.

understand its context until fairly recently. And that's really because it has only been in subsequent years that I have begun to ask myself whether my own philosophical work and life take up seriously enough the real challenges of the human suffering in our world. Sartre's demand in that interview is that we simply not "ignore reality and the fundamental problems that exist. The world's hunger, the atomic threat, the alienation of man" (62). And, though I had been taking up these problems in (what I now view as) a more abstract way in several of my courses, it has only been in the past five to ten years that I have come to confront them in a much more concrete way.

Surviving as a kind of palimpsest in the later drafts of *Words* is the idea of a radical conversion. Indeed, the earlier drafts represented a particularly vicious attack on literature—the life of words—in favor of political action, and enough of this language survives in the published text that Bernard-Henri Lévy has actually read it as a Maoist text. But the later drafts of the book, while not completely obscuring the earlier attack, show that this reading is misguided. In the epilogue (part of the later additions), Sartre gives his readers an attenuated version of his earlier frontal assault on writing and claims that he will in fact continue to write, because "one gets rid of a neurosis, one doesn't get cured of oneself" (253–54).[4]

This tension in *Words* leads Sartre's interviewer in *Le Monde* to ask whether he renounces his previous work. Sartre responds, "Not at all. What I wrote about this in *Les Mots* has been misunderstood. There is no book of mine that I reject. That does not mean that I find them good" (62). He goes on to criticize himself for having lacked a "sense of reality," but claims that he has changed in the intervening years: "*J'ai fait un lent apprentissage du reel,*" he says. "*J'ai vu des enfants mourir de faim. En face l'un enfant qui meurt,* la Nausée *ne fait pas le poids*"; roughly: "I've served a slow apprenticeship with the real. I've seen children dying of hunger. Over against a dying child, *Nausea* cannot stand as a counterweight" (my translation).

The interviewer goes on to ask the astute next question: "What work would act as a counterweight?" (62). Sartre's response is that this is precisely the writer's problem. And I would suggest that this problem arises for the writer (and teacher) of *philosophy*, no less than

---

4. See Whitmire, "Double Writing," esp. 64, 68.

other kinds of "literature." In fact, it's a question that I myself have frankly struggled with a great deal over the course of the last several years. I've had moments when I have wondered whether teaching and writing (that is, scholarship in the usual, academic sense) really are the best use of my time, or whether I should be more directly engaged with the world. The sentiment has slowly grown in my own life that I'm not doing enough, that perhaps I can *never* do enough, at least qua philosopher and teacher (although perhaps this sense owes as much to Emmanuel Levinas as to Sartre). Did I, too, need to undergo a radical conversion from the life of words to civic and political action of the sort that the earlier Sartre believed was absolutely imperative?

For me, this kind of realization grew in a dialectical relationship with the changes I made in a course called "Religion, Suffering, and the Moral Imagination," often affectionately referred to by my students as "the suffering class." When I first began teaching this class in 2006, it was a fairly standard philosophy course on the problem of evil and theodicy, with a couple of classic literary or religious texts to broaden and diversify its scope in a slightly more interdisciplinary direction, given my interests at the intersection of religion and literature. Over the years, though, it became clear to me that dealing with what I would call the intellectual problem of evil was not enough—for me or my students. And so I began to experiment.

During that first trial phase, I reframed the course as a series of attempts from excerpts of great works in philosophy, religion, and literature, to deal not just with theodicy and the classical problem of evil, but with human suffering more broadly—with the fact, for instance, that every single day roughly 16,000 children under the age of five die[5] from malnutrition, preventable diseases, issues stemming from water and sanitation, and other problems for which there are actual, existing solutions; and the number two cause of death for girls ages fifteen to nineteen is childbirth and other maternal causes.[6]

---

5. According to UNICEF data. See https://www.unicefusa.org/mission/survival.

6. See http://apps.who.int/adolescent/second-decade/section3/page2/mortality .html. Girls Not Brides (www.girlsnotbrides.org) estimates that 15 million girls are married before the age of eighteen each year. The lack of physical development of these girls, not just a lack of medical care, also contributes substantially to persistent recurring health problems (such as fistulas), as well as maternal and child deaths.

I wanted my students not to lose sight of this kind of concreteness, as they were clearly doing occasionally, while engaged in the sometimes overly theoretical (though no doubt still important and valuable!) exercises of philosophy of religion. And I wanted them to engage with this concreteness on a deeper, more substantive level than just dealing with the numbers, as well.

So, as I altered the course, I tried to reframe it around two guiding questions: (1) whether and how we can make sense of the tremendous extent of human suffering in the world, and (2) what we should do about it, in our own lives (i.e., our own suffering) and/or the lives of others. Some of our course texts respond to the first question, others to the second, and some to both. Later on, I selected one concrete problem to which I could devote special attention, in order to give more focus to the course. As Ivan reminds us in *The Brothers Karamazov*, there are numbers of questions, and I too wanted to take one that made the situation terribly clear. To do so, I later added a few readings about the empirical situation of women and girls in the developing world, so that my students would have somewhat better narratival purchase on these issues, as well.

•

For my student Sue,[7] the course helped guide her toward her current research agenda as a counselor educator. She came to view grieving as an "individual construction—influenced by many things, but ultimately unique to the individual experiencing suffering in their loss." She tells me she felt free to construct her "own ideas and responses to the history, philosophy, and religious foundations that influence our views of suffering. Now, as an emerging educator, I am striving to allow my students to feel similar freedom in their learning."

•

---

7. Although each of the named students in this piece has provided consent to use their words and/or stories, their names have been altered in the interests of maintaining their privacy.

But this more concrete and interdisciplinary approach still wasn't enough: it was still too abstract and cut off from many students' day-to-day lives. As an existential philosopher, I wanted my students to experience something like the "apprenticeship with the real" that Sartre describes in the interview. I wanted them to really understand, for instance, that in western North Carolina, where I teach, the food insecurity rate is over 15 percent, and overall in North Carolina more than a quarter of our children struggle to have access to three nutritious meals each day.[8] I wanted my students, as Kierkegaard puts it, to make this thought a deed, to genuinely appropriate it existentially, as I was coming to do myself in my own work in the community.

So I began experimenting with service-learning, requiring students to go out into the community and actually work with others who could, on most reasonable understandings, be fairly described as "suffering" in some way, and then reflect on that experience to make the texts they were reading more concrete, the numbers they were seeing more personal. This helped, for this is the classic kind of dialectical interplay the pedagogy of service-learning is intended to foster: discussion of texts that illuminate actual experience, and reflection on experiences that, in turn, sheds new light on the texts.

One particular service site has been particularly pedagogically valuable in this context: The Community Table, a local food pantry and restaurant-style soup kitchen in our town, at which I now ask all students to work for the first service module in the course. This service partner often draws into stark relief some of the presuppositions students bring to their service, as the organization's method of service has been consciously designed not just to address the immediate need of hunger, but also to foster a sense of autonomy and dignity in the guests; and a sense of community between the guests and servers. Rather than an old-style soup kitchen line, for instance, the Community Table's guests are seated at restaurant-style tables, where they have menus from which to order, and servers are often able to sit down and break bread with them after bringing their meals to the table. In this context, the guests are able to exercise some measure of

---

8. According to our regional food bank, MANNA: http://www.mannafoodbank.org/hunger-101/map-the-meal-gap-2014.

human choice with dignity, alleviating some of the alienation that is often the companion of poverty.

Students who are new to service-learning often tend to conceive of themselves as the saviors of these "poor souls." But, through our work with the Community Table and other partner agencies, many of my students have come to see aspects of their own lives mirrored in the experiences of the individuals served. In assisting people who suffer from food insecurity, depression, anxiety, and abuse, my students learn something existentially significant for their own lives. Some students report more direct connections, having encountered someone they personally knew, whether a member of their extended family, a child they had seen in a very different context, or even a previous year's acquaintance from the university. These are the kinds of experiences that most students cannot rapidly move past, and as a consequence, their reflection papers—a hallmark of service-learning, over and above the service—mark something similar to Sartre's description of his own experience of discovering "suddenly that alienation, exploitation of man by man, under-nourishment, relegated to the background metaphysical evil which is a luxury. Hunger is an evil: period" (61).

•

Edna, who went on to do a master's degree in humanitarian development work, writes that "the suffering class served as a catalyst that got me into development and poverty alleviation. Before the class, I was very much an armchair activist. . . . I knew there was suffering, on different levels and across different planes, and I knew that I wanted (and should) do something about it. Reading and discussing all the texts in the class helped me with understanding and conceptualizing, while the community engagement part of the class forced me to go out and actually do it. It increased my capacity to not only empathize and to make sense of suffering for myself . . . but to also realize and come to terms with the idea that there might not be a reason at all . . . but I do know that I'm alive and capable of doing something—even if it's not on the global scale. Impact is impact no matter how small. The suffering class gave me the space to go through all of that while also putting me out into my community to put it into practice and actually do something."

•

Although it is certainly not required for students to do so, I endeavor to open the narratival space for them to share their own stories in the context of the class discussions, written assignments, and final presentations, where they are willing and able to do so. And because the course asks students to interrogate their *own* suffering, to the degree that they are comfortable doing so, I often receive reflective assignments describing in powerful and pointed ways students' own past or present food insecurities; mental or physical illnesses; familial losses; and war injuries, self-harms, and other traumas. Their final written reflections are often profoundly moving; and, when they choose to share them, their oral articulations of those experiences in our final session often come with actual tears—their own and others'. The full semester of building a supportive community in the classroom environment is therefore incredibly important, as it is not uncommon for students to choose to share with others, in this final experience, the private details of their own sufferings and the sufferings of others.

Of course, I am not a clinician, so I am not trying to open up a diagnostic space (in the modern psychological sense) in the classroom. Rather, I am attempting to model what I would call a set of existential-Socratic practices such as openness, humility in the face of the stories others share, and explicitly expressed thankfulness when someone does choose to say something—in writing or speech—that may have been particularly difficult for them to express. I remind students in the class not to be glib when they are discussing issues that their colleagues may have actually gone through, and I also provide them—at the beginning of term and crucial moments during the semester—with destigmatized information to access the clinical resources on campus that some of them might need.

The overall structure of the course, as it is currently constituted, involves something like a series of concentric circles into which students navigate into, away from, and back again from global to personal—from reading about suffering in other parts of the world (through both narratives and numbers) to offering real service in local communities (and in some cases, beyond) to a final project that asks them to think through how these experiences, readings, and discussions have impacted their own views on how to make sense of suffering, both globally and personally, and what to do about it.

•

> Valentine, who had significant darkness in her own past, responded—in both scholarly and existential depth—to questions of forgiveness raised in the course. Afterward, she wrote a senior thesis that not only dealt with the academic literature on forgiveness in philosophy and theology, but also took the extra step of bringing this work into dialogue with her own past in a profoundly moving way. She went on to pursue a master's degree in conflict resolution and reconciliation, before proceeding to advanced graduate work, in which she takes up the question of forgiveness. And she continues to do citizen legislative advocacy for humanitarian causes while doing so.

•

I wish that I could say that every student who takes the class will have a deeply existential encounter, either in her service or in her reflections on that service, that every student would see the face of the Other suddenly break through the categories within which she has been tacitly working or realize that there is a different, perhaps better, way to reframe, make sense of, and deal with her own suffering. Of course, that's not the case. And even if it were, would awakening students to those realities be enough? This question mirrors, in a way, what Sartre identifies as "exactly the writer's problem. What does literature stand for in a hungry world? Like morality, literature needs to be universal. So that the writer must put himself on the side of the majority, of the two billion starving, if he wishes to speak to all and be read by all" (62). Because, he goes on to say, "Failing that, he is at the service of a privileged class and, like it, an exploiter" (62).

Despite the fact that, over the past decade, my courses have tried to attend to community needs, I continue to ask myself whether I could do more—whether I am doing the right thing. Is even my own discussion of both this class and my former students exploitative in some way? If I were genuinely going to "put myself on the side of the majority," would that entail giving up the life of "words"—the standard professional model of reading, teaching, writing scholarly articles in the Academy—in favor of something else? And would that even be existentially possible, or would I just be engaged in an ultimately fruitless process of trying to become cured of myself?

·

Carrie has continued her work with a humanitarian advocacy organization since graduation, participating in both organizational and legislative staffer meetings while in graduate school, her own postgraduate academic interests in ethics having also been shaped by work in the suffering class.

·

These kinds of questions have led me, in the half-decade or more since I began to incorporate service-learning into my own pedagogy, to work more with external business and professional leaders through Rotary (www.rotary.org) and to work as a volunteer citizen advocate with the international humanitarian and development group CARE (www.care.org). I've even taken groups of students from my "suffering" class in the western corner of North Carolina to Washington, DC, to participate in advocacy efforts on behalf of U.S. food aid reform, the International Violence Against Women Act, maternal and child health legislation, and humanitarian aid to Syria.

·

Raven is seeking ordination in a Christian denomination, and finds that the course served her well because "a large part of my call is to be present with people who are suffering. Academically, I gained knowledge of a variety of beliefs that both complemented and challenged my personal beliefs. Having this knowledge will be essential working in hospital chaplaincy, as well as in a parish setting." She also, however, notes that the class helped her live more authentically herself, as it was through her "attendance at the national CARE Conference (which focused on ending gender-based violence and sustaining foreign aid budgets), that I first found the courage to voice my own survival of abuse. This courage to name important parts of my identity has extended beyond survival and into other parts of my life, including my sexuality." She says, "[I hope that I] will have been able to grow through my own personal suffering, using my experiences to have better empathy for my fellow human siblings, and inspired others to do the same."

•

From the beginning, I was convinced that this approach was pedagogically sound—after all, participation in this experience helped students fulfill not one, but all five of my own university's meta-level student learning outcomes.[9] But the course is more than just a pedagogical or academic exercise for me now, for some deeply personal reasons. One of these was the experience of watching, in dread, my partner struggle through two incredibly difficult labor and delivery experiences. In reflection—the moral imagination at work—I've come to appreciate that were we to live in another part of the world or in any number of less privileged circumstances in the United States, either she, one of my two daughters, or both, would probably have died in childbirth. Those moments were the spurs I needed to find the "truth which is true for me," as Kierkegaard puts it.[10] I now spend even more time doing citizen advocacy and talking with elected representatives and their staffers (locally in town halls and nationally in Washington, DC). I've tried, as Sartre's interviewer Piatier puts it, to "place [my] pen at the service of the oppressed" (62). But I remain fully aware of how Sartre would assess my efforts. There is only so much an academic philosopher can do from the sidelines. Sartre reminds us: "[B]ut this is the writer's task, and, if he fulfils it as he should, he acquires no merit from it. Heroism is not to be won at the point of a pen" (62).

---

9. Western Carolina University 2020 Vision, Goal 1.2: "to integrate information from a variety of contexts; to solve complex problems; to communicate effectively and responsibly; to practice civic engagement; and to clarify and act on purpose and values." See http://www.wcu.edu/discover/about/wcu-2020-plan/2020-vision -focusing-our-future-wcu-strategic-plan/strategic-direction-1-fulfill-the-educational -needs-of-state-and-region.aspx.

10. Kierkegaard is here referring, of course, to an (objective) truth that provides purpose in one's life, for which one is willing to live and die, not to "alternative facts."

Which brings me back to the same questions. At the end of the interview, echoing the more nuanced account of conversion he articulates in *Words*, Sartre says, "I have changed as everyone changes: within a permanency" (63). But that's precisely the rub, the question of whether that's enough. I have taught students to think more critically about suffering. I have helped them to remove their blinders, so they can see suffering, where before they could not. But does my own "change within a permanency" go far enough to bring about substantive change in the world? That's the question that has grown in my life over the past several years. Is putting my own pen (at least metaphorically) at the service of the suffering enough for me? Is reaching out to work with legislators, staffers, and business and professional leaders in our communities enough? Can the teaching and writing of philosophy—*Words*!, even if socially and politically attuned—confront directly enough the existential realities of life in a fundamentally unjust world, a world where women and children still regularly die of hunger and in childbirth?

"The universe," Sartre says, "remains dark. . . . [But] I believe, I desire, that social and economic ills may be remedied. With a little luck that epoch may arrive. I am on the side of those who think that things will go better when the world has changed" (62). How far, I wonder, can the coherent unity of a life *in philosophy* be stretched or totalized toward the end of bringing light to the darkness of our world? Can my words actually impact the world, or should I abandon that life in favor of some kind of more direct action?

I confess to remaining uncertain of the answers here, and I can say that there have been times I have thought seriously about leaving academia to work more concretely with and on behalf of others who are suffering. Indeed, I suspect that I will continue to struggle with this vocational question going forward, despite my love of the material I teach and the pleasure it gives me to introduce others to it. But I can say this. I don't continue to teach philosophy, now, simply out of the kind of inertia that earned tenure can sometimes afford. I do so, at least in part, because I can read my students' final papers and listen to their final presentations in the suffering course—the closest to my heart of any course I teach. I do so because I have seen some of the ways that interacting with one suffering while discussing ways to make sense of and respond to that suffering can actually change hearts, impact vocational choices, and alter lives, as seen in some of the more personal stories above.

Despite this existential lack of certainty, my experience with service-learning has enabled me—and many of my students—to feel that we are responding to the concluding admonition of Voltaire's *Candide*. It has provided me with a way to think about my own "change within a permanency." After the last of many debates on suffering in this world, not simply to end the discussion, but to recognize the limitations of words (and theory) alone, *Candide* obliquely suggests that we must *also* go out into the world together and tend to the concrete needs of the individuals (including ourselves) who are suffering in it. This sentiment has become a kind of parting admonition at the conclusion of the student presentations in our final course meeting, for it speaks to my own development as well as their work in the course. I tell my friends that what was shared in the presentations was indeed well said. But we must continue to go beyond *les mots*. We must cultivate our garden.

16

Of Games and Confrontations

David C. K. Curry

The State University of New York at Potsdam

DAVID C. K. CURRY began teaching in 1983 at the University of Virginia and then at Wofford College, where he served as a sabbatical replacement immediately after acquiring his M.A. Most of his career has been at SUNY, Potsdam, where he remains a professor of philosophy. The vast majority of his teaching has been to undergraduates, and much of it is in service to general education. For fun he teaches; reads Plato and Aristotle, George Saunders and Percival Everett; drinks beer; hangs with his children; walks his dogs; and listens to lots of music. He received a President's Award for Excellence in Teaching in 2008 and, more meaningfully, was awarded Outstanding Teacher of the Year by Phi Eta Sigma, the Freshman Honor Society, in 2003 and 2009 and Favorite Professor Awards in 2009, 2012, 2013, 2014, and 2016, all determined by students.

I luck out with the first student to arrive in the classroom—or maybe it's not luck—students who show up ten minutes early for their first class are often overachievers. I ask her, as if simply making small talk, if she has had any experience with role-playing games. It occurs to me that this is probably not an appropriate way to start a first conversation with one's student. She takes it well, though, and replies that she did four years of Model United Nations in high school. I hand her a thick envelope and ask her to read its contents. She will be Kora/Lysander. The other students trickle in; each receives an envelope; each opens it and begins reading. Some contemplate dropping the class. (Some will.) This isn't how a first day is supposed to go—no syllabus, no mind-numbing review of the syllabus, no boilerplate "philosophy is . . ." lecture, no early release (in fact, they will likely be late for their next class, if they have one). Strombichides, Cleophon, Dionysodorus, Autolycus, Rhinon, Corinna, Chrysilla, Cassandra, Charis, Archestratus, Solon, Ariston, Ion, Phidippides,

Miltiades, and Lysias are all resurrected and repopulate the *Pnyx*; and the *Ekklesia* begins its deliberations under the direction of the *Epistates*. Less than a mile away, the Spartan commanders, camped with their armies outside the long walls, strategize.[1]

These days, when asked the somewhat awkward question of what I do for a living, I respond by saying that I teach philosophy, not that I am a philosopher. This distinction is, one might argue, a purely artificial one. Put in active terms, one might argue that teaching philosophy just is doing philosophy. And one would, in some world, be in large part right.

But I teach undergraduates in a small public college—often woefully underprepared undergrads who are enrolled solely in search of a few general-education credits. When I teach upper-division courses, they are usually filled with as many nonmajors as majors. It is hard to do much philosophy with folks who haven't the foggiest idea of what it is that philosophers do or how they do it.

I try hard to motivate the philosophical problems we address in class. Often, though, the problems remain too abstract. So, for example, I often use a recreation of the Ship of Theseus problem (stolen from Jay Rosenberg) to show how philosophical problems arise out of everyday experience and to illustrate how thinking systematically about them can lead us to identify and scrutinize the assumptions that lie behind our intuitions. Many of the students in my classroom become quickly engaged. Others appear to remain in a stupor.[2]

> The *Epistates* calls the *Ekklesia* to order. Lysander's army, along with those of his Theban and Corinthian allies, are camped outside the walls. Athens is besieged, her port blockaded, her supplies dwindling. Soon she will starve. But surrendering is hardly more attractive. The Corinthians and Thebans want revenge for Athenian atrocities committed during the long years of the Peloponnesian

---

1. My accounts of Athens game classes are an amalgam drawn from the four times I have taught this course.

2. You would be forgiven for thinking that this is because the problem of identity over time is too metaphysical. But I have the same problem motivating philosophical discussions of race or gender. Students are more than happy to tell me about their own travails, but getting them to approach the issues—even the issues they already care about—abstractly and rigorously is like pulling teeth.

War. They desire to slaughter all Athenian men, rape and enslave the women and children. The situation is bleak, and all options appear untenable. In this climate thousands of Athenian citizens gather on the *Pnyx* to debate their options. In the turmoil, no one notices the slave girl Kora slip over the long walls to freedom.

This scenario, *Athens Besieged*,[3] is a prologue to the role-playing game *The Threshold of Democracy: Athens in 403 B.C.*, one of a number of role-playing games published by the Reacting to the Past Consortium. I toss my students to the wolves on the first day of class. By the end of that first period, they have an inkling of the form of the class' culminating project, for which the next eight weeks will be spent preparing. The second class meeting, more traditionally, lays out the plan for the semester and distributes roles and offices for the involved *Threshold* game. The next three weeks are devoted to an introduction to argumentation. Pretty standard stuff: the aforementioned Rosenberg thought experiment, Anthony Weston's excellent little *Rulebook for Arguments*, exercises culminating in parsing and evaluating extended arguments. Then we launch into the Platonic dialogues.

Reacting games focus on seminal texts and seek to bring them to life by setting them in their historical context. *Threshold* focuses on the *Republic*, supplemented with texts from Thucydides and Xenophon. One presupposition the gamebook makes is that the Socrates of the *Republic* represents the historical Socrates. I complicate the original design of the game by focusing on what I take to be the more historical Socrates of Plato's early dialogues. So we carefully work through the *Apology, Euthyphro, Meno*, and *Crito* and familiarize ourselves with Socratic philosophy, before turning to a reading of the more overtly political, and Platonic, *Republic*. For the *Threshold* class, I focus my students' attention on the moral and political themes in the *Republic*, barely even touching upon the metaphysics and epistemology of Books 5–7. We dwell on Thrasymachus' position and Glaucon's challenge in Book II, the case for censorship in Books III and X, and the Book VIII ranking of governmental types, particularly the critique of democracy.

---

3. Mark Carnes and Naomi Norman, "Athens Besieged" (unpublished manuscript, July 2017).

In the game, each student is assigned to one of five groups: Thrasybuleans (radical democrats), Pericleans (moderate democrats), Solonian Aristocrats (oligarchs), Socratics, or indeterminates without factional allegiance. They are also assigned an individual role (e.g., Thrasybulus himself, Crito, or Lycon—some based on historical figures, others purely fictional). Before launching into the game itself, students write a short paper defending their character's political worldview with arguments inspired by or derived from the primary texts. Each character has, unsurprisingly, an individual agenda, in addition to their factional agenda. The overarching goal is to see one's faction exert its influence over the restructuring of the Athenian *polis* after the fall of the Thirty Tyrants. The faction(s) or individual(s) who best achieve their goals will be declared the winner in a postmortem at the end of the semester.

> Thrasybulus, flaunting his wounds from the battle in the Piraeus, moves slowly toward the speaker's platform. He makes an eloquent plea for justice, for giving those who supported the Thirty Tyrants what they deserve—a fair trial, to be sure, but exile or death for those found guilty of collaboration with the Thirty. Crito, devoted companion of Socrates, relates a conversation he had with the philosopher about the incoherence of returning a harm with a harm. He implies that Thrasybulus and his revenge-driven compatriots are confused about what things are truly valuable. He argues for a general amnesty for all associated with the Thirty. He speaks of the need for all Athenians, regardless of their political sympathies, to pull together for the good of the city as a whole. Callias, wealthy landowner, speaks in support of Crito's proposal, though he elicits a few scattered shouts of "Sparta lover" and "collaborator." Tensions are high. Reputations, influence, power, but more fundamentally, lives are at stake.

I was in Charlottesville, Virginia, over the now infamous August 11th weekend in spite of knowing full well about the scheduled white supremacist rally. I have a long history with Charlottesville and what I can only call, at the risk of being misunderstood, a Southerner's attachment to the place (no doubt amplified by my understanding of the ancient Greeks attachment to their *poleis*). That is to say, I have an attitude toward Charlottesville that I believe positions me to understand, albeit imperfectly, how an ancient Athenian must have felt toward his city. Charlottesville is my *polis*.

Prior to the horrific events of August 11th, 2017, when a counterprotester was killed in what appears to be an act of domestic terrorism, the city was engaged in a debate about how to respond to the immanent influx of hundreds of armed reactionaries dead set on causing trouble. Some urged confrontation, others argued for nonconfrontation, either at the same sites as the supremacists were to gather or at other, removed sites. Some thought it best to let the invaders come to an abandoned city—to pay them no attention whatsoever. Those debates were not, of course, resolved—indeed, they weren't carried out in anything like the manner made possible by the Athenian *Ekklesia*—and so folks acted as they saw fit. Some sought out confrontation, many marched peacefully, many others met for prayer services and counter rallies across town, and very many avoided the scene entirely. None of these tactics kept tragedy from striking. Now the city must confront the possible mistakes of the past and decide how best to move on. They find themselves in a situation analogous to that of the Athenians debating how to move on after the rule of the Thirty Tyrants.

Philosophy's Place in the University

I used to belong in my job. I was paid a living wage to think about, talk about, and teach what I love. Sadly, these days, those activities take up only a small part of my work-related activities. Not that I teach any less, or that the teaching itself is any less enjoyable and rewarding. But teaching has become an afterthought, edged out by managerial time wasting and, so, has become less enjoyable and less rewarding for both me and my students. Assessment reports, "compliance" training, mandatory budget workshops . . . the list goes on. Rather than reflecting on teaching philosophy, I should be grading departmental assessment exams and writing up an annual assessment report, writing a department newsletter or departmental annual report, or composing thank you letters to donors. It is July when I write this. I have become a manager—no longer, or only incidentally, a teacher. More broadly, the university is no longer a community of scholars, but a corporation devoted to churning out students with degrees. I'm not sure where I belong anymore, if anywhere.

Philosophers have been swimming upstream since long before Socrates drank the hemlock, sparring with a recalcitrant public. I suspect this has always been true, and always will remain true. But I also suspect that the degree of recalcitrance has varied significantly over time, and I know that it has had different causes. For much of history, there have been refuges for those who desired to teach and learn philosophy (and history and physics . . .). Plato's Academy was one such place, of course, and there may still be a few left standing. However, most of what remains are degree factories, professional training grounds, such that even the humanities, not to mention the sciences, must sell themselves on their extrinsic, marketable value. The contemporary challenge to the teacher of philosophy is justifying her existence within the corporatized university.

Each year our philosophy club hosts an event unimaginatively titled "Why Study Philosophy?" That there is a need for such a session at a liberal arts institution is evidence of how far the university has fallen from its mission of being a community of scholars. We practitioners have sunk equally low, catering to the fallen: One handout we utilize—"The Cynic's Case for Studying Philosophy"—makes precisely the aforementioned extrinsic arguments. Another makes a more intrinsic argument, but neither makes the case for living the life of the mind as a vocation. That is just too hard to sell.

Throughout thirty years of teaching, I have watched the scales tip in frightening ways, all deeply intertwined, to create a veritable shitstorm for those who view teaching as a calling—a vocation. Raimond Gaita notes the way in which the very term "vocation" now strikes the ear: "At a certain point in our recent history the concept of a vocation became as anachronistic as the concept of virtue."[4] We don't have vocations anymore, academic or otherwise—just jobs. And universities don't prepare students for a vocation, but for a job.

Gaita is clear that the idea of the corporate university is not just imposed by administrators but endorsed by faculty, if only tacitly. The managerial speak that now governs thinking about the mission of the university has become the norm only with our compliance, if not our collusion. Gaita is less curmudgeonly than I. He seems to believe that academics are still driven by a love of truth, the virtue

---

4. Raimond Gaita, "Callicles' Challenge," *Critical Quarterly* 47, nos. 1–2 (2005):48.

that creates and maintains a community of scholars. I agree that we ought to be so driven, but believe that our collusion/collaboration with the managerial class is evident in how rarely the rhetoric of a community of scholars pursuing truth flows from the mouths of our academic colleagues, much less our managers. Gaita again:

> In his *Notebooks* Wittgenstein agonises over whether his work is infected by dishonesty born of vanity. Such agonising, seen in the light of the concept of an academic vocation, is no more than should be expected of one who is lucidly mindful of its requirements. In the light of the concept of a career or a profession it is likely to appear neurotic or precious.[5]

I fear that not just our university presidents and boards, but the majority of our colleagues would fail to understand how Wittgenstein's obsession could be anything other than neurotic or precious. An irony here is that the forces that have led to the notion of a vocation becoming anachronistic often self-identify as "vocational." In effect, "vocation" has been co-opted and reduced to mean "career." Given this hijacking, it is no wonder that the mission of institutions of higher learning has become obscured. The new mission of the university is job training. The result is that professional and pre-professional programs dominate the university landscape, and the traditional liberal arts disciplines have either been forced into their mold (as with many STEM disciplines) or left to die a slow death. Gaita writes:

> That nursing is not a form of the life of the mind is not of itself a reason for excluding it from universities, for universities have always included the professions. People used to argue about whether engineering and even whether medicine or law were properly university disciplines. Those who warm to the expression "elitist nostalgia" point that out again and again.[6]

I actually warm to the expression, sort of like I warm to being derisively called a liberal or socialist. That ain't so bad. But he continues:

> Never before, however, did such professional courses determine the idiom, set so much of the tone, transform the language, and

---

5. Ibid.

6. Ibid., 50.

set the goals of the institutions to whose essential identity they had previously been marginal. For a very long time, the humanities have had to establish their credentials against the prestigious claims to knowledge justifiably advanced by the sciences, and against the attractions of the professional courses—vocational courses, as they are now called. Never before, however, has the need to attract outside funding and the self-evident attraction of courses that will guarantee secure employment so radically transformed the self-understanding of the institutions of higher education called universities. So great is that transformation, so complete the success of managerial-newspeak, that, as I remarked earlier some of the essential disciplines of the humanities and the sciences—philosophy and (even) physics, for example—have become mendicants for a respected place in institutions that should honour them.[7]

All this helps explain why there is, as Gaita notes, "widespread disillusionment among academics" of the sort I expressed in my opening paragraph: such elitist nostalgists "encounter in nearly all aspects of their academic lives the corruption of their deepest ideals."[8]

The Teaching of Philosophy's Place in the University

What does this litany of complaints about the current state of the university have to do with teaching philosophy? The community of scholars is a community of teachers and students—not just pursuing truth for themselves, but helping others to do the same. The most successful of such communities have actively engaged the broader society in which they exist. The scholar's goal should not be truth for truth's sake, but truth put toward the end of improving lives, our own and others. Plato's Academy was a breeding ground for scholars who traveled the ancient world advising *poleis* on their laws. In our own posttruth era, this task is more daunting than ever. Callicles at least recognized the value of studying philosophy in one's youth (though he believed it childish to continue such study in adulthood). Contemporary philistines don't see any use in studying philosophy at all.

Phil Hutchinson and Michael Loughlin make an eloquent case for teaching philosophy in order to provide a kind of therapy direly needed in the contemporary world. I don't particularly like describing

---

7. Ibid.
8. Ibid.

philosophy as therapy (and they don't seem deeply committed to the term), but their general point is well taken. Our students desperately need to develop the skills and attitudes that philosophy imparts, when well taught. They are discouraged from thinking critically not just throughout their K–12 education but in many of their college classes as well. Yet they are more in need of the ability to distinguish the reliable from the unreliable, the true from the false, the fake from the real, now more than perhaps ever before in American history. Hutchinson and Loughlin put it this way:

> As practitioners/teachers of philosophy we are like the makers of the most effective wooden stakes in an environment dominated by vampires, and we also do an excellent line in therapies for those victims of the blood-suckers not already too far gone to want them. Yet many of us spend our time either apologizing for the lack of practical application of our skills, or asserting that they should have no practical application, or groping around for some way to stretch or alter what we do to give it some application, assuming the discipline, in and of itself, to have none.[9]

I fear the authors endorse a false dilemma between the practical and the impractical, or between the useful and the useless. I have argued elsewhere that this distinction is one that chiefly serves the ends of those who deify the practical. The life of the mind is both the most useless, in one sense of useless, and at the same time the most useful of vocations. For while it engages with ideas for their own sake, it simultaneously develops skills required for successful navigation of the world. In order to successfully engage in those activities that add value to a life, we must first acquire the set of skills necessary to engage in those activities well: critical thinking skills, first and foremost. Acquiring those skills well requires engaging with the useless. In order to think usefully, one must work to learn to enjoy thinking about things that may be of no practical use at all. The useless and the useful are two sides of a single coin, neither able to be developed, nurtured, or inculcated well without the other.[10]

---

9. Phil Hutchinson and Michael Loughlin, "Why Teach Philosophy?" in *Teaching Philosophy*, ed. Andrea Kenkmann (London: Continuum, 2009), 41.

10. See David Curry, "Uselessness: A Panegyric," *The Good Society* 22, no. 2 (2013): 236–46 for a more robust defense of some of these ideas.

In *Parts of Animals* Aristotle gives the following account of the educated person:

> For an educated man should be able to form a fair judgment as to the goodness or the badness of an exposition. To be educated is in fact to be able to do this; and the man of general education we take to be such. It will, however, of course, be understood that we only ascribe universal education to one who in his own individual person is able to judge nearly all branches of knowledge and not to one who has a like ability merely in some special subject.[11]

The generally educated person is one equipped to make judgments, that is, to think critically, about nearly anything, whether they have specialized training in the relevant subject or not. This is the most fundamental skill required both to direct one's own living in the world and to be an engaged, informed, and productive citizen. Helping students develop this skill is arming them with stakes, and armoring them with repellants. That is what philosophy teachers do.

So how can those of us still in thrall to the idea that the university should be a community of scholars keep that ideal alive? How can we carry our message into the classroom without losing those students rightly concerned with developing the skills needed to navigate the confusing and complex and contradictory world in which they live? How do we preserve the teaching of philosophy as a vocation in spite of the forces, within and without the university, arrayed against us?

For starters, we have to own what we do, and defend its relevance to our times. Hutchinson and Loughlin rightly suggest, "We have allowed ourselves to be judged practically worthless in terms of conceptions of value that we have good reason to reject."[12] We must push back, and the only clear means I have of doing so, while retaining my vocation, is by convincing my students that we should reject those conceptions of value. We must convince them of the true value of the study of the liberal arts so that perhaps they will go on

---

11. Aristotle, *Parts of Animals*, trans. W. Ogle, in *The Complete Works of Aristotle, Vol. I*, ed. Jonathan Barnes (Princeton, NJ: Princeton University Press, 1984), 639a1–8.

12. Hutchinson and Loughlin, "Why Teach Philosophy?" 46.

to convince others and become those who seek to protect rather than undermine the fundamental mission of the university.

Gaita quotes from Hannah Arendt's prescient essay, "The Crisis in Education":

> Education is the point at which we decide whether we love the world enough to assume responsibility for it and by the same token save it from the ruin which, except for renewal, except for the coming of the new and the young, would be inevitable. And education, too, is where we decide whether we love our children enough not to expel them from our world and leave them to their own devices, not to strike from their hands their chance of undertaking something new, something foreseen by no one, but to prepare them in advance for the task of renewing a common world.[13]

Gaita adds that "teachers deny their students 'their chance of undertaking something new' when they persistently change what they teach to make it 'relevant' to their students' future needs, as they are divined by government committees and their academic advisers."[14] Rather than change what we teach, what we must do is teach in such a way that the relevance of what we do becomes clear to our students.

So how does that translate to the classroom? There is no panacea, of course, but with each iteration, the Athens game has offered me some intriguing lessons about how to achieve that goal.

My Athens game students, thus far, have been honors students. The vast majority of them are STEM or social science majors. Many are upperclassmen who have taken only the bare minimum of humanities courses. And that is why they are in my class at all: they need their critical thinking and philosophical inquiry general-education classes, and if they can get them in an honors class, all the better.

They come in not knowing what to expect from a philosophy course (and often intimidated by the prospect of taking one), and I throw them off balance even further with that first chaotic day of role-playing. We then return to some semblance of normality,

---

13. Hannah Arendt, "The Crisis in Education," in *In between Past and Future: Eight Exercises in Political Thought*, eds. Hannah Arendt and Jerome Kohn (New York: Penguin Books, 2006), 196.

14. Gaita, "Callicles' Challenge," 51.

lecture/discussion, but focused from the start on how to spot, interpret, and evaluate arguments. They see that having good arguments might be helpful in convincing others to adopt one's beliefs. This is a platitude, but it is one of those platitudes that bears repeating. Later, they find, when immersed in the game, that the quality of argument, while important, is almost never the only factor at work in such persuasion. Then we read Plato and Thucydides and Xenophon. They see that having a consistent and coherent sociopolitical worldview might be helpful in convincing others to adopt one's beliefs. And they find that, once immersed in the game, consistency and coherence are hard to achieve, and that even when achieved they often lead to uncomfortable and sometimes even repugnant conclusions.

> Meletus stands before the 300 jurors and asserts that Socrates' obsession with examining whomever he happens to meet is corrupting the youth. The youth love the spectacle of Socrates' openly mocking and humiliating prominent statesmen and intellectuals. Meletus, Anytus and Lycon, democrats all, want him silenced—he poses an existential threat to peace and order.
>
> Thucydides grumbles to his neighbor, "These are the same politicians who praise Athenian *isēgoria* (equal speech) and yet they fear the words of one crazy old man. Of course Socrates won't object to their hypocrisy—he firmly believes, Zeus save us, that only the virtuous should guide the state. The man ridicules the very idea of heeding the many, who are manifestly not virtuous. And the old fart is so stubborn that he will assert that belief to anyone who will listen, until one of them shows him how he is confused. The irony is delicious—Socrates is going to die, because he has integrity—the democrats will win, because they don't."

Since they know who their characters are from early in the semester, and have some idea of the dynamics of the game from our opening session, students steadily immerse themselves in their fictional world as the semester develops. Often, by the time the game actually begins, students are already invested in their characters. They have begun to care about what happens to them. The lessons are personal.

In a required reflection on the semester's events, students almost universally remark on how the Athens game helped them draw connections between the abstract lessons in basic logic; the not so elementary investigations into abstract moral, social, and political questions; and the hauntingly familiar concrete issues that arise in the context of the game.[15] More strikingly, they also see, sometimes quite profoundly, into the ways the ancient context sheds light on our current one. We have our fair share of sophists and rhetoricians, albeit in different garb. The issues of equal rights and *isonomia*, of equal speech (*isēgoria*), of the status of foreign workers and of imperialism still haunt us today, albeit in different manifestations. An understanding of the Athenian political landscape and worldviews is still (sometimes painfully) instructive in contemporary politics. This upcoming semester, some of my students will grasp the irony of fascist appeals to freedom of speech in Charlottesville.

The majority of my Athens game students report that the class helped them develop the skills necessary to think critically about their own problems, but also helped them see how difficult real satisfactory solutions are to find. Most satisfying, perhaps, is the way in which the game makes them reexamine their own assumptions about, for example, the value, and fragility, of democracy. Their eyes are opened in admittedly frightening ways, but they also report that they feel more confident in their ability to confront the problems they are now more fully aware of. They come to see that ideas are not just important, but potentially life altering. In short, they make a first step toward understanding the value of the life of the mind, even if it is not their own vocation. There isn't much more I could hope to achieve in a semester-long class.

I plan to offer such courses to nonhonors sections in the near future and to expand my repertoire of games as well.[16] Modifying these games for use in the philosophy classroom requires a lot of effort.[17] But the rewards are remarkable.

---

15. I would happily supply copies of these narrative reflections to colleagues who might be interested.

16. There are many reacting games available, but those of greatest interest to philosophers are probably, in addition to the *Threshold of Democracy* game, *Charles Darwin, the Copley Medal and the Rise of Naturalism, 1861–64*; *Confucianism and the Succession Crisis of the Wanli Emperor, 1587*; and *The Trial of Galileo: Aristotelianism, the "New Cosmology," and the Catholic Church, 1616–33*.

17. The games don't require such modification, though they certainly encourage it.

For the humanities to survive, for universities properly so-called to survive, we need to do a better job of demonstrating to our students how studying "useless" things is essential to their success as laborers, as citizens, and most importantly as human beings. While it is certainly not suited to every teacher, I have found the Athens game, when carefully balanced with more traditional teaching methods, to be one means of helping students draw that conclusion for themselves.

> Lithicles sails into the *Piraeus* after months in Ionia, victorious fleet at his back. Word in the agora is that the tribute mission was a success, that Lithicles and his fellow generals have brought as many as twenty city-states back into the Athenian sphere of influence. After a relatively bloodless show of force in Chios, most of the other states fell right into line. But now his generals have declared Lithicles sole ruler of Athens, and the landed elites are backing his usurpation. Even some moderate democrats have endorsed his rule, noting that he has promised to set up advisory councils and pledged to allow the *Ekklesia* to continue to meet and deliberate, albeit with limited powers to act. The great Athenian experiment with democracy has hit another bump in the road. Socrates' fears about tyranny, and democracy, may have been prescient.[18]

---

18. Devin Sanchez Curry offered extremely helpful suggestions for editing this piece. The failures of judgment that remain are all mine.

17

Teaching for Our Good

Bob Fischer
Texas State University

BOB FISCHER teaches philosophy at Texas State University. In 2013, he was the Honors College Professor of the Year, and in 2014, he was given the highest pedagogical honor in his own college: the Liberal Arts Golden Apple Award for Teaching. His textbook on moral issues that affect students, *College Ethics*, was published by Oxford University Press in 2017, and he is working on three more volumes for students: *Ethics, Left and Right* (Oxford), *The Routledge Handbook of Animal Ethics* (Routledge), and *Animal Ethics—A Contemporary Introduction* (Routledge). He tries to help students disagree in kinder, more productive ways.

> For in much wisdom is much vexation, and he
> who increases knowledge increases sorrow.
> —Ecclesiastes 1:18

Jess was like many students you've taught. Her family was religious, but not intensely so; politically conservative, but with some wiggle room on certain social issues; deeply practical, valuing hard work as much as anything else. One Monday afternoon, about halfway through my ethics course, she seemed withdrawn. I invited her to drop by for a chat, and not long after she sat down, there were tears. It began with frustration: Why couldn't she convince other students of things that seemed so obvious to her? But as we kept talking, the real problem emerged. "The topics are so heavy," she said. "What if we really are just our bodies? What if nothing matters? How do you sleep at night?"[1]

---

1. For the sake of student privacy, "Jess" is a composite who represents several students I've taught throughout my career.

159

When she left, I confess feeling a bit self-satisfied. "I'm making a difference," I thought. "I'm having an impact." A student's worldview was being challenged, and I was doing the challenging, armed with a host of arguments that she had never considered. But not long after, the glow faded. I taught a class that made a young woman weep in my office. In some sense, I hurt her. And for what?

•

Why, exactly, should we teach philosophy? Assuming that it isn't for our health, it's probably for the sake of the students: we hope to better them in various respects. Of course, that may not be much more than a hope—we know that students retain precious little of what they learn, and a review of the literature shows that we have little reason to think we improve students' critical thinking abilities—but let's set aside such dark thoughts.[2] Supposing that our teaching makes a difference, what sort of difference should we expect?

Most philosophy classes involve complicating things. We show that it's surprisingly difficult to argue for some highly intuitive claims; we present compelling arguments for some highly *un*intuitive claims; we introduce conceptual possibilities that most students have never imagined. And in general, these moves aren't particularly friendly to conservative outlooks on the world. In the philosophy of religion, we consider the arguments for the existence of God, finding them all wanting. We then show that the problem of evil is much fiercer than students might have thought. In the philosophy of mind, we

---

2. If students don't see the significance of the material they're learning, and so don't make connections between the material and the rest of their knowledge, Ebbinghaus' "Forgetting Curve" suggests that they'll retain as little as 20 percent of what they were taught after a month; see J. M. J. Murre and J. Dros, "Replication and Analysis of Ebbinghaus' 'Forgetting Curve,'" *PLOS ONE* 10, no. 7 (2015):1–23. In practice, of course, students often do better than that, but even when they are using information on a regular basis, quite a lot of it goes by the wayside. For instance, one study found that medical students only retain about half of what they were taught a year later; see Eugene J. F. M. Custers, "Long-Term Retention of Basic Science Knowledge: A Review Study," *Advances in Health Sciences Education* 15, no. 1 (2010):109–28. And on the difficulty of teaching critical thinking, see David T. Willingham, "Critical Thinking: Why Is It So Hard to Teach?" *American Educator* 31, no. 2 (2007):8–19.

reveal how hard it is to defend the soul. In metaphysics, we make the case against free will and the existence of a stable, persisting self. In courses that cover some ethics or political philosophy, we offer arguments against conservative views about sex and sexuality, arguments against eating animals, arguments for extensive obligations to the global poor, and so on.

Of course, this isn't *all* we do, and you shouldn't infer that I am here to complain about the dominance of liberal ideas in the humanities. I don't think that most philosophers are intentionally lobbying against conservative commitments, and I'm not necessarily critical of those who do. This essay is not by a disgruntled right-winger, fussing about bias in the classroom. Indeed, I don't think that bias is the best explanation, as the more plausible story is structural. To teach philosophy is to engage in a subversive activity: whatever your assumptions, we try to challenge them; whatever your beliefs, we present arguments that you should have others. And if most students have views that support a conservative outlook on the world—or if most of the editors of textbooks believe that most students have such views—then you'd expect there to be disproportionate attention to lines of reasoning that aren't friendly to conservatism.

In any case, if most philosophy classes involve complicating things in the ways that I've suggested, what sort of results can we expect? A guess: we help our students become a little less dogmatic, a little more skeptical, and a little more liberal.

At what cost? We're good at raising hard questions; we are remarkably bad at answering them—or, at least, we are remarkably bad at answering them to our students' satisfaction. (Cowing them into silence is not satisfying them.) And many people find it difficult to live with the ambiguity that we create. How often have you heard the refrain "I hate it that there are no *answers* in this class!"

We might insist that it's *good* to learn to live without answers, that given our epistemic situation, we can't ask for more. Fair enough. But good for whom? Let's focus for a moment on student religiosity. Whatever you think of particular religious communities, they are very important to their members, and many studies have identified strong correlations between religious activity and various positive outcomes: lower risk of premature mortality, higher overall happiness, greater sense of purpose in life, and so on.[3] But philosophy tends to complicate a person's relationship to her religious community, and it certainly doesn't encourage the nonreligious to acquire new allegiances. Moreover, it does not replace religious communities and their associated benefits with alternatives. It certainly doesn't offer many psychological comforts.[4]

So philosophy may not be good for student health, either physical or psychological. (It certainly doesn't seem that it was good for Jess'.) We might be entitled to risk such harms to students if studying philosophy made students behave more morally, but it doesn't seem to have this salutary effect (or so say the experimental philosophers).[5] Nor does the study of philosophy promise more money, or more sex, or a wider range of career opportunities than other humanities

---

3. For reviews of the literature on religiosity and physical health, see B. Aukst-Margetić and B. Margetić, "Religiosity and Health Outcomes: Review of Literature," *Collegium Antropologicum* 29, no. 1 (2005):365–71; Cotton et al., "Religion/Spirituality and Adolescent Health Outcomes: A Review," *Journal of Adolescent Health* 38, no. 4 (2006):472–80. Cotton et al. cover adolescents specifically. For a review on religiosity and mental health, see Harold G. Koenig, "Research on Religion, Spirituality, and Mental Health: A Review," *Canadian Journal of Psychiatry* 54, no. 5 (2009):283–91. Things are more complex here, because religiosity can also be associated with various psychological disorders, which means that there are risks and benefits of both religiosity and irreligiosity. However, I doubt that any of us consider those trade-offs when making the decision to teach the relevant material. Also, I'd be remiss if I didn't mention that people's religiosity can have both positive and negative effects on the people around them. Those negative effects—such as restrictions of the rights of others—are good reasons to challenge the forms of religiosity that give rise to them. However, I don't think that is in tension with what I'm saying above, which is focused on benefits to the individual religious person rather than to his community. I'll return to this point later on.

4. The same points don't necessarily apply to political conservatism independently of religious affiliation, as the relationship between political ideology and health appears to be weak. However, the best meta-analysis available does suggest that insofar as there is a relationship between conservatism and psychological well-being, it's positive. See Emma Onraet, Alain Van Hiel, and Kristof Dhont, "The Relationship between Right-Wing Ideological Attitudes and Psychological Well-Being," *Personality and Social Psychology Bulletin* 39, no. 4 (2013):509–22.

5. On this point, see Joshua Rust and Eric Schwitzgebel, "The Moral Behavior of Ethicists," in *A Companion to Experimental Philosophy*, eds. J. Sytsma and W. Buckwalter (Malden, MA: Wiley-Blackwell, 2016), 225–33; Eric Schwitzgebel, "Do Ethics Classes Influence Student Behavior?" (unpublished manuscript, 2013).

majors. It isn't even clear that it promotes more intellectual virtue than intellectual vice. Consider, for instance, whether we foster epistemic humility or knee-jerk skepticism. It's relatively easy to teach students how to do destructive philosophy: to teach them how to tear down a view. It's a lot harder to teach them how to rebuild after the fact. So we tend to offer criticisms of p and then survey alternatives to p. But absent a method for choosing between those alternatives, this, in student-speak, means something like, "Believe whatever you want *other* than p." We do, of course, say a few things about theory selection, but some hand waving about simplicity, explanatory scope, and predictive power is a far cry from a decision procedure. How often do your course evaluations say something to the effect of, "This class has taught me that there are no right answers"?

Relatedly, recall that we can't prevent our students from misunderstanding—or misusing—what we say. I've had students argue fiercely for libertarianism about free will, largely because they think that the alternative is more government regulation. I've spent classes talking about reflective equilibrium, and students take that to mean that we should accept any moral theory that appears to permit meat eating. I've simplified a complex debate, knowing that doing so would make one side look stronger than the other, and have then tried to emphasize that they shouldn't make too much of there seeming to be a "winner"—after all, there is still so much more to say. But later on in the course, it becomes obvious that they haven't heeded my warning.

The above makes me doubt that a little philosophy does much to improve our students. In other words, when critters like us are merely *introduced* to philosophy—that is, when they encounter it but don't have the luxury of studying it at length—I don't see compelling reasons to think that the net result for an individual is positive. As a teacher, I find this troubling. Granted, we may not be obligated to make students better off by the end of a course than they were at the outset. But if, in fact, philosophy doesn't improve students' lives, and even leaves some worse off, then we should be able to articulate our reasons for keeping it in the curriculum.

•

Someone might object to my pessimistic outlook about the individual benefits of philosophy. "It can be liberating," the critic says. "It can be transformative, opening up the possibility of new ways of engaging the world. Philosophy creates the opportunity for true autonomy, true self-determination."

Those, of course, were the thoughts behind my self-congratulatory reaction to Jess' tears. "Sure," I thought, "it's rough for her now. But growing pains are so named for a reason, and she'll be better off in time. This is the path to a view of the world that she can claim for her own, one based on following arguments where they lead." These days, however, I see this line of thought as representing an ideal, as a claim about what we hope to accomplish, rather than what we actually achieve. Granted, our ideals need not be achievable: if we know that we would be content with far too little otherwise, we are wise to demand the unattainable. But such ideals don't always serve us well: sometimes they're not just unrealistic, but they blind us to the good that *is* within reach—about which I'll have more to say in the next section. So we've got to figure out when to hang on to our ideals, and when to let them go.

It's very tempting to think that we are benefitting our students directly, and there is certainly some anecdotal evidence of that. They report coming to understand something puzzling; we see them able to handle logic problems they couldn't previously; we see improvement in their written work; they thank us afterward for the perspective-changing experience. These are all good things. But I'm not sure that they have the significance we attribute to them.

Many psychologists are drawn to a dual-process model of the mind.[6] Essentially, Type-1 processes deal with information quickly and unconsciously; Type-2 processes deal with information slowly and consciously.[7] Most of our thought and behavior is—like it or not—largely shaped by Type-1 processes. (Hence the "1.") And

---

6. For accessible and systematic overviews of the ideas that I'm discussing here, see Jonathan Haidt, *The Righteous Mind* (New York: Pantheon, 2012); Daniel Kahneman, *Thinking, Fast and Slow* (New York: Farrar, Straus and Giroux, 2013).

7. If we allow ourselves to be a little sloppy, we'll speak of System 1 and System 2; such talk amounts to a convenient idealization and certainly shouldn't be taken to imply that there are discrete structures in the brain.

because these are fast, unconscious processes—call them "intuitive," if you like—they're hard to retrain. This isn't news. If you think that it's wrong for adult family members to have consensual sex with one another, you might have a good argument to that effect. But it's more likely that you react with disgust at even the mention of incest, and that this disgust is associated with a strong inclination to condemn the behavior, even when the standard explanations for its wrongness have been undermined. (For instance, even if it's the case that the woman will not get pregnant, because the couple is using two forms of contraception, you find the behavior repulsive.)

Admittedly, you can begin to retrain your System 1. But it's hard and time consuming: our natural discomfort with incest is difficult to shake. Moreover, it would be very easy to mistake *progress* for *temporary deference to System 2*. In other words, when you're consciously thinking about the issue, that's System 2 at work, and conscious thought *can* override the deliverances of System 1. But when you *aren't* being prompted to think slowly and carefully about the issue—for example, *when the semester is over*—System 2 devotes its energies elsewhere, and System 1 is again allowed to rule in that particular domain. Indeed, this interplay between System 1 and System 2 explains the constant progress/regression cycle we see even within our own courses. For instance, consider a student who's an incompatibilist and believes in moral responsibility. Why isn't she bothered by my arguments for determinism, especially given her inability to respond to them? Answer: she finds determinism unintuitive, and the arguments I offered in class didn't unseat her intuition.

Unfortunately for philosophy teachers, both systems are subject to all sorts of biases, and they deploy all sorts of heuristics. We know, for example, that people are bad at making inferences with new concepts. As a result, their critical thinking abilities are, by and large, domain specific. They are subject to various framing effects. They make most of their moral judgments quickly and emotionally, and they don't change their views when their reasons are undermined (which were probably confabulations anyway). They have short attention spans. They are terrible at interpreting statistics. They tend to engage in motivated rather than impartial reasoning. The human mind is also ambiguity- and tension-averse; so, for example, given a choice between cognitive dissonance and a simplistic resolution thereof, people are inclined to opt for the latter.[8]

People have a hard time remembering meaningless information—and when you're taking a general-education class, and you know that you only need to hang on to the material for a few weeks at most, then you might just regard philosophical information as mostly meaningless. People's memories are affected by how many simple sugars they consume, by how much alcohol they drink, and by how much sleep they get.[9] (Sound relevant to anyone you know?) After a few years—and probably after a *much* shorter period—our students will not remember much of anything we said.

The upshot is this: people are not wired for the kind of careful, critical thinking that philosophy demands, and they'll probably forget most of what we teach. These are depressing facts. (Or, at least, they're depressing to me.) But we ought to face them squarely. And when I do, I tend to think that we shouldn't teach philosophy because it makes any particular student better off. We should teach it because, insofar as it does anything, it makes students—seen as a whole—better off. We teach philosophy to foster a more open society, writ large.

•

I value careful, clear-eyed reasoning as much as the next academic; I value the challenging of assumptions; I think it is worth asking questions precisely because their answers are generally taken for granted; I don't think that we should shy away from the hardest puzzles simply because we won't be able to solve them.

---

8. On the point about concepts, again see Willingham, "Critical Thinking"; on framing effects, attention spans, statistical reasoning, and resolving ambiguity, see Kahneman, *Thinking, Fast and Slow*; on moral judgment and confabulation, see Haidt, *Righteous Mind*.

9. On sugar, see Hsu et al., "Effects of Sucrose and High Fructose Corn Syrup Consumption on Spatial Memory Function and Hippocampal Neuroinflammation in Adolescent Rats," *Hippocampus* 25, no. 2 (2015):227–39; on alcohol, see Carbia et al., "Working Memory over a Six-Year Period in Young Binge Drinkers," *Alcohol* 61 (2017):17–23; on sleep, see, William D. S. Killgore, "Effects of Sleep Deprivation on Cognition," in *Human Sleep and Cognition. Part I: Basic Research*, eds. G. A. Kerkhof and Hans P. A. Van Dongen (Amsterdam: Elsevier, 2010), 105.

But in my teaching, I'm no longer sure that I value these things for the sake of individuals. If philosophy offers net benefits to individuals, they are indirect. Philosophy seems to be valuable because of what it can do for *us*. Even if it doesn't immediately improve *your* life, it's got a shot at improving *our life together*, and hence each of our lives derivatively. I teach because I think it has a shot at helping to produce better citizens, and in this way to serve the common good.

This is because philosophy encourages traits that are costly for individuals, but are invaluable in a pluralistic democracy like ours. We can't afford to have too many citizens who cannot imagine believing other than they do. We can't afford to have too many citizens for whom all alternatives appear irrational—or worse still, *evil*. A pluralistic democracy requires that I have the ability to see my set of core convictions as one option among many—all of which are to be protected, as long as they do not come to threaten our joint venture. A pluralistic democracy *also* requires me to have the ability to figure out what *our joint venture* comes to—and to work out the implications of having one. Philosophy is particularly well equipped to hone such abilities. But not in the way we expect.

When I'm in the classroom, I'm teaching conceptual architecture: I'm giving my students packages of claims that hang together more or less well, and I'm trying to show them what happens when you put pressure *here*, or remove *that*, or add on an extra piece *there*. I don't tell them which package to adopt. And, of course, I shouldn't: first, it's not my place; second, even if it were, I wouldn't know which to recommend. In doing all this, I'm giving students an appreciation of the variety of belief systems, and I'm also teaching them something about how to think through the implications of such systems.

However, it isn't the skills we teach that do the work; it isn't what we instill about Kant or Hume or the trolley problem. Rather, it's the experience, which is all we can be sure to provide. We can make them articulate their reasons for their beliefs and then criticize those reasons; we can put them in contexts in which they have to disagree civilly; we can make them focus on the foundations of those disagreements; we can make them defend views that they reject; and, of course, we can make them talk about the political consequences of all this diversity and uncertainty. We can bring them to the point where they feel the floor disappearing from underneath them, where they have a sense of vertigo at their inability to defend what seems obvious or to criticize what seems absurd. And then we can talk to them about how we should proceed in the wake of such experiences. What does toleration look like in the wake of such experiences? How should they respond to disagreement? What's a sensible way forward when it's so hard to know the truth?

My guess is that students are much more likely to remember these experiences than they are to remember the different versions of the categorical imperative, or how to formulate arguments in premise-conclusion form, or the role that the evil demon plays in Descartes' Second Meditation. And that's fine. If those experiences stick, that's a step toward retraining their System 1s. It's a step toward the sort of citizen we need in a pluralistic democracy. So while I think there are personal costs to learning about philosophy, I think there are benefits too—for us, as members of an open society. Philosophy can serve that society by bettering the citizenry, even if not each citizen.

•

I've lost track of Jess. But even if I hadn't, I'm not sure that I'd want her to read this essay. Am I saying, essentially, that it was fine to make her cry—and perhaps much more—so that she might contribute, in some small way, to a better community? I suppose I am, though I hate the sound of it. Indeed, I think she'd be right to push back, to argue that the benefits don't outweigh the costs, at least when you consider the low odds of the benefits. And if she did, you might think that she would be showing that I'm wrong about the impact that we can have on students; she would be showing that her philosophical training gave her the tools to defend herself against the thesis of this essay. But I doubt it. She could have done that much without a course in philosophy; we don't need much training to come to our own aid.

I do hope, though, that if that conversation were ever to happen, it would be motivated, at least in part, by the experience she had in my class. I hope that recognizing the shortcomings of her first-year worldview would make her wonder about shortcomings in mine. And I hope that having to give an account of myself, an explanation of what I do with and to students, would better the university community, and so the wider social world of which the university community is a part.

18

Teaching Ethics, Happiness, and The Good Life: An Upbuilding Discourse in the Spirits of Søren Kierkegaard and John Dewey

Alexander V. Stehn
University of Texas Rio Grande Valley

ALEXANDER V. STEHN is an associate professor of philosophy at the University of Texas Rio Grande Valley on the Southern Texas-Mexico border. He specializes in U.S.-American and Latin American philosophies, but is prouder of being a generalist and teacher. He taught for five years as a graduate assistant at the Pennsylvania State University and for five years at the University of Texas-Pan American, before it merged with the University of Texas at Brownsville to form his current institution. In 2014, he was honored with a University of Texas Regents' Outstanding Teaching Award, which recognizes extraordinary classroom performance and innovation in undergraduate instruction among faculty across the UT System's fourteen educational institutions with more than 20,000 total faculty.

"The more ideal the conception of being a Christian, the more inward it becomes—and indeed the more difficult. Being a Christian then undergoes a change that I will illustrate with a worldly analogy. Formerly, there were in Greece wise men, σοφοί. Then came Pythagoras and with him the reflection-qualification, reduplication, in connection with being a wise man; therefore he did not even venture to call himself a wise man but instead called himself a φιλόσοφος [friend or lover of wisdom, philosopher]. Was this a step backward or a step forward; or was it not because Pythagoras had more ideally apprehended what it would really mean, what would be required to call oneself a wise man; therefore there was wisdom in his not even having dared to call himself a wise man."

—Søren Kierkegaard[1]

"To assume an attitude of condescension toward existence is perhaps a natural human compensation for the straits of life. But it is an ultimate source of the covert, uncandid and cheap in philosophy. This compensatory disposition it is which forgets that reflection exists to guide choice and effort. Hence its love of wisdom is but an unlaborious transformation of existence by dialectic, instead of an opening and enlarging of the ways of nature in man. A true wisdom, devoted to the latter task, discovers in thoughtful observation and experiment the method of administering the unfinished processes of existence so that frail goods shall be substantiated, secure goods be extended, and the precarious promises of good that haunt experienced things be more liberally fulfilled."

—John Dewey[2]

The first epigraph above from Søren Kierkegaard ends with a question that is not marked as a question. Regardless of whether it was Kierkegaard, an editor, a typesetter, or a translator who made the mistake, the omission is instructive, because it glosses over a question that philosophy professors routinely fail to ask: "Is calling oneself a *philosopher* rather than a *wise person* a step backward or a step forward?" In this essay, I use Kierkegaard to recover the importance of this question and lay out my response in conversation with (1) John Dewey's clarion call for a recovery of philosophy[3] and (2)

---

1. Søren Kierkegaard, *The Point of View for My Work as an Author*, trans. Howard V. Hong and Edna H. Hong (Princeton, NJ: Princeton University Press, 1998), 137.

2. John Dewey, *Experience and Nature*, ed. Jo Ann Boydston, *The Later Works of John Dewey, 1925–1953, Volume 1: 1925* (Carbondale: Southern Illinois University Press, 1988), 67–68.

3. See "The Need for a Recovery of Philosophy," in *The Middle Works of John Dewey, 1899–1924, Volume 10: 1916–1917, Essays*, ed. Jo Ann Boydston (Carbondale: Southern Illinois University, 1980), 3–48.

my own experience teaching introductory ethics courses over the past ten years. My aim is to produce what Kierkegaard would call an "upbuilding discourse" in the service of what Dewey would call "true wisdom," an opening and enlarging of our ways of teaching ethics, so that we may more effectively fulfill philosophy's precarious promises of good.

While Kierkegaard's Christian existentialism and Dewey's naturalistic pragmatism are rarely read as allies, I am inspired by their shared emphasis on existence or experience as both the starting point and the end of any philosophy worth its salt; they recognize reflection as both the crucial moment of vision and the persistent temptation. Readers of this volume will not need to be convinced of the value of philosophical reflection, but in the context of teaching ethics, I believe that philosophical reflection can actually be harmful, if it is not yoked to spiritual exercises designed to help us experience philosophy as something that must be practiced in our lives and not merely cogitated in our heads.[4] Like anyone else, ethics professors often fail to live ethically, but we face a special temptation: the use of academic philosophy as a compensatory shelter from the strenuous ethical tasks of improving ourselves, our relationships, and the world. There is also the danger that we will transmit this disease to our students, convincing them that philosophy takes place in books, not lives; in classrooms, not communities; and in words, not works.

The essay that follows has three sections: (1) a Deweyan pragmatist's translation of Kierkegaard's religious insights on Christianity, as a way of life, into ethical insights on philosophy, as a way of life; (2) a brief description of the introductory course that I teach most frequently: Ethics, Happiness, and The Good Life; and (3) a narrative exploration of three spiritual exercises from the course: (a)

---

4. Making "spiritual exercises" part of an introduction to ethics is no longer common practice, but it would have seemed like common sense to most ancient and medieval philosophers. See Pierre Hadot, *Philosophy as a Way of Life: Spiritual Exercises from Socrates to Foucault*, ed. Arnold Davidson, trans. Michael Chase (Malden, MA: Blackwell, 1995). Martha Nussbaum's description of the life of a hypothetical pupil across multiple Hellenistic schools provides an especially vivid contrast with the way most students today encounter philosophy. See Martha Craven Nussbaum, *The Therapy of Desire: Theory and Practice in Hellenistic Ethics* (Princeton, NJ: Princeton University Press, 1994).

self-cultivation by means of writing in an Ethics Notebook, (b) an "existential experiment" in which we practice one of Aristotle's virtues for a week, and (c) a fifteen-hour service-learning component.

Relocating Ethics in Existence: Kierkegaard's "Worldly Analogy" and Dewey's Pragmatism

By theoretically exploring the ideal of genuine Christianity, Kierkegaard gained a profound sense of his own practical failings as a Christian. He recognized that as the conception of Christianity becomes theoretically more ideal, being a Christian becomes practically more difficult. Casting Christianity—a demanding way of life that must be practiced in the sphere of existence—into reflection is thus both promising and dangerous: promising because reflection can help one better understand and appropriate a genuinely Christian way of life; dangerous because reflection may perpetually cast being a Christian out of the realm of existence and into the realm of ideas.

When I reflect upon Kierkegaard's "worldly analogy" with philosophy, I am struck by just how demanding the task of being a wise person is, and I am momentarily relieved to claim only the love of wisdom rather than wisdom itself. But then I think about how this distancing can also be dangerous, especially given the background of a mushy cultural understanding of "love" as primarily a feeling, rather than as something to do, something that puts us to work.[5] To combat this problem, Kierkegaard sought to "jack up the price" of Christianity,[6] to present Christ as an ideal prototype whose life must be imitated rather than merely admired.[7] In a similar way, Kierkegaard's "worldly analogy" presents Pythagoras as an ideal prototype who founded the strenuous way of life called

---

5. See Søren Kierkegaard, *Works of Love*, trans. Howard V. Hong and Edna H. Hong (Princeton, NJ: Princeton University Press, 1995).

6. *Søren Kierkegaard's Journals and Papers*, trans. Howard V. Hong and Edna H. Hong, 7 vols. (Bloomington: Indiana University Press, 1967), 3:75–76, 6:72–74.

7. Kierkegaard distinguishes between *admiration* and *imitation* as follows: "Christ continually uses the expression 'imitators.' He never says that he asks for admirers, adoring admirers, adherents; and when he uses the expression 'follower' he always explains it in such a way that one perceives that 'imitators' is meant by it, that is not adherents of a teaching but imitators of a life." *Practice in Christianity*, trans. Howard V. Hong and Edna H. Hong (Princeton, NJ: Princeton University Press, 1991), 237.

"philosophy" (*not* as someone who began a tradition of metaphysical speculation).[8]

The metaphysics that underwrites the reality of Kierkegaard's ideals appeals to many of my students who identify as Christian, but, to address a wider audience, I also speak of the reality of ideals in the Deweyan sense that pervades my second epigraph.[9] I cannot reasonably expect ethical growth from students if I do not earnestly dedicate myself to my own ethical growth, to my own education in a Deweyan sense.[10] Pragmatically speaking, ideals are real to the extent that they inspire and guide conduct. In other words, an ideal is a beautiful possibility that calls us to the personal conviction that we are responsible for realizing it in the twofold sense of thinking it and making it real.

If the existence of an ideal is left unrealized in this double sense—if *either* we fail to thoroughly think through the possibility presented by the ideal *or* we merely think about how to better describe it, while failing to act upon our responsibility to make it real—then we fail to grow, and the ideal is not opened and enlarged through us. This means that if I am to avoid the "unlaborious transformation of existence by dialectic" in the classroom, I must strive to practice and embody the ethical ideals that I reach by the exercise of my intelligence, or I will be unfit to teach my students to do it. I may distance myself from the immediacy of everyday life and conventional mores to reflect on how we should live (a step back), but I must also remember to practice living in a way that is ever more

---

8. Kierkegaard's assessment of the primary philosophical significance of Pythagoras is consistent with both Plato's and Aristotle's assessments, as explained by Carl Huffman: "For both Plato and Aristotle, then, Pythagoras is not a part of the cosmological and metaphysical tradition of Presocratic philosophy nor is he closely connected to the metaphysical system presented by fifth-century Pythagoreans like Philolaus; he is instead the founder of a way of life." See Carl Huffman, "Pythagoras," in *The Stanford Encyclopedia of Philosophy* (summer 2014 edition), https://plato.stanford.edu/archives/sum2014/entries/pythagoras.

9. An excellent study of Dewey's metaphysics that emphasizes the role of the ideal is Victor Kestenbaum, *The Grace and the Severity of the Ideal: John Dewey and the Transcendent* (Chicago: University of Chicago Press, 2002).

10. See the chapter "Education as Growth," in John Dewey, *Democracy and Education: The Middle Works of John Dewey, 1899–1924*, vol. 9, eds. Jo Ann Boydston and Sidney Hook (Carbondale: Southern Illinois University Press, 1985), 46–58.

consistent with my reflections (a step forward). Designing a successful ethics course thus hinges on more than preparing the reading list, the assignments, and the grading scheme: it also depends on my own dedication to practicing what I teach, that is, philosophy as an ethical way of life.

Kierkegaard claims that it is a risk to preach because God "pays close attention to whether what I am saying is true, whether it is true in me, that is, he looks . . . to see whether my life expresses what I am saying."[11] Kierkegaard thinks that most pastors have shrunk back from this risk, ceased risking their personal *I*, and become content to merely offer some observations on the text. Because people in the pews are no longer addressed as individual *yous*, they no longer risk themselves existentially in listening. Real preaching and listening are thus abolished as disembodied utterances cease to be of live concern:

> Whether I [the pastor] do what I say is none of your concern if only the observation is correct; it scarcely concerns me myself. . . . Whether or not you, the listener, do what is said does not concern me, and scarcely yourself; it is observation and at most it is a question of the extent to which the observation has satisfied you.[12]

I believe this same temptation is present when teaching philosophy. There is a danger that I will existentially step further back from questioning and improving the way I live, even as I become more rhetorically adept and theoretically sophisticated in posing the question "How should one live?" Regardless of whether Kierkegaard's all-seeing God exists, I have more than 100 students each semester, and many will certainly pay "close attention to whether what I am saying is true, whether it is true in me . . . whether my life expresses what I am saying."[13] Like my students, I should risk self-reconstruction in the process of examining my own life and the truths of the philosophers each semester.

If I am *not* risking myself, that is, not striving to more fully appropriate and embody ethical ideals in order to continue becoming the teacher that my students would be wise to truly listen to,

---

11. *Practice in Christianity*, 235.

12. Ibid., 236.

13. Ibid., 235.

then I am a twenty-first-century incarnation of Kierkegaard's hated "Assistant Professor," who makes a series of disembodied observations on some dead texts and blocks his students from being existentially transformed by the truth. Kierkegaard yearns for more authentic educators: "Precisely this is the profound untruth in all modern teaching, that there is no notion at all of how thought is influenced by the fact that the one presenting it does not dare to express it in action, that in this very way the flower of the thought or the heart of the thought vanishes and the power of the thought disappears."[14]

In Deweyan terms, by stripping philosophical texts of their existential power, teachers assume "an attitude of condescension toward existence" and thereby make their courses "uncandid and cheap." It is a risk to teach ethics! Or by logical extension: where there is no existential risk to professor and students, ethics is not really being taught.

Kierkegaard wanted his work to be read as a response to a particular context in which everyone already considered themselves to have completely reached or attained what he understood to be the difficult and lifelong tasks of becoming a genuine self, an ethical individual, and a Christian. The pedagogical problem that drives Kierkegaard's work is something like "How can I get individuals to *become* better Christians if they think they already are *fully* Christian?" or (translated into the problematic that guides my course) "How can I get people (including myself) to grow ethically when we think that our ways of living are basically fine the way they are?" In my course, students encounter both secular and religious ethical traditions, but the difficult and lifelong existential task of becoming a better person constitutes the heart of philosophy in either case, which I demonstrate historically using Plato's Socrates, Aristotle, Epictetus, Kant, Mill, Kierkegaard, and Levinas.

I try to infuse my teaching with what moves *me* in their texts, as a way of encouraging students to have their own encounters with these texts and make their own movements. This requires me to subtly bear witness to, testify on behalf of, confess, intimate, or otherwise convey the insights I have won (and sometimes forgotten!) from these texts, but also from my experience. I try not to cross the

---

14. *Søren Kierkegaard's Journals and Papers*, 1:265.

line into rant, and I routinely encourage alternative readings, but I believe that I am more likely to provoke meaningful student encounters with philosophical theories when I can demonstrate how those theories might bear upon or emerge from my own experiences, when I am risking the personal.[15]

The Socratic recognition of one's own ignorance may be the beginning of wisdom (which is why my course begins with the *Meno* and the *Apology*), but this same move can also be the death of wisdom and its love, insofar as knowing the good also involves doing it. Refusing any claim to being wise can serve as a way of practically distancing ourselves from the ethical life that wisdom and its love entail. In contrast, philosophy understood as a way of life calls us to traverse the gaps between our ideals and our behaviors, our ideas and our practices. While it is important for Kierkegaard to consider the ways in which he is *not* a Christian, he must not step so far back that he loses the desire to *become* a Christian—to *practice* Christianity, to *imitate* (rather than merely admire) Christ by performing works of love—a lifelong task.

We can repeat Kierkegaard's religious point in ethical terms: while it is important to consider oneself *not* to be fully ethical (for one often unknowingly or perhaps even knowingly or indifferently does wrong),[16] one must not lose the desire to *become* a better person (which is a lifelong task). Constructing an ethics course that is only a matter of reading texts, taking quizzes, and writing papers may unwittingly extinguish this existential desire in our students. The alternative is not less reading and reflection, but more shifts to writing and practice, so that our reflections on the contours of the world

---

15. I borrow the phrase "risking the personal" from AnaLousie Keating, who used it to describe Gloria Anzaldúa's "innovative use of autobiographical experience as a tool for community building, knowledge production, and social change." See "Risking the Personal: An Introduction" in Gloria Anzaldúa, *Interviews/Entrevistas*, ed. AnaLouise Keating (New York: Routledge, 2000).

16. Kierkegaard claims that Christianity goes beyond Socratic categories when it redefines *sin* to consist of instances in which one knows the right or good yet knowingly does the wrong. See Søren Kierkegaard, *The Concept of Anxiety: A Simple Psychologically Orienting Deliberation on the Dogmatic Issue of Hereditary Sin*, trans. Reidar Thomte and Albert B. Anderson (Princeton, NJ: Princeton University Press, 1980), esp. 14–24.

and the purpose of our lives are yoked to deliberate transformations in our attitudes, actions, and relationships by way of spiritual exercises, or what Dewey preferred to call "experiments."

Unfortunately, professional philosophers today rarely recognize that reflection can be dangerous, insofar as it can lead us to wholly transfer our struggles from the realm of existence to the realm of ideas. Philosophy courses therefore often excel in producing ad nauseum what Kierkegaard termed the "reflection-qualification," reduplicating wisdom in the realm of thought alone, when what is called for is the reduplication or embodiment of wisdom in the realm of concrete existence. This is precisely the call Dewey issued to us 100 years ago in "The Need for a Recovery of Philosophy" (1917), and the need is no less pressing today.

Syllabus Course Description for PHIL 1310: Ethics, Happiness, and The Good Life

This course offers an opportunity to improve or even reinvent ourselves through higher education. The first part of our philosophical journey begins with ancient Greek perspectives on ethics that will help us think about what kind of people we are and would like to become. As we read and discuss works by Plato, Aristotle, and Epictetus, we will be following Socrates' dual philosophical commandments to: (1) know ourselves, and (2) care for ourselves by thoughtfully considering questions of how we should live. Since this course is designed to introduce you to philosophy as a way of life, we will also practice things like virtue and friendship to gain insight into the links between ethics and happiness by experimenting with different understandings of the good life.

Of course, our individual practices of the art of living cannot be separated from the broader values and needs that shape our lives together. In part two of this course, we will consider two of the most important modern philosophical attempts to develop an account of the universal laws or fundamental principles of morality: Kant's duty-based ethics and Mill's happiness-based ethics. We then will consider the implications of these two theories, with respect to the global problem of extreme poverty, which is also a concern here in the Rio Grande Valley. By taking up this problem, we will learn to think more concretely about how we must care for ourselves in the context of an entire world full of others. At the end of this unit, we will write an essay reflecting on our own personal responsibility to people in extreme poverty.

Since many of us are religious and the Judeo-Christian tradition has greatly influenced secular thinking about ethics, the third part of the course will examine the philosophies of Kierkegaard and Levinas, who each develop a religious understanding of our duty to genuinely encounter and love our neighbors. Their perspectives will help us rethink the role that caring for others might play in caring for ourselves. We will end the term with a service-learning project, which will integrate theoretical reflection and ethical practice.

The overarching aim of this course is to theoretically challenge and practically empower us to become better and happier people by developing a more thoughtful understanding of ethics, happiness, and the good life for ourselves and others.

Practicing Ethics, Happiness, and The Good Life: Three Strategies

My course proceeds chronologically and thematically in three parts: (1) Ancient Philosophy as a Way of Ethical Life and The Care of the Self; (2) Modern Moral Philosophy and The Care of Humanity; and (3) Religion as an Ethical Way of Life and The Care of the Other. Each part of the course is driven by an experiential component that links loving wisdom with practicing ethics and ends with a reflective essay that enables us to articulate and evaluate the impact that philosophical training (both theoretical and practical) is having on our lives.

Day to day, we are responsible for keeping up with the class reading and writing regularly in our Ethics Notebooks, which I present as what Foucault calls a "technology of the self."[17] I explain that just as we today shape our offline identities by the way we construct our online identities, ancient philosophers shaped who they were by what they read and wrote about in their *hupomnemata*. In other words, they practiced what Foucault called "self-writing" or

---

17. Michel Foucault, *Technologies of the Self: A Seminar with Michel Foucault*, eds. Luther H. Martin, Huck Gutman, and Patrick H. Hutton (Amherst: University of Massachusetts Press, 1988).

"the transformation of truth into ēthos."[18] Here's the syllabus passage that introduces the Ethics Notebook as an experimental practice or spiritual exercise:

> For ancient philosophers, the ethical and spiritual tasks of taking care of oneself and others were intimately related to the philosophical commandment to "know thyself." To practice these tasks, we will engage in the exercise of keeping an Ethics Notebook, a bound paper journal separate from class notes. Think of your notebook as a powerful technological device that you may use to: 1) further develop your own personal reflections upon course materials; 2) explore who you are, as well as what you think ethics, happiness, and the good life are, 3) get in touch with a better version of yourself, 4) cultivate your actions and character in light of these ideas, and 5) keep track of your own ethical and/or spiritual development as the course progresses. Sometimes, I will provide specific topics or questions, but you should write regular entries on anything that relates your own life, thoughts, and experiences *directly* to the course readings, class discussion, and existential experiments.

Over the years, I've found that if I can get students to intelligently, earnestly, and habitually write in their Ethics Notebooks within the first few weeks of the course, they will likely remain engaged throughout and develop an understanding of philosophy as a way of life. This requires that I devote considerable class time to explaining the notebook and ensuring that students are properly developing the habit of self-writing. I suspect I will tinker endlessly with how to achieve this, but I have tried providing individualized feedback and guidance on the first few entries, projecting examples from brave volunteers and discussing what is good about them as a class, having students exchange entries, and using anonymized entries from previous semesters' students as the basis for class discussion. Above all, students must be convinced that keeping the notebook is a valuable exercise, not so much in terms of their grade, but in terms of their self-understanding and self-growth, which means challenging students to develop a deeper and wider sense of the aims of education. To help convince them that the Ethics Notebook is a valuable

---

18. *Ethics: Subjectivity and Truth*, ed. Paul Rabinow (New York: New Press, 1997), 209.

and worthwhile exercise, I let them know that even though I have already earned my Ph.D., I am keeping my own notebook because it constitutes an ongoing part of my education, and I express my willingness to share what I am writing about with them.

One thing that helps students take their Ethics Notebooks seriously is to have them conduct accompanying existential experiments and write about them first in their notebooks and then in more formal essays. Early in the course, I've had good results assigning the existential experiment of using Aristotle to better understand and practice virtue (or sometimes friendship) in order to evaluate what effect it has on their happiness and the happiness of those around them. Here's a snippet from the assignment:

> Since "we learn by doing" and "we are investigating not in order that we might know what virtue is, but in order that we might become good,"[19] we will conduct an existential experiment for at least 7 days to explore the relationship between ethics, happiness, and the good life. Each of us will pick one of the three virtues that Aristotle talks about the most (i.e., courage, temperance, or generosity) and experiment by cultivating this active-condition in ourselves and writing about the process in our Ethics Notebooks.

The beauty of the assignment is that it gets us to reflect on the ways we are *not* fully virtuous and what we might do, in order to become more virtuous, thereby inviting us to approach philosophy as a way of life. As Dewey writes, "reflection exists to guide choice and effort." Even though none of my students would initially use these terms, I believe that they come with at least some inkling of Aristotle's eudaimonia (as opposed to more fleeting, passive, and feelings-based contemporary notions of happiness) or of genuine friendships (as opposed to having 300 "friends" on Facebook). In other words, students have their own experiences of what Dewey characterizes as "frail goods" in their lives that can be substantiated by practicing philosophy. They bring some preexisting sense of virtue and how it can contribute to happiness, in part by making genuine friendships with themselves and others possible. These are the "precarious promises of good that haunt experienced things,"

---

19. Aristotle, *Nicomachean Ethics*, trans. Joe Sachs (Newburyport, MA: Focus, 2002), 22–23.

and my task is to help the class experience philosophy as a way of life that can make good on these promises by way of "thoughtful observation and experiment."

With these experiences under their belts, students are in a much better position to write thoughtful formal essays, breathing life into the first part of a prompt that might otherwise give rise to disembodied and unengaged papers:

1. Explain the basics of Aristotle's philosophy (especially when it comes to what virtue is, how it's acquired, how it's related to happiness, and how it's related to friendship).

2. After (or while) you explain the basics of Aristotle's philosophy, explain how your active engagement in the existential experiment of practicing one of Aristotle's virtues while writing in your Ethics Notebook has shaped your understanding of virtue, happiness, and/or friendship.

Part two of the course compares what Kant and Mill think about ethics, happiness, and the good life. As we work through deontological and utilitarian frameworks, we pivot back to the concrete, practical, and personal by reflecting on the problem of extreme poverty as it exists both locally and globally (reading and discussing essays by Peter Singer and Onora O'Neil), and we write essays that address these questions: "What is *my* personal responsibility to people living in extreme poverty? Why?" This ensures that our examination of the categorical imperative and the greatest happiness principle poses some risk to the way we actually live, by demanding a personal response to an enormous problem that most people would prefer to believe is not their problem (unless they are in extreme poverty themselves).

In contrast with the way that part one of the course begins with the self and part two begins with the universal, part three begins with the particular: the neighbor or the Other, whom students encounter during their fifteen hours of service-learning, which the syllabus describes as follows:

> Your service-learning project in this class will be to reflect upon ethics, happiness, and the good life as you serve your *neighbors*, i.e., community members who are *not* your friends or family. This will place you into learning situations where you will encounter

new people and have experiences that would never occur in a classroom, but that are nonetheless crucial for considering the issues that we will raise in class.

While many service-learning methodologies require considerable infrastructure and tend to link students up with nonprofits, my methodology prioritizes face-to-face interaction (with Levinas in mind) and reduces institutional mediation. I encourage students to think about (1) who their neighbors are, (2) what kind of help their neighbors might want or need, and (3) what kind of service they might be particularly interested in (or good at) providing. This works particularly well given my institutional context: we are a commuter campus (less than 4 percent of students live in university housing), so students do not live in a university bubble. They come to campus still immersed in a world of personal, familial, and community needs (over 90 percent are from the region and roughly 80 percent receive need-based financial aid).

One aim of the course is to help students develop the *phronēsis* to navigate these frequently competing demands, which is why the locus of inquiry and praxis expands from self to friends/family to humanity (or the wider community) but then contracts back to the face-to-face level of the individual neighbor or Other, and ends where it began: with the self that has hopefully grown in the process. Some students end up serving with nonprofit organizations or helping out at a school, nursing home, or other service institution close to where they live. But many students end up simply knocking on their neighbor's door (sometimes for the first time!) and asking them if they could use any help. This reorientation—whereby we change our existential mode from ignoring almost everyone around us unless we need something from them to keeping an eye out for others whose needs we might be able to meet—is the reorientation sought by Kierkegaard and Levinas, whom we study in the final part of the course.[20] And although we do not read Dewey, this reorientation

---

20. The course's study of Kierkegaard begins with the previously mentioned chapter from *Practice in Christianity* that distinguishes between imitation and admiration of Christ (or any other exemplar of the good life). We then read two chapters from *Works of Love*: "Our Duty to Love the People We See" (which focuses on the work of loving our family members and friends) and "You *Shall* Love" (which focuses on the work of loving our neighbors).

undoubtedly plays a role in the practice of democracy as a way of life, both social and individual.[21]

Concluding Personal Note

To sum up, *becoming* wise in the context of an ethics class is a matter of loving wisdom by practicing ethics, and it is crucial that we learn this lesson ourselves, so that we stand a better chance of teaching it to our students. Since my reading of the philosophical tradition (especially Plato's *Meno*) leads me to believe that this lesson is not something we learn once and for all but rather something that we must perpetually recollect and practice, I aim to not only do all of the readings with my students, but to maintain my own Ethics Notebook, conduct the existential experiments, and engage in the service-learning. This helps me remember that philosophy is a way of life, not just a subject that I teach.

---

21. Dewey's reflections on democracy as a way of life are scattered across many of his works, but a good place to start is "Creative Democracy: The Task Before Us" in *The Later Works of John Dewey, 1925–1953, Volume 14: 1939–1941, Essays*, ed. Jo Ann Boydston (Carbondale: Southern Illinois University Press, 1988), 224–30.

V. Teaching the Teacher

19

Teaching Philosophy to
First-Generation College Students

Bertha Alvarez Manninen
Arizona State University

BERTHA ALVAREZ MANNINEN has been teaching philosophy for twenty years, first as a teaching assistant at University of Wisconsin, Milwaukee and Purdue University, then as an adjunct professor at Miami Dade Community College in Florida and Kirkwood Community College in Iowa, and finally as an assistant and associate professor at Arizona State University (ASU). She has published three books: *Pro-Life, Pro-Choice: Shared Values in the Abortion Debate* (Vanderbilt University Press), *Civil Dialogue on Abortion* (coauthored, Routledge), and the textbook *Being Ethical: Classic and New Voices on Contemporary Issues* (coedited, Broadview Press). In 2012, she received the Outstanding Teacher of the Year award in ASU's New College of Interdisciplinary Arts and Sciences, and in 2014 she received ASU's Founder's Day Teaching Award for her pedological work in biomedical ethics. In 2017, she received an Outstanding Faculty Mentor Award at ASU for her work in mentoring graduate students. Since 2014, she has been the cochair of ASU's Teaching, Innovation, and Excellence Collaborative, which provides faculty members with workshops and other services to help develop their pedagogy. Through her work in teaching philosophy, Bertha hopes to give a voice to students who may think they have no voice to contribute to the world, open their minds to the beauty and power behind being a virtuous human being, and illustrate how the teaching and learning of philosophy is vital in maintaining a healthy and functioning society.

"College students are old enough to appreciate the deeper reaches of intergenerational friendship yet not so jaded as to have ceased looking for warmth and guidance. Under the right circumstances, they can develop rich and caring relationships with their teachers. Though most of these remain temporary partnerships, some grow into lifelong commitments of intense mutual support."[1]

Philosophy saved my life.

I know that may seem hyperbolic to some, but it really is true. And, because it was teachers who gave me philosophy, I can also say with the same level of genuineness that philosophy teachers, especially one specific philosophy teacher, saved my life. When I consider what my life could have been like in contrast to what my life is now, I attribute this radical alteration of my path, and my family's generational tree, to the education and opportunities provided to me by my education in philosophy.

I cannot talk about my teaching narrative as a philosophy professor without first talking about my narrative as a Hispanic, female, first-generation college student (a university student whose parents or legal guardians have not earned a bachelor's degree—such students are the first in their immediate families to go to college). I grew up in circumstances not typically considered conducive to attaining a professional career. As I was such a student, I now teach such students. The student body on my campus contains more than 40 percent first-generation students, many of them racial minorities and many from working-class or impoverished backgrounds. My story is their story. What my teachers did for me, I try to do for them. I use philosophy as a tool to give a voice to students who consider themselves voiceless and invisible. In teaching them to think for themselves, I help elevate the self-esteem of students who often feel that they don't belong in a university. This is the best way I can think of to repay those professors who did so much for me—to show them that their influence extends beyond my life and into the lives of this new generation.

My Story

I am the daughter of Cuban refugees. I was born and raised in Miami, Florida, and am the demarcating line between the members of my family born in Cuba and the ones born in the United States.

---

1. John Lachs, *A Community of Individuals* (New York: Routledge, 2003), 30.

My parents were extraordinarily hard workers. Neither attained a university education, and they always worked blue-collar, physically exhausting jobs. As expected, money was typically in short supply, and oftentimes the threat of eviction from our home loomed over us. It wasn't until years later that I realized that many of the meals I have come to regard as comfort foods (rice with fried eggs, or rice with beans) were fed to me often because they were low-cost options. We survived on public assistance and government-funded housing, as well as Medicaid for all our medical needs. To this day, I am a staunch supporter of social safety net programs because I know what they mean for impoverished families. I can say with confidence that we would have absolutely been homeless were it not for government aid.

The psychological effects of living with financial insecurity never really go away. Even now, as a tenured university professor, I live in constant fear of losing my job, because my parents lived in constant fear of losing theirs. Living in a poor neighborhood also meant I went to poor inner-city schools that suffered from overpopulation, stressed and underpaid teachers, and a dire lack of resources. Our books were held together by tape, and sometimes we had to sit on the floor of the classroom because there were insufficient desks. It wasn't until I started testing for entry into Florida International University (FIU) that I realized how lacking my education was in several areas: I had to take two semesters of remedial mathematics at the community college, for example, before I was able to take math for college credit.

Not having family members who had attended college disadvantaged me in many ways: I had no parental help when it came to filling out financial aid forms, picking a major, making career decisions, or understanding the amount of time and dedication it took to achieve good grades at the university level. My family was always very supportive of my educational goals—they *wanted* me to succeed and to rise up the economic chain—but they couldn't help me get there. They simply didn't know how. The combination of living with financial stress, navigating university life without a guide, having to take remedial courses, and balancing school with working created psychological obstacles that almost prevented me from successfully finishing college. "I don't deserve to be there," I thought. "I can't hack it. I have nothing of substance to offer. My voice doesn't matter. It isn't worth it. There is nothing college can offer me that will substantially improve my life." At night, I would ride the bus home from school in tears. Many, many times, I almost quit.

Almost.

During my first year, I took Philosophical Analysis—FIU's version of Philosophy 101. I fell in love instantly. Our first text was Plato's *Euthyphro*, and I couldn't put it down. The Socratic dialogue and the subject matter (ethics and religion—the fields in which I now teach and research) enthralled me. I loved the class so much that I took the junior-level course Philosophy of Mind the very next semester, and I flourished in that class as well. But although I found a major I loved, I still did not feel very capable and continued to feel demoralized. Paradoxically, I would only find the confidence and drive that I needed to continue in college by taking a class that I found extremely difficult, one taught by a professor who would become my mentor and friend for the next twenty-two years. It was his consistent mentorship that carried me through the roughest patches.

That class was Introduction to Logic, and the professor's name was Paul Draper. As I would later learn, logic was never to be my strong suit; I have struggled in every logic class I have ever taken as an undergraduate and graduate philosophy student. In this class, it was mastering truth tables that almost led to my failure. Professor Draper tutored me constantly, an hour a day, at least three days a week. He never grew frustrated, was always patient, and was always kind. When it came time to take the test for that section, I still struggled, and felt dejected that, after all that work, I managed only a C. The day he returned the exams, I remember waiting until all the students had left and walking up to him to apologize for wasting his time. He answered: "You didn't waste my time. You didn't fail. A C is nothing to be ashamed about, if you worked hard for it."

That was the beginning of what has turned out to be one of the most important and formative relationships in my life. Through all the difficulties, both academic and personal, that threatened to derail me during my college years, Professor Draper continued to mentor me. When I chose to use a Disney film in a religious experience project, he didn't mock me for liking cartoons; he listened to the connections I was making and took me seriously. He helped me become a better writer, a better thinker, and a more critical reader. I revised a paper I wrote for his class several times, under his guidance, and published it in an undergraduate journal. The idea of my leaving home to attend graduate school was never in the realm of possibility for me until he introduced it. To this day, I am the only person in my immediate family who has left the state for school, and the pushback I received from them in this regard was substantial. I was not raised to leave home until marriage, and, even then, I was to live close by. Nevertheless, I had decided that this is what I wanted to do, and Professor Draper helped me fill out applications, revise my writing sample, and study for my GREs.

The day I got on that airplane to leave for the University of Wisconsin, Milwaukee for my master's degree (which was the first time I had been on an airplane, and the second time I had left the state), he was one of the last people to whom I spoke. And throughout my master's and doctoral education, he continued to be there. When I struggled with my dissertation, he would email me words of encouragement. When I started navigating the waters of being a first-time teacher, he would offer me advice. He congratulated me when I graduated with my doctorate, and double congratulated me when I landed my tenure-track position. He sent me a card when I received tenure. He saw me get married when I was twenty-seven. And more than twenty years later, he and his wife and daughter have played and bonded with my children. I never would have guessed that taking Introduction to Logic would be one of the most important and defining experiences of my life.

It is here I need to say that Professor Draper was not the only teacher who cared for me during my college years. I was also an English literature major, and Professors Carmela McIntire and Lisa Blansett mentored me in that subject area for four years. Their care, their guidance, and the time they spent with me discussing Shakespeare, poetry, and British literature helped me feel nurtured, heard, and valued. Though I have written mostly of Professor Draper's influence, because I ultimately became a philosophy teacher, like him, I cannot understate the effect my English professors had on me as well. I remain friends with them until this day, and Professor McIntire has taught my children how to bake the best holiday molasses cookies I have ever tasted.

My mentors have stepped in to provide care for me through-out my career, and it is because of their responsiveness that I have extended this same attention to my students. I appreciate how both professors and philosophical study can transform lives, particularly in the case of first-generation students. Using my mentors as mod-els and my own experiences as a guide, I reach out to young people who are new to the university environment. In them, I see my own struggles and accomplishments.

Teaching Philosophy to First-Generation College Students

The number of first-generation college students is increasing across universities in the United States. According to a 2012 study by the Georgetown University Center on Education, approximately 32 per-cent of today's undergraduate student body are first-generation col-lege students.[2] I teach at Arizona State University's New College of Interdisciplinary Arts and Sciences in the School of Humanities, Arts, and Cultural Studies. According to our latest numbers, 54.8 percent of the students in our college are first-generation college students, of various ethnic, racial, and economic backgrounds. In 2015, it was reported that nearly half of the first-year class entering the University of California system were first-generation students.[3] In 2015, the University of Virginia saw a 12 percent increase in first-generation college students in its freshman class (from 3,179 in 2014 to 3,552 in 2015).[4]

But although universities are seeing this increase, it does not typically translate into more first-generation students in the humani-ties. In general, it's hard to sell a degree in the humanities, let alone a degree in philosophy, to students who are the first in their families

---

2. Ben Galina, "Teaching First-Generation College Students," January 18, 2016, https://cft.vanderbilt.edu/teaching-first-generation-college-students.

3. Nicole Freeling, "Half of New UC Students Are First-Generational College Students," June 22, 2015, https://www.universityofcalifornia.edu/news/half-new-uc-students-are-first-generation-college-students.

4. McGregor McCance, "Increase in First-Generation Students Highlights Applicant Pool for Class of 2019," January 12, 2015, https://www.news.virginia.edu/content/increase-first-generation-students-highlights-applicant-pool-class-2019.

to attend college. The myth of the philosophy degree's low earning potential conflicts with the understandable goal these students have to use their education to elevate themselves out of poverty. The pressure to pick a major with high earning potential can derive from their families, especially their parents, who frequently have struggled to provide the basic necessities for their children. First-generation students are oftentimes very close to their families. Such students want to succeed for their family's sake, to make them proud; and such students recognize that they may one day have to care financially for their parents. All of these concerns conspire to lead students toward both majors and careers that they perceive as useful and lucrative, a set that rarely includes philosophy.

Four years ago, I taught a "great books" class of first-year honor students, and, given my training, I taught it as a philosophy of religion course. We read Plato's *Euthyphro* and *Phaedo*, Augustine's *Confessions* and *On Free Choice of the Will*, excerpts from Dante's *Divine Comedy*, and Confucius' *Analects*. There was one young woman in the class who already had declared her major as premed and who absolutely thrived and loved the course. Two years later, she found her way to my office and told me, in tears, that she hated her major and wanted to study philosophy and religion more. She knew her parents would never allow her to do so, however, and she knew that she needed to find a job through which she could take care of them as they took care of her. Her desire for her own happiness took a backseat to her moral obligations to her family. I saw her very briefly a few months later, at which time she told me that she was doing much better. I do not know whether she changed her major, but it made me sad to think that she was confining herself to a career about which she was neither excited nor passionate.

I've seen firsthand the kind of damage this can do to a person's psyche. My father was an actor in Cuba, and he loved it so much. Even while suffering from dementia, he still remembered his acting days and spoke of them with a smile. He had to quit the profession to find a higher-paying job, but he never stopped pining for those days. He grew increasingly embittered working jobs he despised. I would hate for this student, indeed for *any* student, to end up like this. And yet, I understand why her parents pressured her as they did; I understand her desire to care for them when they get older, and

I understand that none of them want her to be tethered to poverty for the rest of her life.

Here is where I think professional philosophers need to do more to fight against the stereotype of philosophy as a useless major. Philosophers may recoil at the thought of having to justify their intrinsically valuable discipline in these practical terms. But this reaction comes from a place of privilege. For a child who has grown up in difficult financial circumstances, who has parents who want for their child a lifestyle free from the financial worries that plagued them, financial stability is a very real concern. If we cannot explain how a philosophy major can achieve financial security, then we will have lost the potential to attract first-generation students, many of whom have brilliant philosophical minds.

It isn't hard to make this case. Billionaire technology entrepreneur Mark Cuban has recently gone on record saying that "in 10 years, a liberal arts degree in philosophy will be worth more than a traditional programming degree. . . . Knowing how to critically think and assess them from a global perspective, I think, is going to be more valuable than what we see as exciting careers today . . . ."[5] A 2015 report by PayScale noted that philosophy is the top humanities degree, when it comes to midcareer earnings. The median pay for students with a bachelor's degree in philosophy ten to twenty years postgraduation was $84,000 a year.[6] According to a 2016 report from the National Association of College Employers, "Philosophy majors are projected to be the top-paid class of the 2016 humanities graduates at the bachelor's degree level."[7] Indeed, the list of successful executives and CEOs who majored in philosophy as undergraduates is impressive: former chair of the FDIC Sheila Bair, hedge fund manager George Soros, and overstock.com

---

5. Ali Montag, "Mark Cuban Says Studying Philosophy May Soon Be Worth More Than Computer Science." Febuary 21, 2018, https://www.cnbc.com/2018/02/20/mark-cuban-philosophy-degree-will-be-worth-more-than-computer-science.html.

6. Bourree Lam, "The Earning Power of Philosophy Majors," September 3, 2015, http://www.theatlantic.com/notes/2015/09/philosophy-majors-out-earn-other-humanities/403555.

7. National Association of Colleges and Employers, "Philosophy Projected as the Top-Paid Class of 2016 Humanities Major," February 24, 2016, http://www.naceweb.org/s02242016/top-paid-humanities-graduates-2016.aspx.

CEO Patrick Byrne (who actually has a Ph.D. in philosophy from Stanford), to name just a few. When we advertise philosophy to incoming majors and their families, it is imperative that we highlight that philosophy courses develop the skills for which employers are looking: critical and creative thinking skills, writing and reading skills, open-mindedness, and problem-solving abilities. Flickr cofounder Stewart Butterfield, who has a bachelor's and a master's in philosophy, puts it this way to a group of students at the University of Victoria:

> I think if you have a good background in what it is to be human, an understanding of life, culture, and society, it gives you a good perspective on starting a business, instead of an education purely in business. . . . You can always pick up how to read a balance sheet and how to figure out profit and loss, but it's harder to pick up the other stuff on the fly.[8]

These "soft skills" are hard to teach while on the job, but philosophy majors come with these skills honed and ready to go. Philosophy programs can also emphasize our majors' high scores on graduate school exams, including the GRE, LSAT, and GMAT. Finally, philosophy can be sold as a useful "companion major," one that can supplement an existing major like psychology, premed, prelaw, and even business. Indeed, FIU's philosophy department has a major track that is designed specifically to allow students to take philosophy courses as cognates to other areas of study.

Retention rates for first-generation college students are not favorable. Such students are twice as likely to leave college before their second year than students whose parents attended college.[9] According to another study, "Of first-generation students who had enrolled in postsecondary education between 1992 and 2000, nearly one-half (43 percent) had left without a degree by 2000 and one-quarter had

---

8. Carolyn Gregoire, "The Unexpected Way Philosophy Majors Are Changing the World of Business," March 5, 2014, http://www.huffingtonpost.com/2014/03/05/why-philosophy-majors-rule_n_4891404.html.

9. Susan P. Choy, *Findings from The Condition of Education 2001. Students Whose Parents Did Not Go to College: Postsecondary Access, Persistence, and Attainment* (NCES 2001–126). U.S. Department of Education, National Center for Education Statistics (Washington, DC: U.S. Government Printing Office, 2001).

attained a bachelor's degree."[10] A 2005 report from the National Center for Education Statistics notes that, in comparison to students who have at least one parent who graduated from college, first-generation students are more likely to have a lower GPA and are more likely to have to take remedial courses in their first year of college.

The reasons for these lower retention rates are many and various. First-generation college students can be plagued by crippling self-doubt and lack of confidence concerning whether they have the capacity to thrive in college and whether they even deserve to be there at all. They may not know how to access all of the available majors, navigate university bureaucracy, apply for financial aid, avail themselves of opportunities like internships, or build their resumes. Often, these students come from a close-knit family, whose members may not be as supportive of their educational endeavors as one would hope. In general, "First-generation college students receive far less emotional, informational, and financial support from their parents than continuing-generation students. Those less-supported students also reported having higher levels of stress and anxiety than the few first-generation students who did feel supported by their parents."[11] Typically, this is not because the parents do not want to support their child, but because their families need their children to acquire a job and begin to earn money as soon as possible. Holding off that salary for four (or more) years would have to have a demonstrable benefit. Moreover, sometimes having a child attend college disrupts the family system:

> Although perhaps supportive of higher education, their parents and family members may view their entry into college as a break in the family system rather than a continuation of their schooling. In families, role assignments about work, family, religion and community are passed down through the generations creating "intergenerational continuity." When a family member disrupts this system by choosing to attend college, he or she experiences a

---

10. National Center for Education Statistics, "First-Generation Students in Post-Secondary Education," 2005, http://nces.ed.gov/pubs2005/2005171.pdf.

11. Jake New, "The Opposite of Helicopter Parents," August 13, 2015, https://www.insidehighered.com/news/2014/08/13/colleges-struggle-engage-parents-first-generation-college-students.

shift in identity, leading to a sense of loss. Not prepared for this loss, many first-generation students may come to develop two different identities—one for home and another for college.[12]

In situations where a family does support the decision to break tradition and attend college, the expectations that fall on the student's shoulder may be overwhelming:

> It sits in my head every day. It's like I know that I'm the first one to get this far for my family. . . . I know that my mom is depending on me to make a very good example for my little brother. So, I have to do my best at all times.
>
> Sometimes it gets really hard—What keeps me going is that I am the first in my family [to attend college]. And I have four younger brothers and sisters that look up to me. . . . That's what keeps me going instead of just shutting down or throwing a temper tantrum. I just keep going. I can't do anything else but finish.[13]

In general, then, the obstacles facing first-generation college students as they strive to complete their education vary, from insufficient academic preparation, to limited knowledge concerning how to navigate a university system and setting, to familial and cultural conflict, and, of course, financial constraints.[14] University programs designed to help first-generation students often focus only on the financial difficulties, while ignoring the psychological obstacles.

I try as much as possible to address those psychological obstacles in my classroom, and I believe a philosophical education is conducive to doing so. Philosophy encourages independent thought and hones creative and critical thinking skills. In my class, while I present philosophical essays of varying perspectives, I repeatedly tell my

---

12. Linda Banks-Santilli, "Guilt Is One of the Biggest Struggles First-Generation College Students Face," 2015, https://www.washingtonpost.com/posteverything/wp/2015/06/03/guilt-is-one-of-the-biggest-struggles-first-generation-college-students-face/?utm_term=.a58804988cdb.

13. Mark Orbe, "Negotiating Multiple Identities within Multiple Frames: An Analysis of First-Generation College Students," 2004, https://www.brown.edu/campus-life/support/first-generation-students/sites/brown.edu.campus-life.support.first-generation-students/files/uploads/10.1.1.487.2179.pdf.

14. University of North Carolina at Chapel Hill, "First-Generation College Student Success: A Report from the Office or Undergraduate Retention and the FGCS Committee," 2014, http://studentsuccess.unc.edu/files/2014/09/FGCS-Study-2014.pdf.

students that nothing we read should be considered "gospel"; they are encouraged to critically analyze everyone we read and to develop original, well-reasoned arguments in response. When they do so, I often point them in the direction of a philosopher who may have said something similar. My students' eyes light up when they hear me say: "That's a great point! Plato says something similar." When they discover that their thoughts echo the thoughts of one of humanity's greatest minds, it validates their perspective and lifts their self-esteem. After class, they often come to visit me, hoping to read more of that same philosopher.

Students are often surprised that I *want* to hear what they have to say; that I *prefer* to hear their thoughts, instead of the thoughts of those we are reading. However, I don't let them get away with just saying *anything*. They are expected to provide actual arguments for their perspectives. When they criticize other philosophers, students have to point out exactly which premise of the arguments they disagree with and why. The process of having to fill their perspective this way requires fairly robust intellectual work, which makes them feel that much more accomplished when they succeed. I assign argumentative final papers, in which students can argue whatever perspective they wish, on any of the topics discussed throughout the semester, so long as they articulate their reasons. I have had students describe my final as hard work, because "it forced me to think differently," but I also have had those same students say that my final was the first assignment after which they felt that they had created something that *belonged to them*. One woman in my class, who had two kids, described writing her final paper as "giving birth" to a new version of her mind.

While some students end up changing their minds about some of the issues we study in class, I never encourage it. I encourage them to look for reasons for the beliefs they hold dear, even when we are discussing their beliefs about controversial topics in applied ethics and bioethics, and their beliefs about the existence of God. I want them to make their beliefs truly their own, through patient investigation and critical thinking. The result is a student who feels that she has something worthy to say, and one who is now armed intellectually in a way in which she may not have been prior to my class. For students struggling with self-esteem issues, this can really help boost their confidence. Instead of presenting philosophy as a discipline that dismantles one's familial belief systems, I present philosophy as a discipline that can serve to support and defend one's beliefs against external threats.

Finally, it is imperative to note that teaching, for me, is symbiotic. I have learned so much from my students. Their fresh eyes and willingness to dialogue help me view tired philosophical concepts in a new light. They often share personal stories with me that relate to class topics, and this has helped me look at philosophical issues with a new perspective. For example, on the occasions when my students have shared their own experiences with abortion, their views have influenced my research methodology by encouraging me both to consider men's voices and to recognize that many women who obtain abortions often care very deeply about the life that grows within them. These perspectives have added nuance and depth to my scholarly research. Moreover, working with such students in my classes has added a dimension to my teaching that otherwise would be lacking: bioethics students who have actually worked in hospital settings, for example, press us to think about how we might apply abstract philosophical concepts in real-world settings.

You Don't Need to Be a Philosophy Professor

Many of the tactics I implement to help with these psychological obstacles are things any professor in any discipline can do. Lately, I have been sharing with my students that my first grade on my first philosophy paper was a discouraging C+—and I probably deserved an even lower grade. My paper was riddled with spelling mistakes, grammatical mistakes, and sentence structure issues. I use this opportunity to show students that even their college professors were once struggling college kids and how important it is to hone their writing skills. I also emphasize, hearing Professor Draper in my ear, that one's final grade does not matter as much as the hard work it took to improve. Even a student who once earned a C+ in her writing classes can evolve to make a living out of writing.

In researching this paper, I looked back at my undergraduate transcripts, and realized what a mediocre student I was. While I did well in philosophy, I did poorly in the sciences, in math, and even in history. My first inclination was to plaster that transcript on the screen so my students could see it—every C and D was on full display. In going through those transcripts with my students, I emphasized four things: First, if you're struggling, we understand. Don't assume all of your professors started life as perfect students who knew it all. Come talk to us; we wore your shoes once. Second, your grades don't define you. While I want you to get good grades, and will do everything in my power to help you, you aren't doomed by bad ones, and they don't decide the rest of your life. Third, try to learn all you can. Looking back, I wish I had paid more attention in history and the sciences; even a class you don't have to take for your major can have something valuable to teach you. Fourth, appreciate everyone's strengths. While I did well in philosophy, I didn't do well in other subjects, and these are classes in which I am sure many of you thrive. Appreciate your strengths and others' as well. We all have our own unique way of contributing to the world.

If a student works hard and continues to struggle, I try always to remember how I felt when Professor Draper handed back that logic test with a red C on it: the frustration, the shame, the overwhelming desire to quit everything. I also remember how I felt when he recontextualized success for me in a way that helped alleviate that shame and inspired me to do better (I ended up with a B+ in that course). A student may succeed in nontangible ways that aren't immediately obvious on paper. Reminding students of that, as many times as you need to, may help to galvanize many of them when they are running out of energy and motivation. Professors of all disciplines have this power to help students see themselves in a better and more positive light when they are struggling. You never know the impact that one positive word, one act of compassion, care, or solidarity can have on a student who is besieged with their own inner voices of doubt. The fact that I am here in my office writing this piece attests to that. My entire success as a college professor comes down to whether I can do for my students what my professors did for me.

Acknowledgments

I am blessed beyond measure to have three "lifelong commitments of intense mutual support" with college professors. Dr. Carmela McIntire and Dr. Lisa Blansett, your mentorship during my undergraduate years was invaluable, but your friendship all the years since has meant even more. There isn't a piece of Shakespeare or British poetry I read now without thinking of you. Thank you both so much.

Paul, you listened when few would, and you saw me when I was invisible to so many others. You showed me a new path, pushed me to walk through it, and held my hand throughout the roughest parts of the journey. I emerged on the other side of that journey successful because of your guidance, support, and mentorship. This essay is for you.

20

Critical Thinking Can Save Your Life

Elizabeth Jelinek
Christopher Newport University

ELIZABETH JELINEK received her B.A. in philosophy from Welles-
ley College and her Ph.D. in philosophy from Duke University. Her
research explores the intersection of philosophy of science, epistemology, and metaphysics in Plato's natural philosophy. In addition to
publishing her scholarly research in several peer-reviewed journals,
she has published a pedagogical article on small group learning in
Teaching Philosophy. She has taught undergraduate- and graduate-level
philosophy courses at Duke University, Vanderbilt University, and
Christopher Newport University, where she currently teaches. She has
designed courses for majors, nonmajors, honors students, and graduate students at the introductory through the advanced levels. Students
and university administrators have recognized her for her passion and
excellence in teaching: she has won three university-wide teaching
awards over the last five years.

"A re you sure I can write on this?" my grandmother asked. Even
after I reassured her that she could write on the typed document, she still made her marks lightly and in pencil. I was using the
computer upstairs to type up handwritten stories and poems about
her life, and it amazed her that I would go upstairs with a handwritten copy and come downstairs with a typed copy, one I could magi-
cally duplicate several times. To a woman born in 1912, modern
technology was both fascinating and bewildering.

My grandmother Ilse (whom we called "Omi") was writing the
story of how she, my grandfather, and their then two-year-old son
immigrated to the United States from Germany, their homeland, in
1939 to escape Hitler's persecution. My grandfather Walter (whom
we called "Opa") was a philosopher by avocation, but he passed away
when I was only five years old, so I didn't know him well. Nevertheless, their story is my source of inspiration. Opa and Omi never

amassed much wealth, but they gave their children and grandchildren something more valuable than money: an appreciation for the importance of education. After all, their education was the only thing they could take with them when they fled their homeland. Thus, my "inheritance" from my grandparents is my passion for philosophy and my dedication to teaching it. The power of their words and actions has shaped my life, and it is their story that continues to inspire me to teach philosophy.

Part One: Analytical Reading and Confronting Uncomfortable Truths

It was the summer of 1938, a time when German newspapers were controlled by the government. Sure, everyone knew that Hitler hated the Jews; the Nuremberg Laws of 1935 excluding Jews from much of civil society in Germany had already been implemented. But no one thought that Hitler would go as far as he did, committing a mass genocide of six million Jews—two-thirds of the entire Jewish population in Europe. Certainly, none of the German Jews in my grandparents' community thought that Hitler was coming for *them*. Like many German Jews, my grandmother's father had fought for Germany in World War I. Surely Hitler wouldn't kill an upstanding German veteran and citizen like him, and so he didn't even consider leaving the Fatherland. Given the lack of information available to the Germans and the belief that things would get better, not worse, for the Jews, most Jews didn't feel an urgent need to leave.

That summer, my grandfather's doctor advised him to try the famous mineral springs of Carlsbad, Czechoslovakia, as a possible remedy for his gallbladder attacks. Travel in and out of Germany was already restricted for Jews, but since my grandparents' travel to Carlsbad was for medical reasons, they were allowed to cross the border. Their trip turned out to be lifesaving, because it was in Carlsbad that Opa had the opportunity to read foreign newspapers. Omi wrote:

> As we sat there on the veranda of our cozy little villa overlooking Carlsbad and its contentedly strolling summer guests, I leaned back in my deck chair, sunning myself and enjoying that peaceful scene. Walter did not; he hardly talked, while his head was buried in foreign newspapers, Swiss, French, Italian—anything he could

read well enough to understand. And it was always the political news he looked for, while the sports page, entertainment, and local gossip remained untouched. Between sips of Carlsbad's healing waters he read and he brooded, he brooded and he read.[1]

My grandfather never just read. He always pored over what he read and analyzed it thoroughly. He quickly realized that reading foreign newspapers wasn't enough to truly understand and confront what was happening at the time. He had to dig deeper. Confronted with the popular assumption that Hitler's *Mein Kampf* was merely empty rhetoric, Opa procured a copy of *Mein Kampf* while in Carlsbad, so he could read it and draw his own conclusions. He read, he analyzed, but, most importantly, he had the courage to confront uncomfortable truths. My grandparents were already aware that life in Germany was becoming increasingly dangerous for Jews, but my grandfather's careful study of the material he read in Carlsbad impressed upon him the urgency of the situation. It became clear that they had to escape. To this day, I wonder if I, too, would have had the courage to face reality head-on rather than hide in the comfort of denial.

One of the skills we philosophy teachers aim to cultivate in our students is that of analytical reading. Reading analytically requires that you reread the same material several times, and then read several other sources until you've deepened and enhanced your understanding of the topic from multiple angles. Often, reading analytically forces you to question long-held assumptions and confront views with which you disagree. It was my grandfather's study of philosophy that taught him how to read analytically, and ultimately, that is what saved their lives.

Part Two: Acting on Your Principles

Throughout his life, my grandfather's philosophical convictions drove his actions. He was never afraid to act on his principles even if doing so was inconvenient, impractical, or at times, dangerous. In 1938 Carlsbad, it was his vehement objection to what Hitler stood for *philosophically* that ate away at him the most. Living according to my grandfather's philosophical convictions, in this case, meant risking his and his family's lives to escape. He sent a letter to a distant

---

1. Ilse Riesenfeld, "It Can Be Done" (unpublished memoir, 1999), 10.

cousin who lived in the United States at the time and asked him if he would be willing to send an affidavit that would allow my grandparents to immigrate to America. The whole process was slow, and so their one-week visit to Czechoslovakia turned into a several-month stay. It wasn't until January 1939 that my grandparents finally had the opportunity to leave Czechoslovakia, travel to France, and catch the very last refugee boat leaving France for the United States. Only two months later, Hitler's troops marched into Czechoslovakia and rounded up all of the Jews, Gypsies, and dissidents, most of whom later died in concentration camps.

Acting according to your principles takes courage. My grandparents had to leave behind their parents, their entire extended family, their careers, their money, their language, their culture, and their customs. Their only child, at two years old, was smuggled out of Germany by a Polish maid and reunited with my grandparents just in time before the boat left the dock. They were off to America, never to return to their former life. All they had with them was a suitcase of summer clothes, ten dollars, their education, and their commitment to their personal principles.

This wasn't the only time my grandfather acted on his principles. He consistently led his life that way. During the early days of the rise of Hitler, when travel out of the country was heavily restricted for Jewish adults, Opa risked his life by chaperoning Jewish children out of Germany and into France, in hopes that the children could escape Hitler's tyranny. This was prior to the famous *Kindertransport* of German Jewish children to Great Britain in November 1938, but similar in nature. If it was clear at the time that German Jewish children needed to escape, it also must have been clear that it was risky for a German Jewish adult to chaperone them. Such risks didn't deter my grandfather. If he could save another person's life, he did, whatever the cost.

After my grandparents had lived in the United States for a while, Opa was fortunate enough to get a job in a factory that manufactured airplane parts. Like any factory, there were certain production guidelines in place intended to ensure that once the parts were assembled, the airplane would be safe for flight. But the foreman wanted to increase the rate of production in his factory, and so he loosened the safety standards to make production more efficient. When my grandfather learned of this, he confronted the foreman, troubled with the knowledge that the lack of precision in production could render the planes unsafe. Unfortunately, the foreman didn't care about the potential risk to human life; he only cared about his profit margin. Opa was the only wage earner in the family, and the money he made was barely enough to survive on. But this was irrelevant to him. It was more important to live according to his ethical principles. After his conversation with the foreman, Opa quit his job on the spot. He was always one to reflect critically on his actions, and it was his philosophical training that equipped him to do so. But philosophy leaves its students with more than just the power of critical reflection. Opa had courage. Once you can see things clearly and distinctly, it becomes difficult not to act.

The modern education system discourages us from discussing students' personal codes of ethics, but studying philosophy gives students the tools they need to develop principles that can guide their actions outside of the classroom.

Part Three: Never Stop Learning

My grandfather read and wrote about philosophy until his death in 1984. Just recently, on a whim, I googled my grandfather's name, not expecting to find anything except perhaps a link to a commercial genealogy website. To my amazement, one of the hits from my Google search was the website for the Bertrand Russell Archives, housed at McMaster University in Ontario, Canada. The website provided a list of all of the names of the fans and colleagues with whom Russell had corresponded, and among those names was my grandfather's. I opened the pdf and showed my mother, and she instantly recognized Opa's distinctive handwriting. Following his letter was Russell's response, dated April 29, 1957. My grandfather had asked Russell about his book *Unpopular Essays*. I am lucky enough to have inherited Opa's books, including his own yellowed copy of *Unpopular Essays*. One of the passages he had starred in the margins of the book reads:

> The result of this [absence of knowledge] is that the human race becomes divided into rival groups of fanatics, each group firmly persuaded that its own brand of nonsense is sacred truth, while

the other side's is damnable heresy. Arians and Catholics, Crusaders and Moslems, Protestants and adherents of the Pope, Communists and Fascists, have filled large parts of the last 1600 years with futile strife, when a little philosophy would have shown both sides in all these disputes that neither had any good reason to believe itself in the right. Dogmatism is the enemy to peace, and an insuperable barrier to democracy. In the present age, at least as much as in former times, it is the greatest of the mental obstacles to human happiness.[2]

It was dogmatism that had forced my grandparents out of Germany and murdered the family they left behind. While democracy had given them the chance to survive, my grandparents weren't dogmatic about their belief in democracy either. It was not democracy per se that had saved them. Rather, it was my grandfather's insistence upon reading and learning the truth. My grandparents knew that not even democracy is failproof. After all, Hitler was elected by the people. My grandmother, a poet and teacher, wrote a poem called "Choices" about what Hitler's rise to power can teach us about the importance of being a well-informed voter:

> There is a lesson
> And it is grim:
> It was the people
> Who voted for him.
>
> Let's never make
> The same mistake,
> And think, for our
> Country's sake:
>
> "Are they right, are they wrong
> Are they telling the truth?"
> Before you enter
> Your voting booth.[3]

My grandparents knew that even a democracy could yield dangerous results, and so they made a point of impressing upon us that education, not political or national allegiance, is our most powerful shield.

---

2. Bertrand Russell, *Unpopular Essays* (New York: Simon and Schuster, 1950), 26.

3. Ilse Riesenfeld, *Silver-Haired Thoughts* (Kearney, NE: Morris, 1999), 4–5.

Part Four: An Unlikely Source of Inspiration

Seventh grade was a defining year for me. I lived in New Jersey during the early 1990s, also known as the Era of Big Hair. Rachel Jones was the prettiest, most popular girl in the school, and of course, not coincidentally, also the girl with the biggest hair.[4] Stocks for the company that manufactured Aqua Net hairspray must have been as high as Rachel's bangs. She must have used a can a day to hold that hairdo. Rachel and I never spoke. She was popular and I, clearly, was not. With pink-rimmed glasses and a mouthful of metal braces, I was the kind of kid who was so focused on acing the next math test that I hardly noticed whether my socks even matched, much less whether my bangs were the right height.

I did notice, however, that Rachel was running for student president, and this deeply concerned me. Rachel Jones was not a good student nor a particularly responsible one, so how could she possibly be qualified for a position of such gravity? Surely, my peers would realize this too, but unfortunately, no one was bold enough to run against her. We needed a class president whom the teachers respected, one who was skilled enough in math to balance the student council budget and intelligent enough to know what direction to steer the ship. I didn't want the job myself. I was much happier studying math. Though I thought the presidential position would be tedious I realized that it would be better to serve as president myself than to be ruled by an unqualified winner.

And so my campaign for class president began. While Rachel lured voters by playing Top-40 songs on her boombox during homeroom, I took the more practical route and distributed pencils engraved with my campaign slogan: "Betsy is your best bet." I took the campaign quite seriously, planning out who should serve on my cabinet and what my first agenda item would be. Thus, I was crushed when the election results arrived, and I found out that I had received all of five votes. Was it a coincidence that the mothers of the five students who had voted for me just happened to be friends with my mother? I'll never know. While I was upset about my own lost election, I was downright depressed once I realized the deeply worrisome implications of this election result: if my own seventh-grade class was

---

4. Names haves been changed to protect anonymity.

wooed by big hair and sensationalistic campaign promises, instead of actual proficiency, then perhaps adult American voters were equally vulnerable to such sophistry. Our country, I realized, was doomed.

It was shortly thereafter that I discovered my grandfather's treasure trove of philosophy texts. I picked up a book titled *Plato's Complete Works*, and upon noticing that it was full of dialogues, I thought it would be more interesting than the book with the word "Kant" on the cover, which, by the way, was not only misspelled but also missing an apostrophe between the "n" and the "t"— clearly, whoever wrote *that* book was not very smart. I didn't understand all of what I had read of Plato, but I read enough of the *Gorgias* to guess that Plato wouldn't have liked politicians who used hairspray either and enough of the *Republic* to notice that Plato was about as worried about democracy as I was. Imagine my excitement: finally, someone who understood me! I was head over heels—the same way most kids swoon over boy bands—and I've been a fan ever since. I carry that childlike enthusiasm about philosophy to this day, and I love helping my students discover that same joy. The challenge of making philosophy come alive for my students the way it came alive for me fuels my passion for teaching philosophy. And, thanks to Rachel, I recognize the importance of educating students to be responsible citizens, well-prepared for democratic participation.

Part Five: Give, Give, Give

Even when my grandparents were too poor to give anything to others in need, they generously gave the one thing they could give: the gift of education. Opa was always eager to discuss philosophy with anyone who was interested, and Omi taught music to anyone willing to learn. They would have appreciated what Isabel Allende says about giving:

> Give, give, give—what is the point of having experience, knowledge, or talent if I don't give it away? Of having stories if I don't tell them to others? Of having wealth if I don't share it? I don't intend to be cremated with any of it![5]

---

5. Isabel Allende, "In Giving I Connect with Others," in *This I Believe: The Personal Philosophies of Remarkable Men and Women*, eds. Jay Allison and Dan Gediman (New York: Henry Holt, 2006), 15.

My grandparents taught us why it was important for *us* to become educated, but they also taught us the value of sharing our knowledge with others. After all, in a democracy, it makes little difference if one person is educated; it makes all the difference if many people are.

Opa taught because he was compelled by his philosophical conviction that education is important. While Omi also shared this conviction, she was a bit more lighthearted and practical than Opa, and her main motivation was the sheer joy that teaching provided. Regardless of their motivations, they both embraced the philosophy that teaching others need not take place only in a formal classroom setting and that anyone, no matter their background or walk of life, could learn.

When they first immigrated to the United States, they didn't know any English, so my grandmother communicated with others through music. Wherever they lived, Omi would quickly figure out who in the community was musically inclined and create a band, orchestra, or choir from there. If you had no background in music, she would gladly teach you the basics. After receiving her master's degree in teaching, she taught at a kindergarten for developmentally disabled children. The students whom she couldn't reach with words she could always reach with music.

My Uncle Joe, my grandparents' firstborn son, had an intellectual disorder that we now know as autism. His disability became apparent at a time long before most people knew what autism was, and certainly well before public schools knew how to accommodate autistic children in the classroom. Because of this, my uncle attended public school only through the eighth grade. After that, my grandfather took responsibility for my uncle's education. My uncle could not write an essay or wax philosophical, but he had a savant-like memory for numbers. My grandfather opened a small neighborhood convenience store so my uncle could learn to work as a cashier. Teaching and learning doesn't have to happen in the classroom, and education isn't something that only the elite can enjoy. In my grandparents' eyes, you didn't need to be a published philosopher or a concert pianist; all you needed to be was willing to learn. It is not only my passion for philosophy that I inherited from my grandparents, it is also my steadfast commitment to sharing this passion through teaching.

Part Six: My Philosophy Classroom

My introductory level, ancient Greek philosophy course is one of the most challenging—yet most important—courses I teach. The course fulfills a general-education requirement at the university at which I teach, and there are no prerequisites for enrollment. At this university, incoming freshmen do not choose their fall courses, and whenever the registrar runs out of classes in which to enroll freshmen, I volunteer to increase the enrollment limit in my philosophy classes to make room for those students. While I do get some students who are genuinely interested in philosophy, I also get plenty of students who clearly don't want to be in a philosophy class. After all, how could learning about a bunch of old dead guys be the least bit enjoyable, much less relevant to a seventeen-year-old's life? But this is precisely why it is my favorite course to teach. I enjoy the challenge of drawing connections between ancient Greek philosophy and today's world, so I can show my students that philosophy is exciting, valuable, and relevant.

In the beginning of the semester, I have my students read the introduction to Simon Blackburn's book *Think*. One of the sentences I emphasize to them reads: "Success [in philosophy] will be a matter not of how much you know at the end . . . success will mean taking seriously the implications of ideas."[6] My grandfather wasn't compelled to flee Nazi Germany simply because he had mastered the content of Descartes' *Sixth Meditation*. But reading Descartes' *Meditations*, as well as a panoply of other philosophical works, taught my grandfather how to think through a position and anticipate its consequences. Studying philosophy gave him the tools to develop his own ethical principles, which then informed and guided his actions. In my own teaching, these are the skills I hope to cultivate in my students.

Years after my students have taken my philosophy class, they might not remember which philosopher was Socrates and which philosopher was Aristotle. But I hope that what stays with them is an understanding of the value of philosophy and the ability to apply our texts in practice. My grandfather's desire to learn and his sharp analytical skills are what saved him and his family from persecution. Philosophy taught him to read widely; to spend time developing

---

6. Simon Blackburn, *Think* (Oxford: Oxford University Press, 1999), 5.

firm principles; to defend those principles with reasons, instead of power; and to act on those principles courageously, when threatened. I am driven to teach my students philosophy, because I believe that, someday, it just might save their lives.

Acknowledgment

This work was supported by a grant from Christopher Newport University, Newport News, Virginia.

21

This Is Teaching

Jane Drexler
Salt Lake Community College

JANE DREXLER is associate professor of philosophy at Salt Lake Community College (SLCC), in Salt Lake City, Utah, surrounded by mountains and canyons. She earned her Ph.D. from SUNY-Binghamton, specializing in social and political philosophy and ethics. At SLCC, she teaches Intro to Philosophy, Intro to Ethics, Environmental Ethics, and Informal Logic and Argumentation. She has served as president of faculty senate and in several other capacities within SLCC's shared governance system. She has published essays on philosophy in peer-reviewed, academic publications and in general-audience journals. She won a national Blackboard award for her design of an online course in environmental ethics and has won the SLCC Foundation Teaching Excellence award. She was awarded sabbatical leave for academic year 2016–2017 to work on a project about the role and value of philosophy at a community college.[1]

> Tell all the truth, but tell it slant.
> —Emily Dickinson[2]

There's a kind of romantic ideal of the teacher who loves their craft: they make personal connections and inspire life-changing breakthroughs with their appreciative students, their eyes twinkle with a passion for inspiring others, and they are remembered long after they've departed from this earth.

---

1. Thanks go to Katerina Salini, Claire Peterson, Lisa Reynolds, and Jason Pickavance for early assistance with this essay helping me find some order and clarity in my excessively complicated thoughts. Special thanks too go to Lynn Kilpatrick for a whole sabbatical year of conversations about teaching, scholarship, and writing—and for making our writing retreats so fun and productive.

2. Emily Dickinson, "Poem 1129," in *The Complete Poems of Emily Dickinson*, ed. Thomas H. Johnson (Boston: Little Brown and Company, 1960), p. 506–7.

That image of the Dead Poets Society professor who embodies the love of teaching is certainly inspiring to see, and it has moved many people to seek teaching careers. But I think it has also done a disservice to our understanding of the love of teaching. It has encouraged us to think of the "love of teaching" as a simple thing to identify and articulate. It has encouraged many good professors—including myself—to question whether we have picked the right line of work, when we do not manifest that passion, when we fail to fit the mold.

I definitely don't fit that mold. I'm not the kind of professor who remembers personal stories about individual students, or who makes a lot of personal connections. I am the kind of professor who likes to have fun during class. I like to tell a good story and dig into concepts. I like to talk about serious matters, without being grave. I enjoy spending time with students when we get to catch glimpses of the scary and beautiful markers of the human condition and a life of meaning. And I am exhilarated after a great discussion or lecture. But I also get utterly demoralized by the unrelenting, burnout-ensuring workload, and the constant attempts, from multiple corners, to demand more from us, while simultaneously de-professionalizing what we do. I resent the exclusionary nature of our philosophical tradition and the petty undermining that can occur between professionals. I feel unmotivated in the isolated halls of academia, where philosophy gets squirreled away from the real-life experiences and human lives it was designed to engage. I hate that I am often so tired.

It's safe to say that I do not feel one particular way about teaching philosophy, and that teaching philosophy is not one particular kind of experience for me. Most of the time, I feel confused and frustrated, mired in tensions impossible to resolve.

So what the hell am I doing writing an essay on why I love teaching philosophy? I'm writing because my mixed feelings here are probably not unique. Only Mary Poppins or Pollyanna love their work unreservedly. So, if we love teaching philosophy, it must be a complicated love . . . , you know, one infused with a bit of rage. It must not always look fun or happy. Love must include sleepless nights filled with regret, doubt, and anger, and days of exhaustion and boredom.

In 2005, David Foster Wallace gave a commencement address at Kenyon College that began with this story:

There are these two young fish swimming along, and they happen
to meet an older fish swimming the other way, who nods at them
and says, "Morning, boys, how's the water?" And the two young
fish swim on for a bit, and then eventually one of them looks over
at the other and goes, "What the hell is water?"[3]

Wallace's point was that the most obvious, everyday realities of our
lives are often the most unnoticed and unacknowledged. For the
graduating seniors he spoke to, his message was an invitation to find
sacredness and meaning in the "boredom, routine and petty frustrations" of the day-ins and day-outs that would characterize the rest
of their lives. The value of their education, he argued, was that, with
it, they could cultivate an attention to, and awareness of, the sacredness in the ubiquities of their world; that, with it, they could keep
reminding themselves: "This is water. This is water."

So, as I reflect on the complicated, everyday love of teaching—
what teaching looks like and where we find meaning and value in
it, I am reminded of Wallace's invitation to *see* the water—to see the
broad context in which we teach—to reflect on it honestly. Only in
doing so can we see teaching's sacred-mundane and articulate what
it means to love it.

This is Teaching. This is Teaching.

Everything Has Two Handles

My college's convocation is an event that I find disruptive and shock-
ing. On the day before classes start—that is, on the last day to scram-
ble to get my syllabi finished and copied, to build my course websites,
to prep my first class activities, to formulate a coherent overview of
my courses' purposes and design, and to enjoy a last day of freedom,
before the crush of a heavy, 5-5 community college load—my college goes ahead and schedules a mandatory full day of welcome back
events and meetings. Returning from the summer to assessments,
strategic planning, and completion agendas feels foreign and intense,
like I sort of (but don't quite) remember the language into which
I've been suddenly reimmersed. And though I'm an introvert, whose

---

3. David Foster Wallace, "This Is Water," Commencement Address for Kenyon College, May 21, 2005, https://web.ics.purdue.edu/~drkelly/DFWKenyonAddress2005
.pdf.

human interactions have been limited to close friends and family for four months, convocation pushes me to socialize with hundreds of returning colleagues. By the end of the day, if I hear another word about outcomes and initiatives, if I field one more question about my summer or my plans for the semester, I might explode.

But convocation is also an event I secretly love. After weeks of rising feelings of dread and panic about the new semester, the college asks me to pause for a minute; be among others who are in the same boat; remember why we are here, and what possibilities exist. Tomorrow we are going to be in the thick of it, so let's spend today remembering what we can (and do) accomplish under the weight of those day-ins and day-outs.

In my mind, convocation is grounded in a kind of Stoic recognition, best captured by Epictetus: "Everything has two handles. One by which it can be borne, one by which it cannot be."[4] The stoic knows that our capacity to carry our burdens largely rests on the way we pick it up: do we pick it up by the handle that is painful and wearying, or do we pick it up by the handle that connects us to the meaning and purpose at the heart of the struggle? Epictetus said, "If your brother has done wrong, don't grasp this by the 'wrongdoing' handle—it can't be borne by that one—but by the 'brother,' the 'brought-up-together' handle, and thereby you will be able to bear it."[5] For Epictetus, the weight of the burden matters much less than how we choose to carry it, and it is up to us to choose the handle we can manage.

And so, to me, convocation is about taking the opportunity to set down our burden for a moment, before we have to carry it for sixteen weeks, in order to explore the different handles it has, and to choose the one we are going to carry it with.

And make no mistake, it is a burden. Most philosophy professors who teach at community colleges teach five classes a semester, each class with thirty or so new students, each at differing levels of college readiness. Our students come from varying social locations: the first-generation college student; the vet; the middle-aged,

---

4. Epictetus, "The Enchiridion," in *The Moral Life: An Introductory Reader in Ethics and Literature*, eds. Louis Pojman and Lewis Vaughn, 3rd ed. (New York: Oxford University Press, 2007), 527, para 43.

5. Ibid.

laid-off worker returning to "retrain" for a new career; the gifted, straight-A student interested in saving money; the recovering addict; the distressed; and the full-time mom with a full-time job taking a full-time load.

We are expected to repeatedly create extraordinary and transformative experiences for our students, and to reflect in depth on our teaching methods and continuously develop our pedagogical and disciplinary creds. We teach in an age when we are expected to identify, codify into measurable units, track and assess each course outcome in triplicate. We are expected to work on committees that serve the larger institutional mission and to be able to articulate, at any moment, how our classroom efforts fit into those larger goals. We are expected to substantively evaluate each other, and hold each other accountable to the professional standards we set (which routinely ask us to specify how we will do *even more*—how we will progress to the next level—in the years to come).

We are expected to do all of this in an environment where we are underpaid and where our disparate disciplines too often fight opportunistically for FTEs and scarce resources. Our broader cultural environment, rather than serving as a supportive backdrop, too often is decidedly anti-intellectual, filled with hostile forces that dismiss the value of humanities and complicate our work by exploiting our society's basest fears.

And did I mention the grading?

The sheer weight of it all threatens to bury us daily, and so it really does matter how we carry it. Does it destroy us to the point that we simply lose the will to carry it anymore? Do we carry it so bitterly that we can no longer see anything good in it? Do we carry it so secretly that from the outside it looks easy while our knees are buckling? Or do we find the handle that makes it possible to bear. What does that handle look like? Where do we find it?

I'm always searching for that bearable handle, because I regularly experience the demoralizing pain of the unbearable ones. And so I particularly liked this year's convocation keynote speaker, Phil Hanson, a talented visual artist who reimagined his life and work after nerve damage left him with a trembling hand. His overall argument was that creativity and wonder often occur when we are burdened by pain and limitation. Constraints can move us in new directions. In a eureka moment, Hanson asked himself, "What if I can only draw with a tremor, what could I do with that?" His answer evolved into some truly spectacular projects designed to explore the possibilities within limitations.[6]

Hanson's insights about looking for greatness in what appears, first, as hopelessness is a bit like what it means to love teaching: finding possibility within the constraints. To borrow from Dickinson, looking at it "slant." Maybe the love of teaching comes from considering it sideways when the head-on will hurt too much. Following the Stoics, then, Hanson's keynote reminds me that we choose our handle: we can decide how we feel about teaching, despite the often difficult circumstances in place at open-access colleges. Our love of teaching is not so much an emotion, then, as it is an attitude we choose. The attitude doesn't arise naturally from the role we inhabit or the context in which we work. On the contrary, those roles and contexts are our constraints. But these everyday, ubiquitous burdens are the water in which a rare love swims. Anyone can love what's fun and joyful. Choosing to love the overwhelmingly difficult: that's the real trick.

A Tale of Two Janes

In the crunch of midsemester, my closest faculty friends and I often commiserate about what our Past Self has done to us. When we are buried under the pile of new papers that Past Us wrote into the course requirements, or preparing brand new lectures that Past Us thought were essential changes to a course, it has become a running joke about the abuse that Past Us constantly levels upon our overworked present selves.[7]

Past Jane—that Jane last summer who was all gung ho and refreshed—set up unreasonable expectations for Future Jane: Past Jane revamped our intro class, because she envisioned something

---

6. https://www.ted.com/talks/phil_hansen_embrace_the_shake.

7. Daniel Goldstein's neuropsychological model of temporal selves explores how we think about our Past Self and Future Self: https://www.ted.com/talks/daniel _goldstein_the_battle_between_your_present_and_future_self. In this essay, however, my purpose is not to say something about how our minds work per se, but how we might employ the idea of temporal selves to reflect the difficulties we have in living up to the expectations we create for ourselves.

grand, leaving a bunch of to-be-determined readings and unfinished lectures and assignments. She wrote that impossible sabbatical proposal, confident that Future Jane could actually produce an entire book manuscript, change her institutional organization, and design a new program in one year. Past Jane signed up for the three committees on which Future Jane would serve. (Indeed, it is Past Jane that committed Future Jane to writing this essay.)

It's clear here that Past Jane thinks that Future Jane is amazing. Past Jane thinks Future Jane has all the time in the world. She thinks that Future Jane has a totally set routine, and uses all her time efficiently. In Past Jane's mind, Future Jane is eating nutritious, nonbloaty STET foods that don't cause food comas. She only drinks one relaxing glass of wine in the evening, and that's as she's sitting by the fire reading students' papers with an engaged spark of appreciation for the unique souls and mental processes of all 150 of them. Future Jane has an exercise regimen that is motivating and effective, and her personal relationships are all untroubled and energy giving. Future Jane is the smartest, most capable, well-adjusted, efficient, stable person in the world!

God love 'er, Past Jane thinks the very best of Future Jane. But for her part, *Actual* Jane, the Jane buried under the weight of all these old optimisms, thinks Past Jane is a bitch.

Past Jane was ambitious and optimistic, but *Actual* Jane is overburdened and sleep deprived. Past Jane saw the joy and vision of teaching, Actual Jane is in the middle of triage grading. Past Jane shouted, "Yes We Can!" Actual Jane is whimpering a desperate, "Please, May We Not."

The trouble is—and here's why this tension is unresolvable—you want Past Jane to stay optimistic. You don't want Actual Jane's naysaying to make its way too far into Past Jane's world. You don't want to settle for the pessimistic view of what is possible. You don't want the onslaught of deadlines and burdens to become the place from which you imagine the future.

So, while Past Jane is the sadist of this drama, she's also kinda the hero. After all, Past Jane's relentlessly confident conception of Future Jane is precisely what enables Actual Jane to more and more become the person that Past Jane thinks Future Jane is. Because I feel obligated to Past Jane, I really do end up begrudgingly doing the work that makes me into the kind of person that Past Jane thinks I will become.

So, what does this constantly recurring drama help me to understand about the nature and love of teaching? The most obvious lesson is that teaching is not any one, static thing. It is a constant interplay of the pessimistic and optimistic, the tired and energized. It is a temporal experience of moments in time that, like a pointillist drawing, look like something coherent only when I'm not in it.

So as I try to think about what my love of teaching looks like within this temporality, my first thought is that my love is always displaced. Past Jane can only anticipate my love for teaching, while Future Jane is never really present to experience anything. And Actual Jane: often I can only see the joy and meaning of what I do retrospectively, after I've stepped back far enough from the deadlines to see something coherent.

At best, then, in the context of this temporality, my experience of my love of teaching—of the fun, joy, exhilaration, meaningfulness, contentedness, and peace—come only as flashes—flashes that disappear whenever I try to see them directly or collect them into a box.

There (in that student's smile of understanding).

There (in that hard-won point of persuasion).

There (joking with a colleague).

There (running into a graduating student at the cafeteria).

There (getting home from a long day).

There (laughing at a remembered moment in class).

There (turning in final grades in May).

This is teaching.

The Spectacle(s) of Philosophy

A couple years ago, I was at a general-education conference, sitting on a panel with faculty in various disciplines from several Utah institutions of higher education, discussing whether and how we should think differently about designing the introductory courses that introduce our majors, on the one hand, and the introductory courses that serve as general education and, thus, as the only courses students will take in our fields, on the other.

This isn't something I thought about until a few years ago. My standard operating procedure kept me focused on my own classes, my own department, my own field. Moreover, as a junior faculty member, there wasn't a whole lot of time to consider the broader, institutional perspective. But once I received tenure and then became faculty senate president, I started gaining a more holistic point of view. I found myself working on our General Education Program committee, charged with developing a model of general education that went beyond disparate "menu" items and offered, instead, an *integrative* program.

At the community college, general education is what we do. Though we are trained to teach in a discipline, that training doesn't fit the institutional context in which we teach. Community colleges have what might be called "premajors" that prepare students to transfer to four-year colleges, but it's only rarely that I ever see a student sign up for a second course in philosophy. I get students for sixteen weeks, and then I don't see them again. Given this, I gradually started to allow myself to interrogate and reimagine the traditional introductory course in philosophy. I stopped asking, "What skills and content should one teach in a typical intro class?" And I started asking, "What are the most important philosophical ideas and skills that I *could* teach in sixteen weeks for students who, in all likelihood, will never take a second course in philosophy?"[8]

Because I was working on these questions, I was invited to participate in that panel on the pitfalls and promises of approaching general-education courses differently than introducing-the-major courses. I focused my comments on assignment redesign—how to encourage students to draw creative connections between philosophy and their talents, interests, and other areas of study: art, video, poetry, graphic design, or whatnot. Because of a last-minute change, one of the other panel members was also a philosophy professor, from a research institution, and we ended up having a bit of a back-and-forth for a while. He was worried about the "watering down" of expectations in intro courses for nonmajors. He said that he was always careful to treat nonmajors with the same expectations as majors and that it was a disservice to conclude that nonmajors can't handle the rigor of a typical philosophy course.

---

8. See Jane Drexler, "Philosophy for General Education: Teaching Environmental Ethics to Non-Majors," *Teaching Philosophy* 38, no. 2 (2015):289–305.

But I pushed back on the idea that teaching differently means "watering down." I did so by arguing that the conceptual tools we bring to an object of inquiry become the lens through which we see that object. I used an example from an essay by Byron Good called "How Medicine Constructs Its Objects."[9] In it, Good traces a familiar Foucauldian line. When medical students learn to take patient histories, they are inadvertently acquiring the lens through which they conceive the patient: As they fill out those history charts more and more, they begin to walk into the patients' rooms with those categories and questions emblazoned on their minds. And while, of course, those lenses are crucial to the patient's diagnosis and treatment, they also limit what the medical practitioner is able to see about the patient. The patient becomes an object that is viewable *only* through those categories and questions.

Similarly, our discipline's focus on a particular kind of assignment—the critical-analysis paper—becomes a lens that limits how we experience philosophical texts. Though such papers can develop students' skills in using evidence, critiquing an argument, and identifying presuppositions, they also limit the questions you can ask and the understanding you can glean. You might miss the moments of wonder, inspiration, connection, and resonance—the moments in which an idea enters our world and in which our world fits into an idea. In short, it's the critical-analysis paper that "waters down" philosophy.

In my courses, we still write a few traditional papers—I teach critical analysis and argument development. But I also assign more creative work: my students have submitted comic strips and advertisements on key philosophical concepts; they've written songs about the Allegory of the Cave and Descartes' *Meditations*; they've created videos on logical fallacies. If we are willing to unshackle our course assignments (and content) from the tradition of the discipline just a little bit, we might be able to grind a few new philosophical lenses, recapturing the fullness of philosophical inquiry and engagement and cultivating an appreciation for the multiplicity of ways we can say, "This is philosophy."

9. Byron J. Good, "How Medicine Constructs Its Objects," in *Medicine, Rationality and Experience: An Anthropological Perspective* (Cambridge: Cambridge University Press, 1993), 65–87.

Building Philosophical Muscle

A few years ago, I started writing articles on philosophy for the *CrossFit Journal*. It seemed a totally natural thing to do: I was a professional philosophy professor and an avid CrossFitter, and I was beginning to see philosophical insights and principles everywhere in the gym and within the CrossFit community. The first article I wrote suggested that Aristotle's virtue ethics were reflected in the culture of CrossFit. Aristotle's "overall point is that when we 'train'—physically, morally, intellectually—(and, indeed, when we don't), we are molding not just our bodies or behaviors, but also our very characters."[10] The last article I wrote presented CrossFit as a kind of stoic training: "Let others practice lawsuits, others study problems, others syllogisms; here you practice how to die, how to be enchained, how to be racked, how to be exiled."[11]

Of all the *CrossFit Journal* articles I published or drafted, the easiest one—on Camus' reading of Sisyphus—was the best.[12] CrossFit workouts tend to have these super-Sisyphean moments, where we must struggle along, even when it seems we can't do any more. In these moments, we tend to see only despair. But Camus found freedom and happiness in the in-between moments, when, with "heavy but measured step," Sisyphus turns around and walks back to continue his unending struggle.

At bottom, this article—like the others—wasn't really about CrossFit. I wrote it with my good friend in mind. She was a CrossFit coach and a newish mom who was experiencing an existential crisis from which she couldn't find escape. CrossFit offered a shared frame through which I could express an idea I wanted to share with my friend:

> What if we thought of our other life activities like that: the going-to-work, paying-the-bills, grounding-the-children, eating-the-right-foods, cleaning-the-kitchen activities? What if we imagined that some of the most important moments in our lives are those

---

10. http://library.crossfit.com/free/pdf/CFJ_Aristotle_Drexler_FINAL2.pdf.

11. http://library.crossfit.com/free/pdf/CFJ_2014_02_Stoicism_Drexler.pdf.

12. It only took me a couple hours to write—I woke up one morning not only with an epiphany of an idea for it, but also with it already mentally written (which is the first and only time that's ever happened to me).

moments in-between—those vulnerable and quietly triumphant moments—when we, with heavy but measured step, choose willfully to continue walking?[13]

As it turned out, my articles were a welcome contribution to an ongoing exploration of the mind in the *CrossFit Journal*. The philosophical aspects of CrossFit resonate with its varied membership: returning vets, public service professionals, soccer parents, and recovering addicts, among others. My articles received thousands of "likes" on Facebook and several thoughtful comments from bloggers. *CrossFit* readers posted comments like the following to the journal's website and Facebook pages:

> When I first found CrossFit, or should I say it found me (way back in 2005–6), it had a wonderful, quasi-intellectual bent to it. There were always pithy aphorisms posted directly below each day's [workout]. . . . New experts were regularly introduced, and offered their insight and experience in article and/or video format. Sometimes these experts even debated one another, openly, on camera. Definitions were created(!) For a brief time . . . inspirational literature and (mostly classical) music were linked on the mainsite for us to discover, right there with the Pose Running Technique. For a lifelong fitness guru like myself, who always thought of exercise as mostly about the body, and less about the mind, CrossFit was, in a word, Revelatory.[14]

Comments like these remind me that the "life of the mind" matters to people. We all engage in philosophical reflection, looking for meaning, purpose, and the strength of will for a heavy lift, a numbing PTA obligation, or an overwhelming teaching load.

But professional academic philosophers tend to think (with a spark of pride, even) that philosophy is too intellectual for the masses. Indeed, these essays were dismissed by many of my peers and colleagues as "lowbrow"—a hobby, rather than part of my job. Where was the peer review? Where was the prestige? But that kind of arrogance suggests that the lived experiences that philosophy was meant to engage are irrelevant. The most prestigious "scholarly" articles I

---

13. http://journal.crossfit.com/2013/03/crossfit-a-sisyphean-endeavor.tpl.

14. J. Susa, Comment 1, http://journal.crossfit.com/2014/02/the-greek-and-the-games.tpl#comments.

have written feel as if I have written *about* the world, but not *within* it, unable to speak meaningfully to anyone who was not already specially trained in my vocabulary and canon. What I gained from the *CrossFit Journal* experience—of sharing something meaningful to a broader audience, but receiving a bit of ridicule for it—was, thankfully, a bit of immunity from other people's views about what constitutes "real" philosophy. Writing these articles was, for me, about giving myself permission to revise my conception of my job and to find that this, too, is teaching.

With Heavy But Measured Step

In the end, there is no tidy way to articulate the meaning and love that I find in teaching philosophy at a community college. I have only the handle with which I choose to carry it, the flashes of contentedness and joy, and the ways I make room in my job for my broader definition of it. Given the burdens and limitations of my job, it's not possible or preferable for me to articulate my work as being about some clear purpose or end. Sometimes my work is about turning around "with heavy but measured step," and choosing willfully to continue walking.

Or, perhaps, swimming.

This is our water.

22

Teaching as a Humanism

Russell Marcus
Hamilton College

Over the past thirty years, RUSSELL MARCUS has taught in high schools in New York City (mathematics and computer science) and Costa Rica (history, math, literature, and writing); in community colleges (mathematics), and in four-year undergraduate institutions (philosophy). A board member of the American Association of Philosophy Teachers, he is now Associate Professor of Philosophy at Hamilton College, where he has taught since 2007. Russell's main area of research is the philosophy of mathematics, and he has published articles in top journals and a monograph, *Autonomy Platonism and the Indispensability Argument* (Lexington), as well as coediting *An Historical Introduction to the Philosophy of Mathematics* (Bloomsbury). His *Introduction to Formal Logic* and *Introduction to Formal Logic with Philosophical Applications* were recently released by Oxford University Press. At Hamilton College, Russell received the John R. Hatch Excellence in Teaching Award, in 2011, and the Class of 1963 Excellence in Teaching Award, in 2016. Russell believes that a teacher's job is to help each individual student move from wherever they are to the next step.

The autumn after I barely finished college, I found myself teaching mathematics at Jamaica High School, in Queens, New York. It was a sprawling, noisy old building with 4,000 students, a struggling school in a struggling neighborhood. I was suddenly faced with responsibility for 170 children—five, thirty-eight-minute classes of thirty-four students each day. I had no practical training, just a few liberal arts theory courses. But my dad was the chair of the math department at another New York City high school, so I had resources.

I had only two preps that fall of 1988, two sections of ninth-year math and three of a remedial course called Fundamentals of Mathematics. Every day, I would get to school by six-thirty and teach my classes and monitor a hallway for one period. Then I would walk out of the building, get into a hand-me-down 1976 Buick Apollo, cry for ten or fifteen minutes, and drive home to collapse. I was learning what it meant to be an adult, and it hurt.

•

A dear colleague, speaking recently about why she teaches, said that she wants to change the world for the better. Her claim first struck me as pretense, a view she seemed self-consciously to share. I wish I could say that I'm working to improve the world. But I fear that my work is not that important.

I love philosophy. I love reading Quine's *Word and Object* or Berkeley's *Principles*, or anything by Plato except the *Phaedo*, especially after a year or two away from it, and discovering more in there than I saw before. There's so much to learn, and I keep growing. When I see a smart new move, or a distinction that helps me frame the world anew, there's a self-indulgent thrill.

But certainly, my research is of little consequence. I've published a little, largely defending an unpopular metaphysics (platonism in mathematics), and an even more contentious epistemology (rationalism). I'm pleased to have received some encouraging feedback from others. But I can't help but wonder how much of that is a way of aggrandizing their own work. So little in the real world depends on whether there are mathematical objects or whether we have a priori knowledge that it's a little embarrassing even to try to make the case that it matters. People live and die, work and thrive, love or fight, suffer and die, in the same way, whether or not there are mathematical objects, whether or not physical theories require them. Even mathematicians don't and shouldn't care too much. Philosophy of mathematics doesn't really matter.

And if the content of what I'm teaching is unimportant, then it can't really matter whether students learn it. I've taught, to some modest acclaim, for nearly thirty years, mostly useless topics that most students mostly forget soon after they receive their final grades. I'd love to improve the world, but that may be beyond my ken.

•

I expect that many of my teachers would be surprised that I ended up as a competent academic, or as any kind of success at all. Of the many low points of my academic life, I remember especially my pre-calculus teacher saying that I wouldn't go anywhere interesting in life; the look of disappointment on the face of my history professor after he read my final paper: "I expected better of you"; my depression at the ends of school breaks; how I would stay up all night watching TV and sleep through the torture of the next day's classes.

I went into teaching mainly because I couldn't figure out anything else to do after college. I went to an employment agency in New York City right after graduation; they had no idea what to do with me. I sent a letter requesting advice from Roger Angell, who wrote compellingly about baseball in *The New Yorker*, two of my favorite pastimes; I got no reply. At least with teaching, I would have some support and potential mentoring, and a salary. And as a twenty-two-year-old, I did want to change the world for the better.

This was a lesson I learned largely from my dad. My paternal grandfather, a Romanian Jewish immigrant to New York, had built a small business. He had a "factory" (three women with sewing machines in Jersey City) producing curtains, which he delivered to retailers on Orchard Street and elsewhere on the Lower East Side. My dad helped his father with deliveries as a kid, but found the dishonest, self-serving negotiations of commerce repugnant. He wanted to teach mathematics, and to do some good, and he started his career, just out of City College in 1959, at James Monroe High School in the Bronx.

In 1968, at the hospital after his second heart attack, my grandfather said to my dad, "So now you'll come back and take over the business."

"No, Pop. I'm a teacher."

"Is *that* what you're going to do?" my grandfather spat. "Spend your life teaching the niggers and the spics?"

"Yeah, Pop. That's what I'm going to do."

My father, in his seventies now, after a forty-three-year career teaching in the NYC public schools, can still feel the sting. His father had constructed, ambitiously, a new life in a new country, a business, with visions of passing it to his son. My father rejected that ambition, choosing instead what seemed to his father to be a mundane and useless career. He had to learn to live as a disappoint-ment to his father.

At the end of my college career, I wasn't a disappointment to my father, but I wasn't exactly a proper object of pride. I finished my col-lege career with about a C average, despite a relatively strong senior year. I had no concrete prospects or plans.

·

The Mishna is a collection of the ancient Jewish oral tradition, illus-trating and explaining the commandments of the Torah. One aspect of the Mishna is called *tikkun olam*, or repairing the world. It has mystical roots and can be interpreted, traditionally, as guidance to adhere to Jewish law. It is widely understood today as a responsibility to others, to social justice. I didn't think of teaching as *tikkun olam* explicitly, then. But it played an implicit role, pushing me away from more promisingly profitable pursuits, toward something worthy of my family, and of myself.

My dad is an amazing teacher, and I cannot say enough about his influence on me. Among the broad lessons I learned from him are:

• In designing curriculum and individual classes, focus on stu-dent needs.

• Any class is a good class if the students and the material are well matched.

• Your job as a teacher is just to move the students from wherever they are to the next step.

• When in doubt, shut up, and let the students work; teaching is service, not self-aggrandizement.

• Abstract pedagogical theory is almost always a waste of time.

At Jamaica High School, I started to learn how to design a les-son. Start with a short motivational exercise that builds on what the students have learned, challenging them to the next step with a twist they haven't seen. You can subtract 4 from 8, but what about subtracting 8 from 4? You can factor $x^2 - 3x - 4$, but what about $2x^2 - 3x - 4$? Create demand in your students' minds. Get them to want to learn. If you ever need an introductory activity for a high school math lesson, ask my dad. The guy is a master at thinking out the little steps students need to get themselves through their work. It was a delight to peer into his mind as I started to learn my craft, to understand his experience and skills.

I wasn't a good teacher, then, of course. No one walks into a classroom for the first time as a good teacher. It's a skill, *areté*, and requires honing. I saw my inadequacies daily. Teaching at Jamaica could be especially tough. The city closed the school in 2014, citing a stagnant graduation rate well under 50 percent. In the semester I was there, a student was shot and killed on the front steps. I saw the drop slip a week later. My remedial classes, which started with addition and subtraction, were frustrating, both because the students were seeing the same material for years on end, and because they could not master it. Many stopped coming to class, especially the one held in the boiler room next to the cafeteria. Tyrone Alexander offered to throw my motherfucking ass out of the fucking window, rather than do the class work one day. I made mistakes, and students let me know. But I was young, and cared about them, and was sort of okay for a white guy. I didn't lecture them on how much better the students used to be, or get uptight about late or missing homework. I just tried to help them get from where they were to the next step. I showed up every day, and held myself responsible, even when it took all of my courage to get up in the morning to face the exhaustion. I wasn't trying to revolutionize anything. I was just trying to do my job and get better at it.

•

My father's vision was focused on the close-at-hand: students who needed to learn in the hopes of living productive and fulfilling lives. His father had wanted to build something beyond him. While my interest in teaching is closer to my dad's view, my interest in philosophy is closer to my grandfather's: a pursuit of eternal truths, a world that goes beyond ourselves, sub specie aeternitatis.

But my love of philosophy really came from my mom, and my mother's mother. My mom taught me poetry, and the love of words. I had heard that ontogeny recapitulates phylogeny, that metonymy is the generic form of synecdoche, and the "Love Song of J. Alfred

Prufrock" as a child. Her mother loved chewing on ideas, obsessing over them. But we didn't know much about philosophy. Her brother-in-law, my Great-Uncle Barney, would talk about philosophers, Nietzsche especially. But he was dismissed as pretentious and annoying, a pontificator.

My father turned me on to the existentialists when I was a teenager. He handed me *The Stranger* one evening when I was fifteen. "I think you might be ready for this." I fell asleep on it, and cut school the next day to finish it. But my dad and I didn't really talk about it, or much of anything, when I was that age.

My grandmother and I would talk about everything. I mean everything, including how my grandfather used to visit the prostitutes over in Red Hook. "Every generation thinks they invented sex." She saw philosophy as continuous with the Jewish tradition of learning. Her father, a peasant communist, had escaped Russia and made a life as a tailor in Brooklyn. My grandmother was bright and independent, but graduated from high school in 1929 and had to work to help the family survive the Depression. She finally got to college after my grandfather retired, graduating from Queens College at age seventy-two, with a bachelor of arts in Yiddish studies. With her, I could talk Aristotle and Plato and Maimonides. She lived close to Jamaica High School, and I would sometimes pick up a kosher pizza and have dinner with her after my after-school cry.

·

I was excessed from Jamaica High on the first day of the spring term. A transfer arrived twenty minutes before my first class, and I was the least senior math teacher. I substituted in various schools for a month before finding an opening at Newtown High School in Elmhurst for the rest of the term, replacing a teacher who needed brain surgery. Again, I had some tougher classes and some better ones. But after a year of being an adult, I was tired. I had no job for the fall, and I was both eager for a different kind of excitement and hoping to find an easier way to live.

I enjoyed working with students, and I had learned already the exhausting thrill of good teaching. You invest yourself emotionally, starting each class with the hope that you figured out how to construct the lesson that will finally get a student to succeed, to develop the self-confidence they need to meet the next challenge. Sometimes it works, and it feels great: *tikkun olam*. But then there's disappointment when they fail, which means that you, the teacher, have failed. There are no student failures, they say, only teacher failures, and I know that's not true or useful. But I can't let it go, because it is true, and it is useful. Explain that lesson a different way. Use more concrete illustrations. Have the students explain it to you, or to each other. Give them more practice problems. Cajole. Beg. There's always something else to try, some other way to help a student to succeed.

All of this emotional investment enervated me that first year. Plus, I had to figure out how to navigate the system and to work with the angry older teachers. The year felt like a lifetime. I had a girlfriend with a sense of adventure, also a math teacher in the city and also ready for something new. We moved to Costa Rica with our summer salaries.

•

After a couple of months in San José, we ran anxious without concrete plans and low on money. A private school near San Antonio de Belén called Costa Rica Academy (CRA) needed a couple of teachers, and we were in the classroom again. This time I taught social studies, convincing the headmaster that a bachelor's degree in philosophy was sufficient preparation.

In New York City, the curriculum was worked out by others and given to teachers, which was great for getting started. Now, with the freedom of a small private school, I caught the curriculum design bug. I was able to dream about how to structure and teach different courses: literature and statistics, journalism and AP Language and Composition. By my third year teaching, I had found my voice.

But my second year was still rough, and I was making lots of mistakes. I had a world history class with a mix of maybe twenty tenth and eleventh graders. They were good kids, but they recognized my inexperience and they played with it, naturally. A group of about five boys called themselves Los Locos, and prided themselves on their collegial rambunctiousness. I banished at least one student a day to the principal's office, or just to sit outside the classroom.

It was a futile show of strength, ineffective in the long term. But it had a small positive effect, enough to earn me a few quiet minutes of instruction. The ostracized student felt the sting a little, though it was also a small point of pride. The rowdiness of the class was contagious. Even Erica Jiménez was banished once, and looked at me with understanding and pity as she left. I was at a loss for better classroom management strategies, and we all knew it.

One day, as I entered the sixth-period class, I heard the students laughing about something which sounded like "jock-a-cheemba."

"What's that?" I asked.

"What's what?"

"Jock-a-cheemba."

"Oh, that," said Ramon Rodríguez, one of the Locos, pensively. "It's just, kind of . . . it's a greeting."

"Like 'hello'? Huh. I've never heard it."

"Yeah, like 'hello.' It's just a little Costa Rican slang."

These were the kids who taught me that *pura vida* was strictly for tourists; *tuanis* was hipper. *Mae* was literally like "idiot," but used for friends. Thanks to the Locos, I could say, *Oye, mae ¿Que tal?* And get back, *¡Tuanis!* But these were all phrases I had heard elsewhere, unlike "jock-a-cheemba."

"So, how is it used?"

"You just say it when you greet someone," Ramon explained, as the Locos nodded agreement. "When you come into class, you can say, 'Jock-a-cheemba, Locos,' and then we'll say, 'Jock-a-cheemba, Profesor Marcus.'" (CRA students used the Spanish *profesor*, with the accent on the final syllable.)

That's how it went, for the rest of the term. I would enter the class, and say, "Jock-a-cheemba, Locos," and Ramon and Miguel and William and the other Locos would look up with gleeful, respectful smiles, and reply, "Jock-a-cheemba, Profesor Marcus." And then we'd get to work.

Look, it wasn't that I didn't have suspicions. It was clear that something was off about our little dialogue. But I had no idea what the problem was, and using the new script was pedagogically effective. I had shown a little trust in my students, a little vulnerability, which helped them to feel empowered. Classes were quieter. The tension of wondering who would be the arbitrary target of my exasperated frustration was mitigated. We started with smiles. I just avoided looking at Erica and Maria during the introductory jock-a-cheemba play. I did not report my class greetings to my Costa Rican friends.

It wasn't until my last year at CRA that my curiosity overwhelmed my fear. Ramon, who had graduated the previous year, came back to visit, and I asked. Turns out, yes, it's as bad as I feared. *Chimba* is slang for a woman's genitals. What I heard as "jock-a" was in fact ¡*Diay, que! Diay, mae, ¡Que chimba!* The best English equivalent that I can muster is, "Man, what an amazing pussy!" The original had been aimed at one of the young women in the class, of course. And then, well, I just started each day in World History II with an exclamation about the amazing pussy in front of me.

Yeah, I was still making mistakes. Despite this, something, in even my most challenging early classes, was working. The students understood that I cared and respected them, that I wasn't out to wield my authority. My focus was on their learning, and if I wanted them to behave in certain ways, to pay attention or to do their homework, it was because I thought it would be useful to them and because I cared about them. I wouldn't waste their time, at least not consciously so, and I would listen to them, and hear them, and be honest with them. I had to learn more creative teaching methods, better classroom management, and how to craft more thoughtful assignments. I saw all the warts on my teaching. But my supervisors were puzzlingly (to me) encouraging. And I was starting to see more clearly why education is so important, a lesson you can't learn really well until you teach for a while, until you see the effects on students and feel their appreciation and trust and start to share their hopes and frustrations.

Even on reflection, I struggle to say what worked, what transferable lessons I learned. At the risk of offering useless abstract pedagogical principles, perhaps it was commitment and caring, about the students and the material, loving what I do and doggedly trying to figure out how to get the students to love it too. Being there, consistently, accessibly, and reliably, also cannot be underestimated. We share with our students the desire for them to succeed. Making that happen is just figuring out who and where they are, respecting their own ends, and then helping them to see the utility of others.

I left Costa Rica after three years, returned to New York City for one more year as a high school teacher, and then started graduate school in philosophy at the City University of New York. I stayed in touch with a few folks from CRA, including Dan Schwartz, who had taught there my first year. Dan hadn't liked working at CRA, but he loved the Costa Rican men, and the thriving, underground gay scene there. The machismo culture and proscriptions against gayness were strong, though the drag show to which Dan took me at a finca in the hills above Heredia is still my favorite.

Anyway, Dan ran into one of my former students in a gay bar a few times after the student had graduated. It took Oscar some time to come out to Dan, despite repeatedly meeting him in the relevant places. Eventually, they talked candidly about their mutual discomfort at CRA. Oscar told Dan that my history class, the jock-a-cheemba class, was the one place he felt comfortable in his time there. I don't remember the incident during which I made it clear that the casual homophobic talk in class was unacceptable, but apparently it was heard. It wasn't all mistakes.

•

At Cardozo High School, where I spent the year between Costa Rica and graduate school, I jumped at the chance to teach an honors geometry class and an AP computer science course. I challenged my geometry students to construct proofs about three-dimensional figures. My computer science students and I worked on a program to find the most efficient path between any two classrooms in the school, a 1993 prototype for Google Maps. I took a couple of practical education classes, on cooperative learning and on avoiding confrontations in the classroom. The former led to my first published article. Education classes often get a bad rap, but there's nothing better for a young teacher than listening to good teachers talk about their craft.

Good teaching is hard work, and I worked hard, out of love and necessity. I'm not generally very good at thinking on my feet. I often overprepare, which may explain why I spent thirteen years in graduate school. But I fell in love with the puzzle of figuring out how to connect these students with those concepts. I've always loved puzzles. One year, my wife planned a vacation for us: three days in Paris, France, eating crêpes and walking in the parks and museums. I planned the next year's excursion: a weekend at the Stamford, Connecticut, Marriott for the American Crossword Puzzle Tournament.

Each class is a puzzle about how to organize the content and present it in a way that clicks with this group of students. Every class is different, because every person is different and all of their interpersonal interactions are different. You need a lot of tools to reach them all.

But the preparation is more for me than for the students. In evaluating my courses, students tend to remark on my enthusiasm, not my hard work, on the infectiousness of my love for philosophy. Enthusiasm is not fully a virtue, and the word is not always praise. But it fits my teaching and it explains, at least partly, why I returned to philosophy. I like math, and I loved teaching math. But I didn't love math as I love philosophy. Good teachers love what they do and care for their students, and they commit to solving the puzzle about how to bring it all together. And we suffer when it doesn't work.

•

Starting graduate school, I was way ahead of my peers in teaching experience and skills, and way behind them in philosophy. I had more enthusiasm than commitment in college, and no idea how to manage frustration and anxiety, how to take charge over an assignment or organize my work and time effectively. Teaching had given me the skills I needed to be a proper student, though, so I thrived for a few years.

Nearly everyone has difficulty in graduate school, in one way or another, though every unhappy student is unhappy in their own way. Some of my issues were just personal, including another in a series of disappointing breakups of long-term relationships. I struggled to develop a dissertation topic, finally settling on the indispensability argument in the philosophy of mathematics and a supportive adviser, Jerry Katz. But then Jerry's cancer returned and he died, terribly sadly, a year into my writing. I still miss him whenever I'm working on my research. I had a jerk for a second adviser, and, when he dumped me, I took a long time to recover. I wouldn't have completed the degree had David Rosenthal not held my hand, kicked me in the pants, and pointed me back to the trail. Words cannot express my gratitude to David.

Along the way, I finally met the right woman. We married and had two children. The first was born right before Jerry died, and the second was born just before the jerk told me that I would never be able to finish my dissertation. With Emily in the workforce, I spent invaluable time changing diapers, hanging out in the playgrounds, and generally making a home. I continued to teach at various colleges, including Queens College, alma mater of both my mother and my grandmother. It was poorly paid adjunct work, mostly, and I didn't know enough philosophy then to be really good. But students enjoyed my classes often enough, and I was always proud of the amount of material I could march them through.

Finally finishing my degree, I received a postdoctoral fellowship at Hamilton College, and then a tenure-track job here three years later. I experiment with curriculum and teach classes filled with students who actually do the readings (at least mostly, at least eventually). There aren't many philosophers of mathematics in places like this, and I feel some pity and puzzlement from colleagues at conferences. But I couldn't be happier, professionally or personally. I hope never to take my good luck for granted.

Still, I found myself standing in front of my logic class on the morning after the 2016 U.S. presidential election, failing to introduce relational predicates, and failing to hold back the tears. I had made a big mistake in my life. This isn't where I am needed. Teaching at Hamilton has nothing to do with repairing the world. "I'm in the wrong place," I sobbed. "You don't need me."

•

That was a tough day for me, as it was for many of us, and I was overreacting. But it is true that most of my students here don't really need me. That's another lesson from my father: in any class, you'll have some strong students, who will learn the work without much help, and some weak students, who need more help than you can give them. A teacher's main responsibility is to the middle of the class.

Students at Hamilton are selected because they have all been at the tops of their classes. They don't need me, by definition.

Still, I do have the ability to do some good here. Many of our graduates go off to Goldman Sachs or McKinsey, wielding great influence. If I can help them to think more clearly, to make decisions that are more grounded in good and thoughtful reasons, then I have some indirect ability to affect the world.

My goal is not to ensure that students retain the subtleties about the semantics we study, or the logic or the metaphysics. Even most of my best students don't fall in love with philosophy or find it really transformative. I can get them to enjoy studying it with me, to come along for the ride and like it. But mostly what they get from me are transferable skills: to read difficult material with confidence, to interpret with charity and clarity, to speak clearly about challenging ideas. That's a little *tikkun olam*.

More importantly, I hope to model a life not rooted in commerce or fear, a life of trading in ideas and ideals rather than material goods. I want my students to see how to resist immediate social exigencies to take a longer and deeper view of what's meaningful in life, a heartfelt and respectful engagement with lasting questions. The content of philosophy is an indulgence, but it's useful just because it's useless, because it's not about relentless consumption. We can't all be philosophers all the time; we need to grow the food, distribute it to the hungry, and care for the ill. But the way we all live is not the way that we have to live, and I hope that I help my students see alternatives. A world with more thinking and less buying and selling and consuming would seem repaired to me, or on its way.

I'm not under the illusion that I can make the world fully according to my ideals of equity and justice. But I do help the students I meet to grow and challenge themselves. And it is only really possible because I really love what I do, both the teaching and the philosophy.

Can good teachers not love their work, and not be emotionally committed to the successes of their students? Can teachers who love their work not be any good? Sure. There are no necessary and sufficient conditions on good teaching. We all have to find our own voices.

•

Two years ago, I taught a new seminar on Wittgenstein's work. There were nine of us, with varying strengths. The class was an unremitting pleasure. We struggled with the material, challenging and supporting each other. Everyone was engaged, every time we met. It was as good a class as I could imagine, a long way from teaching remedial mathematics at Jamaica High School. I've learned a lot since then about classroom management, curriculum design, and structuring a lesson. But these skills were in the deep background during the seminar. We all just sat around talking philosophy, walking around the Academy, seeking the forms. And there I was, on the last day, crying in front of the class, telling them how much of a joy and a privilege it was to study with them, to think about philosophy with students who are interested in seeing a life they don't see much in the outside world. "When I tell colleagues at conferences," I choked out, "that working with my undergraduates is as challenging and rewarding as working with graduate students at top programs, they're skeptical. But in the future, whenever I tell them that, I'll be thinking of you."

23

When Our Students Die

Nick Smith
University of New Hampshire

NICK SMITH is a professor and chairperson of the University of New Hampshire Department of Philosophy. Before coming to UNH, Smith worked as a litigator for LeBoeuf, Lamb, Greene, and MacRae and as a judicial clerk for the Honorable R. L. Nygaard of the U.S. Court of Appeals for the Third Circuit. Smith published *I Was Wrong: On the Meanings of Apologies* (Cambridge University Press, 2008) and *Justice through Apologies: Remorse, Reform and Punishment* (Cambridge University Press, 2014). Smith regularly appears in the media, including in interviews with Diane Rehm, the *Wall Street Journal*, the *New York Times*, the *Chronicle of Higher Education*, the *Guardian*, NPR, BBC, CBC, CNN, *Fortune*, *Salon*, *Philosophy Talk*, and others. He has received teaching awards from UNH and Vanderbilt.

John was the first.

Professors can forget what it feels like to begin college. I've been through dozens of Septembers on both sides of the desk, and it takes some effort to remember the electrifying cocktail of independence, anxiety, opportunity, and exponentially expanding social and intellectual horizons that characterize what we label "undergraduate education." College is intense, and on this late summer afternoon in coastal New Hampshire I felt pangs of nostalgia for my own lurching start to college decades ago. The weather, the grounds still in bloom, the well-rested students fresh from summer, and faculty at their least grouchy all contributed to my very good mood—here I am, a professor in a beautiful place. Comedians and philosophers have a lot in common, and Jerry Seinfeld talks about how as a young adult the idea of making a living doing comedy was, for him, like heaven: getting paid to be weird and make people laugh. Even if he could only earn enough for a loaf of bread per week, that would be the life for him. Philosophy is a lot like that for me. I still feel like I somehow tricked the world into paying me to do this job so full of life. I had just emerged from teaching an advanced undergraduate course in Continental philosophy where we debated Nietzsche versus Kant on the purpose of philosophy. The students were an all-star group drawn from my previous courses. I had only been here a few years, so this felt like the first group of *my* students who had gone from introductory to advanced philosophy under my wing. Overcaffeinated, giddy from channeling Nietzsche, and riding the teacher's high, I walked over to the department office.

I asked Alexis, our administrative assistant who was also the social hub of the department, if she could pull up what John was taking that semester. He had taken two other classes with me—including my very first class at UNH—and I thought he would enjoy this course. John spent a lot of time in my office chatting about philosophy and life. He would, in earnest and without any pretension, read and engage with everything I assigned. His friendly enthusiasm made him a fun interlocutor. I probably spent more time talking with him outside of class than any other student during that period. His passionate ideas seemed to erupt out of him, yet he always expressed his thoughts with tenderness and diplomacy. He listened to his classmates, and he made a point of learning their names. He improved my classes and gave me confidence as a young professor. He seemed to deeply appreciate what I did for him as a teacher—always an extra "really, thank you" on the way out—and he tried to return the favor by sharing films and hardcore music with me and asking if he could help me in any way. I made some progress in encouraging him to add philosophy as a second major, but we hadn't sealed the deal.

Alexis remembered John, hadn't seen him around recently, and entered his name into the database as I organized the pile of papers from class. I could overhear a group of students in the hall continuing the discussion from class. Alexis gasped and put her hand on her heart as John's registrar entry came up. She looked at me and then back to the screen. "It says *deceased.*"

I closed my eyes. Students in the entryway argued about whether philosophy should be more like math or poetry. Alexis made some discrete calls and confirmed. John had died over the summer. Sometimes I'll be in front of a class and think to myself: "Look at me! I'm a professor!" I experienced a similar moment of self-awareness here:

"Here I am, learning of the death of my cherished student." A small group gathered outside my door for office hours, still bantering about Nietzsche and reading from a class handout: "No one can construct for you the bridge upon which precisely you must cross the stream of life, no one but yourself."[1]

•

When I was in early adolescence, several of my relatives passed away over a short period. I think of them whenever I'm asked why I chose my career. Because philosophy seems like an unusual vocation, we're often asked a version of "How did you decide to become a philosopher?" The deaths of my family members stand as landmarks in my developing personality. A series of funerals at a formative age burned into the foundations of my identity questions about existence, finitude, meaning, values, and justice. These weren't academic questions. *I wanted to know* the answers, and I grew increasingly dissatisfied with the way religion used platitudes to stick corks in such lines of inquiry. Here we are, with something like infinite space in every direction and slim explanations about why any of this exists. We walk around as if everything makes sense. We maintain the illusion that humans know what we're doing, but, for me, those deaths punctured the veneer.

Where I grew up, we did not have anything like the precollege philosophy programs emerging now. Those would have been a godsend for a kid like me. I stumbled toward philosophy by way of what I perceived as edgy literature: Orwell, Burgess, Vonnegut, Plath, and even Ayn Rand. At the end of nights with friends where we felt in-the-know because we realized that the Cure song was about a Camus story, those family deaths kept me awake. Death is an omnipresent menace, and philosophy shadowed and sometimes challenged it.

Those deaths in my family marked me, and John's death had a similar impact on my identity as a teacher. I hadn't thought through the death of a student before John. I appreciated that teachers of philosophy can be powerful allies to their students, as they confront profoundly difficult and potentially life-altering questions. My job, as I have understood it from the outset, is to help each student gain the

---

1. Friedrich Nietzsche, *Untimely Meditations*, ed. Daniel Breazeale (New York: Cambridge University Press, 1997), 129.

intellectual and emotional courage needed to engage the problems of philosophy, first with me at their side, but ultimately on their own. When a class session or semester ends, its discussions should extend into students' personal lives without missing a beat. Good teaching, as C. Roland Christensen describes it, is a humble exercise.

Effective classrooms are illuminated by shining students rather than by a professor's brilliance, and I try to remember to measure pedagogical success by my students' achievements rather than by my own erudition. This is obvious but easy to forget: if you want to see how things are going in a class, look at your relationships with your students and at the relationships between your students. Mastery of the material is often easy compared to the work of building the sorts of "safety nets" that Christensen describes as "enabling participants to walk the high wire of adventuresome thought and argument with daring bolstered by a sense of security."[2] I do not think of my students as an audience for my show, but as people under my care. Humans are all weird and vulnerable, and by the time they come to a formal philosophy class, they have often built up defense mechanisms against the very questions we chase in philosophy. Knowing this, we should be prepared for feelings stirred up by ideas we introduce.

Philosophy teachers build relationships and environments where it feels safe and even exhilarating to do philosophy. One of the greatest joys of teaching philosophy to college students comes from sharing these transformative ideas with dynamic young people who otherwise would not enter your life. College students remain young, energetic, and hip, and as time passes the generational distance between student and teacher grows. If we didn't have something as valuable as philosophy to offer, students wouldn't come around. The opportunity to interact with this demographic wouldn't exist. Being around people at the beginning of their independent lives provides me with a renewed sense of purpose every semester. This also means that there is a good chance that professors will experience some of these lives ending prematurely.

•

2. "Every Student Teaches and Every Teacher Learns," in *Education for Judgement: The Artistry of Discussion Leadership*, eds. C. Roland Christensen, David A. Garvin, and Ann Sweet (Boston: Harvard Business School Press, 1991), 152–72.

Workers in many vocations experience the deaths of young people. But because of the nature of the questions we ask and the conversations we have with our students, philosophy professors often know these young adults in ways that few others do. I will often know my students' deepest values, their passions, their vision of a good life for them and others, and how they comport themselves in challenging and sometimes uncomfortable discussions. I help them envision and take steps in the direction they want their lives to go, and I am invested in their success. Achievement in my life's work as a teacher is entwined with their success.

Philosophers often do not like any associations between their discipline and religion, and many will balk even at administratively combining philosophy and religion departments. (Be advised not to browse a "metaphysics" section of a typical bookstore with an academic philosopher.) We often protest any such associations between philosophy and religion or "spirituality," but permit me this: because of the conversations we have with our students, philosophy professors can have an existential connection with them. At the risk of derision, we might say that we have a uniquely spiritual access to the people we teach. When we ask our students to seriously consider, for example, their reasons for believing in God, truth, gender, or justice, we reach out across emotional boundaries. It can become quotidian for us—just another day at the office breaking down Pascal's Wager or the male gaze or the simulation argument in ten minutes. But, occasionally, we notice the look in their eyes or the tone in their voice. *Oh my god*, they sometimes think, *I will never see things the same way again.*

The day I learned that John had died, I wrote a letter to his family. I shared many things I genuinely appreciated about him. I explained how John "brought wit, modesty, and genuine laughter to the class on many mornings" and how "he had a way of illuminating complex philosophical and emotional issues with a silly, somewhat self-deprecating story." "Everyone in my classes learned from and enjoyed him," I wrote. His parents called me a few days later. Even though I appreciated the opportunity to talk about John and provide some solace, a father sharing the pain of losing his only child still haunts me. I have three children now. I often ask myself when making pedagogical decisions: What would I want a philosophy teacher to do for my child? That question, in this situation, scars the imagination.

After this experience, I found myself scanning my classrooms—even on the first day of the semester—imagining life trajectories for each student. Some will go to prestigious graduate schools or land fancy jobs earning a lot more than me. Some will study abroad with me and share platters of cakes and moments of awe as we traverse Central Europe. Many will struggle at some point. Some will marry each other (a topic for a different essay). I will watch some of their kids grow on social media. A few will get rich and return to reminisce and even donate money. Some will come to my retirement party, or my funeral. Some will share John's fate. This unknown future and my ability to impact it inflects my relationship with each of them. Just as awareness of the horizon of our own finitude adds urgency to what might otherwise feel like a succession of dull days, we can treat our time with our students either as a chore to dispatch or as something considerably more meaningful. Here we are ants on a ball of rock in space, spiraling around the drain of a supermassive black hole, trying to make sense of it all. Any one of us might not make it to the next semester, or even next Thursday. There is nothing original here, but it does require tenacious focus on the basic question from the existentialists: What do we do, together, with this brief time? Other traditions might think of that question as something of a mantra or prayer. But it is also philosophy.

·

I learned of Elias' death shortly after John's. Driving north for a family vacation, I received a call from another student about what happened. Sitting on a rocky Winslow Homer beach outcrop, I remember looking at the sea and thinking: *This is going to keep happening. This is part of the job.* I attended the service to celebrate his life, and I very much appreciated my colleague offering the eulogy so that I could keep my composure. The prayer card with Elias' photo lives in the top drawer of my desk, a memento mori on the way to class. *Take time with each of these students*, I remind myself. *Be present for them. Care for them. This is what I'd most want a philosophy professor to do for my child.*

I sometimes joke that my own children serve as existential amplifiers or "meaning machines." When you have little ones, you appreciate that you have only a few years of them at each stage of development, and you only get about fifteen or so years with them as *children* who will play with you and view you in certain fleeting ways. One's adult life can drift into stretches without significant milestones—it does not matter so much if you take a major trip on your fortieth rather than your forty-fifth birthday—but the temporal compression in children adds urgency. Experiences meaningful for a five-year-old can seem babyish to a ten-year-old. The moment becomes ripe for certain developmentally appropriate activities, causing parents to curate age-specific family bucket lists for every summer. We feel our lives as parents unfolding before us. Sending a child on the bus to kindergarten or dropping her off at college feel so difficult, in part, because these events mark endings: that stage of your relationship with your child—that stage of your life—is over. There are only a few stages, and so too with our students.

We have fourteen weeks or so with them in an introductory course. Certain experiences and gestures resonate best in those moments, and then that course is over. Perhaps the relationship continues into another class or project, with new opportunities and teachable moments. In the barrage of the academic year, the opportunities—classes, meetings, commenting on papers, letters of recommendation—might seem endless, but really they are just fleeting opportunities in a young person's development. The time we spend with them or a genuine compliment we offer can change the trajectory of their lives. A seed we plant and nurture might grow. And after a few seasons, they move on. Their communications will be less frequent after graduation. A new group will replace them. Years later they write to tell us what that seed became.

I often teach Kant's hypothetical imperative in my introductory courses, as a way to think about values and meaning. A hypothetical imperative, in short, is a means to an end, or a tool. For example, if I want an A in a course, I have to stay up all night and work on this paper. If I want to go to heaven, I must be honest. If I don't want a divorce, I shouldn't cheat on my wife. From this perspective, we do all of these things to get something else. As Kant says of hypothetical imperatives: "Here there is no question whether the end is rational and good, but only what one must do in order to attain it."[3]

This conversation tends to trouble students who feel that life is full of nothing but things done for the sake of getting somewhere else: work on a paper and miss a family event because you want a good grade for that assignment. You want that good grade on that paper because you want a good grade in the class. You want a good grade in the class because you want a high grade point average. You want a high grade point average in order to get into law school. Law school accelerates the process even more intensely for three years. You get a good job and the means-to-an-end lifestyle intensifies as you try to please your boss, earn promotions, and make more money. So you skip your grandmother's birthday party to study because of the benefits this might confer somewhere down a long and nebulous road. Every day feels lived for tomorrow, and when tomorrow comes we live it for the next day. We invest moments in a future that never quite arrives. Then, we die. Our life is filled with means always competitively racing from Point A to Point B, but with no idea where Point B ultimately will lead us or if that place is good.

For students, that can seem a little too applicable to their achievement-focused lives. What really are the best and most important things in life—the true and best ends? What should our values be? Where should we be headed, personally and as a civilization? Is it hubris to trust that STEM will lead us toward good places, when STEM seems like another tool incapable of thinking what makes for a good life? College students hunger for these conversations, and this motivates why we read Kant and other ethical philosophers. In class, we tarry with the issues of true ends, the meaning of life, and how many means will camouflage themselves as ends to lure students in. Here I explain what happened to Laura.

Laura took this very class with me, I tell them. We had this very conversation about means and ends and about what ultimately should orient one's life. She became one of my best students over several courses, and she double majored in economics and became a leader in campus politics. She earned one of the university's highest

---

3. Immanuel Kant, *Grounding for the Metaphysics of Morals*, trans. James Ellington (Indianapolis: Hackett, 1993), 25.

awards, and I show a picture of her with the president of UNH. She enrolled in a top-five law school and excelled there. She had a job at an elite Boston firm waiting for her. As she rode home in a taxi a few weeks before her law school graduation, an intoxicated driver crossed the center line and killed her in a head-on crash. When students hear this story—many of whom dream of working their way to Laura's accomplishments—it makes an impression.

I might follow up with a similar example, explaining that I still find myself making expressions like Benji, one of my funniest students ever. Benji graduated, climbed mountains around the world, and worked in some of the best kitchens in the country. His philosophical and tech-savvy mind landed him a job as a security analyst at Google. Just as he settled into a lucrative Silicon Valley dream job, doctors diagnosed him with a blood disease that killed him at twenty-nine.

Students see that telling these stories is emotional for me. The questions pour out of them. Would Laura have done things differently if she knew she would die so young? Does an early death negate such accomplishments in some way, or are they inherently valuable? When I die, which parts of my life will have been the most meaningful? College students can feel invincible and can live without much thought of their own mortality. Here we are in these moments, in a classroom together, on the edge of our seats discussing Kant and the meaning of life. Sometimes students ask how I can live and go about doing normal things, while thinking about philosophy all of time. The best answer I can give is trying to model being a thoughtful, compassionate person who can have a laugh even when—and perhaps especially when—things are almost too heavy.

Sometimes I show students a picture of Laura next to Cody at a department party. Cody reminded me of a cross between a young Allen Ginsburg and Eugene from Gogol Bordello. Poetry, music, insight flowed from this remarkable person. He never majored in philosophy, but he could comfortably participate in advanced courses and steer things in the most interesting directions: profound, amusing, and sometimes even profane while sensitive. His creative spark could light a room with fun, and I really enjoyed being his teacher. He died of an overdose shortly after graduation. The students have all heard about the opioid problem in our region, but seeing his grin and striped shirt and knowing that even his flame could be extinguished makes everyone a little more aware of their mortality. Patrolling the student-teacher boundaries can prove especially challenging for philosophy professors. Because of the nature of our classroom discussion, I might be one of the student's few trusted adults. Sometimes I am another pair of eyes, watching for issues. The more present I am, the more I see. I am not trained to give many of these students the help they need, but I do keep a list of counseling services in my top drawer next to Elias' prayer card.

It might seem as if a disproportionate share of my students have passed away, and that this rare experience has focused my attention disproportionately on this subject. But I suspect, again, that this is just part of the job that we internalize without much discussion or preparation. My stories here are neither the most interesting nor the most dramatic. One of my colleagues advised David Foster Wallace as an undergraduate. Another friend led a small study-abroad group that included Sean Collier, an officer shot and killed pursuing the Boston Marathon bombers. Such high-profile student deaths bring interviews, publicity heroizing the deceased, memorials, and thoughts of why some losses garner more attention than others. After the Virginia Tech and Sandy Hook mass shootings, teachers remain and continue teaching. Many readers will have their own list of casualties and experiences where we have been in leadership positions mourning with others in the emotional blast radius of student deaths.

•

I hope this essay does not appear maudlin or cheaply sentimental, like I have narcissistically compiled these loses into an essay about my teaching to make it seem more dramatic and important. This is something like sacred material for me. It is difficult to convey the full significance.

Our students are not our children. They are not our grandchildren, nor nieces or nephews. Nor even the children of our close friends. But our students exist close to the center of our sphere of concern. Some students will, at least for a time, receive more attention than some family members. Over a career, there will be hundreds, if not thousands, of students who concern us, often very deeply. We are not prepared for this, and we do not speak of it because it sounds inappropriate given our inadequately nuanced conceptions of care and affection, but we often have some form of *love* for our students. Even in writing this, it still feels wrong to be putting this into words and hard to believe that these students do not exist in their adult lives somewhere beyond campus, like all of my other students. I can imagine them appearing in a dream and having an easy conversation about their jobs, young children, and what they are reading. Then I would remember: *Wait, you don't live anymore.*

Sometimes I see their names on social media and, for a moment, forget, only to be reminded by a photo posted by a friend or a happy birthday wish sent by a parent into the ether.

Philosophy professors are not clergy. We do not sit bedside or offer last rites. But we are guides who share conversations with students about the very deepest issues in their lives. If we are to take seriously the claim that questions about "the good life" lie within our jurisdiction and our areas of expertise, and that we are the right people to teach such subjects, then we should be prepared to be impactful in our students' lives. Many of us can relate to how philosophers have helped us through difficult times, and I appreciate various turning points in my own life where philosophical texts have colored my understanding of what was happening and what I should do. When it comes time to die, our students will often think of the philosophies that most influenced their self-understanding. And, in these moments, they will also think of us teachers, just as I think back with overwhelming gratitude to the teachers who took time with me and who introduced me to ideas that, in a very literal sense, make me who I am. As my own teachers retire and write their final chapters, I need to find a way to make this appreciation part of their stories. A footnote of thanks won't do.

I dedicated one of my first publications to John, and recently his best friend from high school tracked me down via that paper. She just emailed me to say hello and to thank me. Fifteen years ago, and it still gets me. I look around at all of my current students. With an even deeper pang, I look at my own children. And I sense the opportunity and urgency of spending time with all of these young people doing philosophy, thinking with compassion and in solidarity about what all this means and what we should do.

24

A Teaching Life

Martin Benjamin
Michigan State University

MARTIN BENJAMIN is professor emeritus of philosophy at Michigan State University, where he received the Teacher-Scholar Award (1973); the Senior Class Council Recognition Award (1978); the Distinguished Faculty Award (1995); and the Paul Varg Alumni Award for "outstanding teaching and scholarly achievement" (2003). He also received the Award of Merit for Outstanding Leadership and Achievements in the Teaching of Philosophy from the American Association of Philosophy Teachers (1998), as well as a Special Lifetime Award for Achievement and Leadership (2006). He initiated a graduate seminar on teaching philosophy at Michigan State, and, for years, taught a condensed version of the course for advanced graduate students at the American Association of Philosophy Teachers Biennial Workshop-Conference. A former member of the APA Committee on Teaching, he has also taught philosophy to elementary and high school students and practicing health professionals. He now teaches retired senior citizens. His publications include *Splitting the Difference: Compromise and Integrity in Ethics and Politics* (1990), *Philosophy & This Actual World* (2003), and, with Joy Curtis, *Ethics in Nursing: Cases, Principles, and Reasoning*, 4th ed. (2010).

Bebop clarinetist Tony Scott once characterized himself as a jazz musician who played clarinet, rather than a clarinetist who happened to play jazz. In Aristotelian terms, his musical *essence* was as a jazz musician; that he played clarinet was mere *accident*. In much the same way, I think of myself as a teacher who teaches philosophy, not as a philosopher who happens to teach.

In 1962, immediately after graduating as a college English major, I entered the Peace Corps. With only brief training, I was assigned to teach ninth-grade English in Gondar, Ethiopia. It was there that I learned, first, that I enjoyed teaching and, second, that

I was reasonably good at it. The following year circumstances led to my teaching tenth- and eleventh-grade math and history. Though I was far from expert in either, the principal determined that students in these courses would learn more math and history from me than anyone else he could have placed in their classrooms. I worked hard mastering the relevant material and managed to bring my students to grade level or higher.

At the same time, I was teaching myself philosophy. As a college senior, I had become more interested in philosophy than in literature, but it was too late to change majors. So before flying to Ethiopia, I spent most of my Peace Corps clothing allowance on philosophy books and had them shipped to Gondar, where I would have time to read them. I applied to philosophy graduate programs from Ethiopia, and in 1964 enrolled at the University of Chicago.

Four years later I began what would become thirty-seven consecutive years as a full-time philosophy teacher: two at Miami University and thirty-five at Michigan State (MSU). My wife and I retired in 2004 and moved to Oakland, California, to become "hands-on" grandparents. In 2007, I obtained a part-time position as visiting professor at nearby Mills College, where for the next eight years I taught one course a semester. Overall, then, I've taught philosophy in colleges and universities for forty-five years.

But when I reflected on what I might contribute to this volume, it occurred to me that much of my teaching has ranged beyond the college and university classroom. I've also taught philosophy to elementary and high school students, to practicing health professionals, and now, at age seventy-seven, I'm teaching retired senior citizens. In what follows, I describe these efforts and encourage others to venture beyond the college or university classroom.

Teaching Elementary and High School Students

When our daughter Kirsten was in third grade, her elementary school invited parents with special expertise to propose grade-appropriate presentations in various classrooms. At an early age, Kirsten was exposed at the dinner table to age-appropriate philosophical questions. She seemed capable of participating in such discussions and enjoying them. So, I proposed meeting in a classroom in her school once a week for about thirty minutes to discuss adaptations of the moral dilemmas found in Jean Piaget's *The Moral Judgment of the Child*.[1] A fourth-grade teacher who had been having discipline problems mistakenly assumed I was a psychologist (though I had clearly identified myself as a philosophy teacher) and, thinking I might be of help, invited me to meet with her class.

The results were quite good. The students were able and willing participants in discussing moral choices and reasoning arising for children like themselves. Subsequent publications by, for example, Gareth Matthews and the Institute for the Advancement of Philosophy for Children at Montclair State University, have shown that children, even young children, are interested in and quite capable of discussing age-appropriate philosophical questions at a reasonably high level.[2] The teacher seemed pleased, and meetings with her class continued for several weeks.

The next year I came across a notice in an American Philosophical Association (APA) publication by philosopher Matthew Lipman about a novel, *Harry Stottlemeier's Discovery*, he had written for eleven- and twelve-year-olds that was designed to teach elementary logic and foster philosophical reasoning and discussion.[3] Copies (at the time in reproduced typescript) were available from Lipman for anyone who requested one. I wrote Lipman and he sent me a copy.

Lipman's book was just what I needed for a fifth-grade class taught by Jean Medick, an outstanding teacher who understood and appreciated the value of philosophical discussion and Lipman's work. Lipman's novel centers on a group of eleven- or twelve-year-olds who discover and discuss (in model fashion) various matters of philosophy. The first discovery, an element of Aristotelian logic, is made by

---

1. Jean Piaget, *The Moral Judgment of the Child*, trans. Marjorie Gabain (New York, The Free Press, 1965).

2. Gareth B. Matthews, *Philosophy & the Young Child* (Cambridge, MA: Harvard University Press, 1982); Gareth B. Matthews, *Dialogues with Children* (Cambridge, MA: Harvard University Press, 1992); Institute for the Advancement of Philosophy for Children at Montclair State University, https://www.montclair.edu/cehs/academics/centers-and-institutes/iapc.

3. Matthew Lipman, *Harry Stottlemeier's Discovery: Reasoning about Reasoning* (Upper Montclair, NJ: First Mountain Foundation, 1985). See also Ann Margaret Sharp, Ronald F. Reed, and Matthew Lipman, eds., *Studies in Philosophy for Children: Harry Stottlemeier's Discovery* (Philadelphia: Temple University Press, 1992).

one of the students, Harry Stottlemeier (get it?—"Harry Stottle"—
say it fast). Harry's classmates are taken by, and extend and explore,
the nature, limits, and value of Harry's discovery.[4] They then turn
to other questions of logic and ethics. The discussions in Jean Medick's class of the various discoveries and discussions among Harry's
classmates were rich and in many cases as philosophically interesting and adroit, given the subject matter, as I would encounter in a
good freshman or sophomore class at MSU. In fact, one of Lipman's
own discoveries was that certain aspects of logic are easier to teach
to eleven-year-olds than to college freshman, because their thinking
has not been corroded by an additional seven years of poor "mental
hygiene."

I continued to read and discuss *Harry Stottlemeier's Discovery*
with Jean Medick's fifth-grade classes for about six years, including
those that included our daughter Kirsten and then our son David. By
the time David was in fifth grade, Lipman had come out with *Lisa*, a
sequel to *Harry*, and I started teaching that as well.[5] The first chapter
of *Lisa* centers on a difficult moral dilemma for Lisa, a classmate of
Harry's. Lisa loves animals. She also loves her mother's roast chicken.
When she recognizes the apparent inconsistency, she's troubled. What
should she do? Give up eating chicken or admit that she doesn't love
animals as much as she thought? She and her classmates model what
Lipman conceives as a Peircean "community of inquiry" in discussing
the dilemma. I introduced several of Peter Singer's arguments into
our discussion as well as an account of factory farming. The resulting
give-and-take was nearly as rich and complex as one would have with
beginning college students. I became worried, however, about possible fallout. What if some of Jean Medick's students went home and

---

4. Harry's initial discovery (an aspect of Aristotelian logic) is that "[a] sentence can't
be reversed. If you put the last part of a sentence first, it'll no longer be true. For
example, take the sentence 'All oaks are trees.' If you turn it around, it becomes
'All trees are oaks.' But that's false. Now, it's true that 'all planets revolve about the
sun.' But if you turn the sentence around and say that 'all things that revolve about
the sun are planets,' then it's no longer true, it's false!" In discussion, his friend Lisa
provides a counterexample ('No eagles are lions'), requiring Harry to modify his
discovery, but he and his friends' discoveries about logic and language are then off
and running. Sharp et al., *Harry Stottlemeier's Discovery*, 1–4.

5. Matthew Lipman, *Lisa* (Montclair, NJ: Institute for the Advancement of Philosophy for Children, 1976).

refused to eat meat or chicken because of what they'd learned from their "philosophy teacher"? But, much to my relief, I never heard a word of complaint from a parent or from Jean Medick.

Years later, when David and his good friend Jeremy Scott were in tenth grade, they asked if the three of us could meet for philosophical discussion. Thomas Nagel had just published *What Does It All Mean?* In the introduction he writes,

> I suppose most readers will be of college age or older. But that has nothing to do with the nature of the subject, and I would be very glad if the book were also of interest to intelligent high school students with a taste for abstract ideas and theoretical arguments— should any of them read it.
>
> Our analytical capacities are often highly developed before we have learned a great deal about the world, and around the age of fourteen many people start to think about philosophical problems on their own.[6]

So I purchased copies of Nagel's book for David and Jeremy, and we agreed to discuss a chapter a week after dinner on Sundays. Our discussions were at least as deep and probing as would occur in a good introductory college course. They led, in the following year, to David and Jeremy starting an extracurricular philosophy club at East Lansing High School with me as advisor. Here a group of about twenty of what David called "thinkers" (as opposed to exclusively A students) went through Nagel's book, a chapter a week, and discussed other philosophical matters as well.

At about the same time Mat Lipman, now codirector with Ann Margaret Sharp of the Institute for the Advancement of Philosophy for Children (IAPC) at Montclair State College[7] and editor of the journal *Thinking: The Journal of Philosophy for Children*, invited me to review Nagel's book. I made a counterproposal: two reviews from different perspectives, one review by me and one coauthored by David and Jeremy. Mat liked the idea and the two reviews were published

---

6. Thomas Nagel, *What Does It All Mean?* (New York: Oxford University Press, 1987), 3.

7. Now Montclair State University.

side by side.[8] Subsequently, at the invitation of the APA Committee on Pre-College Instruction, David and Jeremy made presentations at the 1990 Central Division APA Meeting in Chicago on starting and maintaining a high school philosophy club.[9]

Thanks to the work of Mat Lipman, Ann Margaret Sharp, and others, there are now many national and international efforts to introduce philosophy in elementary and secondary schools.[10] At MSU, my former colleague Steve Esquith has for many years facilitated several efforts involving graduate students in philosophy introducing aspects of the IAPC materials in local grade and middle schools. More recently, in his role as dean of MSU's Residential College in Arts and Letters, he has initiated an ambitious international program in which undergraduates integrate aspects of teaching philosophy for children in Michigan with educational efforts cultivating peace-building in Mali.[11]

Teaching Practicing Health Professionals

A year after teaching the first philosophical bioethics course at MSU in 1975, I was invited to become a member of the Interdisciplinary Task Force on Death and Dying of the Michigan House of Representatives convened by Representative David Hollister. Membership was open and included individual physicians, nurses, lawyers, senior citizens, representatives of various medical, nursing, legal, religious, and senior citizen agencies and organizations, and two other MSU philosophers, Bruce Miller and Howard Brody. After

---

8. Martin Benjamin, "Thomas Nagel's *What Does It All Mean?*" *Thinking: The Journal of Philosophy for Children* 7, no. 4 (1988):26–28; David Benjamin and Jeremy Scott, "Thomas Nagel's *What Does It All Mean?*" *Thinking: The Journal of Philosophy for Children* 7, no. 4 (1988):28–29.

9. See David Benjamin, "Philosophy in High School: What Does It All Mean?" *Thinking: The Journal of Philosophy for Children* 8, no. 4 (1990):43–44.

10. See, for example, Institute for the Advancement of Philosophy for Children at Montclair State University, https://www.montclair.edu/cehs/academics/centers-and-institutes/iapc; Thomas E. Wartenberg, *Big Ideas for Little Kids: Teaching Philosophy through Children's Literature*, 2nd ed. (Lanham, MD: Rowman & Littlefield, 2014).

11. Stephen L. Esquith, "Philosophy for Children: Peace Building from Michigan to Mali," presented at Biennial PLATO Conference 2017, Social Justice: Where Do We Go from Here? University of Chicago, June 23–24, 2017.

addressing regulations for emerging hospice organizations, the Task Force turned to what at the time were called "living wills" as a possible solution to the problem of life and death decision-making for formerly competent adults who, due to illness or injury, could no longer accept or refuse medical treatment.

During more than two years of monthly deliberations leading to what the Task Force called the "Medical Treatment Decision Act," Miller, Brody, and I served mainly as philosophy teachers. As we ourselves learned about law, medicine, nursing, psychology, the perspectives of senior citizens, legislative politics, and so on from other members of the Task Force, we explained the nature and philosophical foundations of concepts like autonomy and rights and principles like utility and "respect for persons" (the second formulation of the categorical imperative) and stressed the importance of certain distinctions, such as the difference between a legal right to refuse lifesaving medical treatment, on the one hand, and a legal right to be dead, on the other. (There was at the time no such legal right. Whether there is now such a limited right in states permitting physician-assisted death is an interesting open question.)

At one point Brody, Miller, and I introduced an alternative to the living will proposed by Georgetown bioethicist Robert M. Veatch.[12] Better than a written document, Veatch argued, would be the appointment of a trusted proxy or agent who would be legally authorized to accept or refuse medical treatment on one's behalf if, due to severe illness or injury, one could not do so oneself. The Task Force brought Veatch to Lansing to present and discuss his proposal with the group.

The Task Force then found itself divided; roughly half of the members preferred the living will and half preferred Veatch's alternative. So Miller, Brody, and I suggested we form two subgroups: one assigned to draft a paper stating and making the strongest case for the living will, the other assigned to draft a paper stating and making the strongest case for appointing an agent. Then, with both documents before us, the entire group would debate their respective merits. This was carried out, and Veatch's alternative (investing

---

12. Robert M. Veatch, *Death, Dying, and the Biological Revolution: Our Last Quest for Responsibility* (New Haven, CT: Yale University Press, 1977).

legal authority, as Representative Hollister put it, in a "living person" rather than a "dead document") ultimately prevailed. The result, House Bill 4058, was endorsed in 1979 in an editorial in the *New England Journal of Medicine* (though it took more than ten additional years for a variation of the bill finally to be passed by the Michigan Legislature).[13]

Testifying to our success as philosophy teachers was the impatience of longstanding members of the Task Force with newcomers unfamiliar with concepts, principles, and distinctions that Miller, Brody, and I had previously identified and explained. It was mildly amusing to observe them shaking their heads or rolling their eyes at newer members who, for example, didn't understand the nature of a *utilitarian* argument or the difference between a right to refuse lifesaving treatment and a right to be dead.

In an article examining the focus of ethics teaching and testing in medical schools, philosopher William Ruddick proposed that teachers try to produce and test for a capacity he called *discursive moral competence*. By this he meant the ability to discuss in appropriate moral terminology a variety of routine and rare cases with the variety of people likely to be involved in these cases. Thus, a physician with discursive moral competence would be able to use such distinctions as *active* and *passive* euthanasia, *harm* and *wrong, coercion* and *persuasion*, as well as such moral principles as *The Golden Rule* or *Double Effect*. The physician should also be able to discuss a variety of cases with other physicians, nurses, patients, relatives, lawyers—however different their moral concerns and principles from the physician's own. . . . Not only will physicians become more acute reasoners in moral matters, they will also become more acute listeners, more sensitive to the moral issues that are either ignored or garbled in anxious, hurried discussion.[14]

I think Ruddick is right and would add only that, in some cases, philosophers will also have to bring to the interdisciplinary table some aspect of their specialized training that illuminates a contentious issue. Consider, in this connection, an aspect of the theory of

---

13. Arnold S. Relman, "Michigan's Sensible 'Living Will,'" *New England Journal of Medicine* 300, no. 22 (1979):1270–72.

14. William Ruddick, "What Should We Teach and Test?" *Hastings Center Report* 13, no. 3 (1983):21.

action and agency that distinguishes between a person's simply not acting, on the one hand, and his or her performing a negative act, on the other. This distinction is employed in a widely anthologized article by James Rachels on whether there is a morally relevant difference between active and passive euthanasia.[15] It is also examined at length in a volume published by the President's Commission for the Study of Ethical Problems in Medicine and Biomedical and Behavioral Research.[16]

As years passed, I continued to learn about the world and decision making of practicing health care professionals while reciprocally cultivating their capacity for discursive moral competence. I participated in and sometimes organized ethics case conferences in Lansing area hospitals (for which physicians received continuing medical education credit). I began coteaching a MSU course on nursing ethics with nursing professor Joy Curtis. Dissatisfied with the available texts, we subsequently wrote a book of our own.[17] We made a presentation, "Ethics in Nursing: Issues and Inquiry," to the Central Division APA meeting in Milwaukee in 1981. In 1982, we conducted a five-week National Endowment for the Humanities (NEH) Summer Seminar on Ethics in Nursing for nursing faculty from around the country. And in 1983 we participated in an NEH Summer Institute on Moral Philosophy and Nursing Ethics directed by philosopher Tziporah Kasachkoff at Tufts University.

In 1986, I was appointed chair of the Ethics and Social Impact Committee (ESIC) of the Transplant and Health Policy Center of Michigan, a state-funded organization located at the University of Michigan Medical School. The interdisciplinary ESIC included transplant surgeons, transplant nurses and coordinators, lawyers, state policy planners, clergy, transplant recipients, a psychiatrist, and another philosopher, Carl Cohen of the University of Michigan. One of the

---

15. James Rachels, "Active and Passive Euthanasia," *New England Journal of Medicine* 292, no. 2 (1975):78–80.

16. President's Commission for the Study of Ethical Problems in Medicine and Biomedical and Behavioral Research, "Reexamining the Role of Traditional Moral Distinctions," in *Deciding to Forego Life-Sustaining Treatment* (Washington, DC: U.S. Government Printing Office, 1983), 60–77.

17. Martin Benjamin and Joy Curtis, *Ethics in Nursing: Cases, Principles, and Reasoning*, 4th ed. (New York: Oxford University Press, 2010).

first things I did as chair was to have the center purchase a copy of James Rachels' *The Elements of Moral Philosophy* for each member of the committee and schedule a daylong retreat for us to discuss it.[18] Rachels' book, which models discursive moral competence, set the tone for the philosophical reasoning and analysis that characterized the committee's deliberations in the years that followed.

In 1987, the ESIC took up a question then much in the news: whether, with the informed consent of both sets of parents, it was morally permissible to transplant the heart of an anencephalic infant into the chest cavity of an infant born with a likely fatal defect of the heart. After months of informed, disciplined discussion with a small residue of reasonable disagreement, I asked each committee member to write a short paper stating and defending his or her position, after which each paper would be photocopied and read by every other member. This would ensure, among other things, that each member's position would be given a fair hearing. What was remarkable was that, after everyone had to state and defend their views on paper, nearly all important differences among the committee members disappeared. The emerging qualified consensus provided a basis for a committee-authored paper published in the *Hastings Center Report*.[19] Later, after extensive, careful, and mutually respectful give-and-take discussion, the ESIC drafted and published two additional papers on controversial topics in prestigious medical journals.[20] One of them ("Alcoholics and Liver Transplantation") has influenced policy and has been reprinted in many bioethics texts.

Finally, as a member of the ethics committee of the United Network of Organ Sharing (UNOS), a private, nonprofit organization

---

18. James Rachels, *The Elements of Moral Philosophy* (New York: Random House, 1986).

19. Ethics and Social Impact Committee of the Transplant and Health Policy Center and Martin Benjamin, "Anencephalic Infants as Sources of Transplantable Organs," *Hastings Center Report* 18, no. 5 (1988):28–30.

20. Carl Cohen, Martin Benjamin, and the Ethics and Social Impact Committee, "Alcoholics and Liver Transplantation," *Journal of the American Medical Association* 265, no. 10 (1991):1299–1301; Martin Benjamin, Carl Cohen, Eugene Grochowski, and the Ethics and Social Impact Committee of the Transplant Policy Center, "What Transplantation Can Teach Us about Health Care Reform," *New England Journal of Medicine* 330, no. 3 (1994):858–60.

that manages the nation's organ transplant system, I was appointed to a subcommittee charged with developing a set of principles for allocating the limited supply of transplantable organs. As a member of this subcommittee (that also included Robert M. Veatch), I drew on aspects of a book I'd written[21] to propose language and a rationale for accommodating both Kantian and utilitarian considerations in the final set of principles.[22]

In all these interdisciplinary settings, individuals from different backgrounds and specializations taught and learned from each other. I learned about medicine, nursing, law, and related matters. I taught by modeling and cultivating discursive moral competence and, where useful, drawing upon and making accessible to nonphilosophers more technical aspects of academic philosophy. The result was informed interdisciplinary moral reflection and recommendations of a high order.

Teaching Retired Senior Citizens

In 2016, I came across a *New York Times* article about the more than 150,000 older, mostly retired, men and women who were taking noncredit courses in a variety of subjects through one or another Osher Lifelong Learning Institutes (OLLI, pronounced "Olly").[23] The more than 119 OLLIs are mostly affiliated with colleges and universities. I found the website for the OLLI at nearby California State University, East Bay, and submitted a proposal for a course titled "Martin Luther King, Jr. and the Trial and Death of Socrates." Three times in King's justly celebrated "Letter from Birmingham City Jail" he appeals to Socrates. So I proposed a course meeting two hours a week for four weeks in which we would first read and discuss King's "Letter" (available online) and the concept of civil disobedience. We would then read and discuss Plato's "Euthyphro,"

---

21. Martin Benjamin, *Splitting the Difference: Compromise in Ethics and Politics* (Lawrence: University Press of Kansas, 1990).

22. 1991 Ethics Committee, United Network for Organ Sharing, "General Principles for Allocating Human Organs and Tissues," *Transplantation Proceedings* 24, no. 5 (1992):2227–35.

23. Harriet Edleson, "Older Students Learn for the Sake of Learning," *New York Times*, January 1, 2016.

"Apology," "Crito," and a short excerpt of "Phaedo" and relate them to King's references to Socrates.[24]

I taught this course in the fall of 2016 and followed it with a five-week course on "Issues in Bioethics" in winter 2017 and a five-week course in "Justice and the Health Care System" in spring. The courses were a joy to teach. The participants included retired physicians, lawyers, nurses, dentists, several homemakers, and representatives of other occupations and professions. All were bright, serious, and engaged. They completed and reflected on the reading assignments with care and were articulate, reasonable, and tough-minded in discussion. For those of us who enjoy the college and university philosophy classroom at its best, OLLI courses offer the rewards of teaching with none of the essential but burdensome requirements of reading and extensively commenting on papers, testing, and grading. I've been exhilarated at the end of every class meeting, and the feeling stayed with me throughout the twenty-two-mile drive home and into the evening.

For years at MSU I taught a successful course titled "Philosophy in Literature." The course allowed me to combine my interest and college major in literature with my interest and graduate training in philosophy. In fall 2017, I taught a five-week OLLI course at Cal State, East Bay, titled "Philosophy in Literature: *Candide* and *The Death of Ivan Ilych.*" The first class meeting provided philosophical background about a priori versus a posteriori knowledge, rationalism and empiricism, and the problem of evil. We then examined how these are embedded in and required for fully understanding Voltaire's *Candide.* After this we read excerpts from Leo Tolstoy's *My Confession* to discuss his personal spiritual crisis regarding the question of whether, and if so how, our lives can have meaning in the face of mortality. We then turned to *Ivan Ilych* to see how seven years later Tolstoy turned both the question and his own answer into literary art. The course went well and I followed it with a course titled "Philosophy in Literature: 'The Grand Inquisitor' and *The Plague.*" In spring 2018 I will teach an introduction to Rawls titled "Justice as Fairness."

---

24. Plato, *The Trial and Death of Socrates*, trans. G. M. A. Grube, rev. John M. Cooper, 3rd ed. (Indianapolis: Hackett, 2000).

I have also, through OLLI, given lectures at various retirement residences in the East Bay. I made three presentations of "Defining Death in a Technological Age: The Interface between Medicine and Philosophy" in spring 2017 and made two presentations of "Obligations to Future Generations" in fall.

At my age, I no longer plan too far ahead in too much detail. So I don't know what I'd propose to teach if I'm still around and healthy after this. But if I am around and reasonably healthy, you can be sure that I'll find something to teach in an OLLI course that will interest both me and, I would hope, those who enroll in it.

A Teaching Life

In 1879, Tolstoy became obsessed with the question of whether his life could have a meaning that would not be destroyed by death. "If not today then tomorrow," he wrote,

> sickness and death will come . . . to everyone, to me, and nothing will remain except the stench and the worms. My deeds, whatever they may be, will be forgotten sooner or later, and I myself will be no more. Why, then, do anything?[25]

One plausible answer to Tolstoy's question is that a person's life acquires a meaning that will not be destroyed by death if much of that life is devoted to a valuable practice or project that began before the person was born and won't be completed, if ever, until long after he or she is dead. In becoming an integral part of such a practice or project—in critically and creatively linking its past with its future—a person's limited lifetime acquires a kind of secular transcendence. Teaching philosophy, I believe, is one such practice.[26] It goes back at least as far as Socrates, Plato, and Aristotle, all of whom, recall, were teachers as well as great philosophers.

As a graduate student, I learned in four years some of the accumulated wisdom of more than 2,500 years of philosophical inquiry.

---

25. Leo Tolstoy, *A Confession*, trans. David Patterson (New York: Norton, 1963), 30.

26. There are many other such practices, including, for example, the practices of medicine, raising children, and working to make social and political institutions more just. For further development of the main ideas of this section, see Martin Benjamin, *Philosophy and This Actual World* (Lanham, MD: Rowman & Littlefield, 2003), 170–87.

No individual or individual generation could produce from the ground up the complex combination of knowledge, skills, and understanding that constitutes contemporary philosophy. It's been centuries in the making. We are its beneficiaries and are indebted to those who contributed to it.

As a teacher I then began sharing, modifying, and expanding what I had learned, first with college and university students, then with elementary and high school students, then with practicing health professionals, and now with retired senior citizens. Philosophical inquiry and understanding, I believe, make significant contributions to a liberal democratic society and to the lives of its members. Philosophical inquiry has also given birth to many other important disciplines, and it's an integral part of what's best in the larger culture.

As I face up to my mortality, I take some satisfaction in thinking that some of my former students will, as citizens, parents, health professionals, teachers, scholars, or in other capacities, continue and improve the practice of philosophical inquiry by modifying and adding to what they have learned from me and other philosophy teachers and then passing the practice and results on to their friends, family, students, or readers, some of whom I hope will do the same after my former students are dead, and so on. In contributing to and becoming part of the ongoing practice of disciplined philosophical inquiry—serving as a connecting link between its past and its future—the life of a philosophy teacher acquires a degree of meaning and value that outlives his or her finite existence. The aim of this chapter, then, has been to show that philosophy teachers can *increase* the meaning and value of their lives by extending their efforts beyond the traditional college or university classroom—to elementary and high school students, to practicing health professionals, to retired senior citizens, and to many others.